AF539431

TEACHER MORALE IN SECONDARY SCHOOLS

TEACHER MORALE IN SECONDARY SCHOOLS

By

DR. KUNDAVARAPU VENU GOPALA RAO
M.A., M.Sc., M.A., Ph.D.
Siddartha College of Education
Vijayawada, (A.P.)

Editor

DR. DIGUMARTI BHASKARA RAO
M.Sc., M.A., M.A., M.Ed., Ph.D.
R.V.R. College of Education
Guntur—522006, (A.P.)

2000
DISCOVERY PUBLISHING HOUSE
NEW DELHI—1100 02

First Published–2000

ISBN 81-7141-551-2

Published by

DISCOVERY PUBLISHING HOUSE
4831/24, Ansari Road, Prahlad Street,
Darya Ganj, New Delhi-110002 (India)
Phone: 3279245 # Fax: 91-11-3253475
E-mail:dph@indiatimes.com

Printed at:
Tarun Offset Printers,
Delhi-110053

PREFACE

Teacher Morale, in an educational set-up, indicates the conscious commitment of the teacher to his profession in order to promote effectiveness of teaching and to provide qualitative education in the society. Identifying the importance of teacher morale, a study was designed to identify the morale in the secondary school teacher population.

For the purpose, a teacher morale opinionnaire was constructed giving prominence to teacher factor and environmental factors. The teacher morale in the teachers working in about one hundred secondary schools seems to approximate to the pattern of normal probability distribution. Probably, the environmental factors contribute relatively more to the teacher morale than the teacher factor.

The tool, the results and the recommendations of this extensive investigation will be of great significance and use. This work will help many policy planners, administrators, researchers and teachers in enhancing the academic efficiency.

For their generous co-operation and support, thanks are extended to Prof. P. Mohan Rao, Sri. K. Satyanarayana, Sri G. Sundara Rao, Dr. D.S.N. Sastry, Sri R. Jesupadam, Sri C. Venkateswarlu, Sri K. Nageswara Rao, Smt. K. Rama Ratnam, Smt.Y.S.N.L. Annapurna and the managements and colleagues of Siddartha College of Education and RVR College of Education.

Dr. K. Venugopala Rao

Dr. D. Bhaskara Rao

January 26, 1999

50th Republic day of India

CONTENTS

1

INTRODUCTION

INTRODUCTORY

"Peace Eludes Us... . The Planet is Being Destroyed... . Neighbours Live in Fear... . Women and Men are Estranged from Each Other... . Children Die".

(Prabuddha Bharata, May, 1994)

This is an observation made by the centennial—and second—1993 Parliament of World Religions which met at Chicago, from August 18 to September 5, 1993 in commemoration of the first one held in 1893 with Swami Vivekananda. They issued in 1993 a Declaration towards a 'Global Ethic', their recommendation in a nut-shell was that "Earth cannot be changed for the better unless the consciousness of individuals is changed first...".

"After two world wars and the end of the cold war, the collapse of Fascism and Nazism, by the fifties and the shaking of foundations of Communism in the nineties, humanity has entered a new phase of history".

But still, "Our world is experiencing a fundamental crisis: a crisis in global economy, global ecology, and global politics... . Hope for a lasting peace among nations slips away from us. There are tensions between the sexes and generations. Children die, kill and are killed."

Verily a new consciousness is essential in us in order to face our challenges in a concerted manner. We must have both a 'will and a way' to meet them.

'Morale' is perhaps one important consideration for us in a world full of the above atmosphere. We should develop it positively in us and use it in these days of our diminishing ethics. Unless and until, we plan to do so on a top priority basis in the present-day society which is charged with the above atmosphere, we may not at all move towards the goal postulated and enunciated by the above-said Parliament of Religions.

The Related Problem in Education

Moved by the above situation and by applying it to the world of Teaching, the investigator regretfully notes that the teachers' value-system too is at crossroads in the present-day society. The values cherished by a Teacher as well as his pupils in the present system in which they work for Education are nothing but commercial and political. These values are manifest even in almost all situations of the day-to-day working of an educational institution, in matters concerning pupils' behaviour with one another, teachers' behaviour with one another and also with pupils as well as their parents, administrators and others. More time and resources are spent in these institutions under the present system with lot of examination-mindedness so that their examination results would be high. So, no lofty ideals of an ethical or intellectual nature could be pursued in these institutions.

Pondering over such a situation in the world of Education in the light of the one depicted above at the global level, the investigator has reasons to believe by means of his experience in the Teacher-Education at B.Ed., level for the last 10 years, that though the material working conditions of Teachers seem to have become better than before in the recent years, particularly in our country, yet the quality of education which they impart has not risen much; on the other hand, we have also a people who are too hypercritical of the falling standards in both teaching and learning, depicting their pessimistic outlook which naturally affects adversely the morale of all the concerned. Added, we have a system of Education, where we measure the performance of a pupil as well as his Teacher, by means of the examination-results they get. What the, is then use of blaming the present-day world and the present day generation, as a worthless stuff? We resort therefore to a philosophical statement to the effect that "Earth cannot be changed for the better, unless the consciousness of individuals is changed first". Similarly, should we blame the present-day Teachers alone, for their ostensibly low morale which they manifest even after the material conditions of their working in Educational Institutions have improved through several measures like the State Revised Scales of pay introduced in 1993 in the case of School Teachers and the revised U.G.C. scales of 1986 in the case of College Teachers? Can we say that mere increase of salary, etc. would improve one's morale?

Whatever the answers to these questions might be, only to create a healthy academic atmosphere in educational institutions all facilities to the possible extent were provided by the Government with a fond hope that these would help them to enhance the Teacher's morale.

> *All the nations in the world have duly recognised the importance of Education and its Materialistic and Non-materialistic contribution.*

Also we cannot think of a negative approach in the matter, by thinking these incentives would not promote Teacher Morale. But also these incentives don't seem to have promoted it. So, it is imperative that we study what would promote it. On the other hand there has been a lot of realization that Education has an immense value in serving as an In-put for a good human Out-put. That is why we find emphasis on aspects like universalisation of Education, compulsory Education, its qualitative improvement etc. Hence the huge expansion in Education in this century.

Having thus realised that the prosperity and well being of a nation exclusively depends upon the quality and quantity of Education that it possesses, all the nations of the world are taking steps for the development of education . This is so even in those countries which have hiterto paid scant attention for the development of Education. The contribution of Science and Technology has become an inseparable part of this nation-building process. So, Education at 10+2+3, that provides to our future citizens a general background of knowledge should be improved, Furthermore, the learning at the School and Intermediate levels would serve as the foundation for the training of most of our Technicians.

Consequently every nation in the world has been voting crores of rupees through its parliament for the development of Education. The importance of Education for the peaceful existence of humanity has been time and again raised by many scholars throughout the world. In this post-sputnik age, development is taking rapid strides. Every country should keep pace with this fast development. So, investment on Education has become inevitable in any country. Consequently due to the public pressure and these fast developments all the countries are forced to establish educational institutions in a large number.

In our country too, a lot of educational expansion has taken place after Independence in 1947. Compared with 191.5 lakh children in classes I-V in 1950–51, 834 lakh children attend schools today. In classes VI to VIII, in 1950-51, 31.2 lakh children attended schools; now 450 lakh children attend schools. In classes IX, X and XI, in 1950, 12.2 lakh children attended schools, now 420 lakh children are in schools. Nearly 27.91 lakh teachers are employed...20.72 lakh men and 7.19 lakh women. The total number of primary schools today is 4,66,332 as compared to 2,09,671 in 1950-51. Upper Primary Schools today number 94,214 while they were 13,596 in 1950-51. Similarly the number of High/Higher Secondary Schools today is 43,800 while they were 13,596 in 1950-51. The number of universitities too has increased from 27 to 105 and enrolment in institutions of higher education increased from 2,00,000 to 34,00,000. India has risen to the third place in the world in terms of college enrolment, immediately following the United States. The total expenditure on education is about 3 per cent of the Gross National product. The Education Commission (1964-66) recommended that it should be 6%. In view of the mounting expenditure which has risen subsequently, it should increase further.

We have now in India the New Education Policy since 1986 with some laudable objectives, one of which is to take our country into 21st century, in order to help her to occupy her rightful place in the world of Technology in the 21st century. Accordingly, the Government of India and State Governments have taken necessary steps, by identifying our National targets in Education and New curricular trends that need emphasis under the New Education Policy (N.E.P.) However one large thrust in our Educational Expansion in Post-Independent India is therefore an increase of the number of children whom we have to educate; it is perhaps needless to reiterate the need for a thrust on qualitative improvement too, in Education. And a few more thrusts would be (i) strengthening the existing compulsory scheme of Primary Education (6-11 years), and (ii) universalising Education upto the, age of 14 years as per our constitution, which would only add to the existing quantitative expansion.

The number of institutions which are thus fast developing have increased today the strength of their staff and students, enormously. In order to quench the quest of public for acquisition of modern knowledge and for the development of education, the private institutions are increasing day-by-day raising the strength of their staff and students. Consequently the contribution of the Government and the private organizations has increased, which in turn makes the system of education huge by raising their in-take capacity, their infrastructure and the required teaching and non-teaching material, creating also certain academic and administrative problems in managing them. Proper management of these institutions has become a problem in the present days. But yet the state is taking all possible measures for the smooth running of these institutions. The successful functioning of an institution throughout the academic year will certainly give an opportunity to yield good results.

The very purpose of an educational institution and its existence will be evaluated to a maximum extent on the basis of its products. So, for obtaining good products from an educational institution all the factors should contribute their share satisfactorily; some of these factors are the reading and writing materials made available to it, its infrastucture, the teaching aids, proper financial assistance etc. But almost all the institutions are being equipped in one way or the other with the required facilities, but yet the results are not very satisfactory.

The system of education has become therefore a target for public criticism for its inability in not producing the required man-power required by the society.

> *But as a matter of fact the system of Education may not be in a position to provide what the society demands but it has to provide at least what the society needs.*

Neither of these objectives is met by the system of education in modern times. Why, are the institutions not producing the best students? Where does the problem lie?

Importance of the Present Investigation

A lot of research has been made to analyse the factors contributing positively or negatively to the successful functioning of the educational institutions. The contribution of academic, administrative, psychological, sociological and economic, factors has also been analysed in detail to measure their degree of contribution in making an institution successful. Almost all the aspects contributing to the successful functioning of an Educational Institution were studied to identify their share, but the contribution of the teacher who is the king-pin in the system has not been evaluated satisfactorily.

The teacher and his personal traits apart from his conscious commitment to his profession must also be treated as a major factor that contributes to determine the destiny of the institution. Whatever be the other factors like teaching aids, audio-visual equipment and financial assistance they are all subsidiary when compared with the teacher and his commitment. A committed teacher is an asset to the system. The contribution of a committed teacher will certainly override the absence of other factors to a large extent. Ample evidence is available in Indian Educational system, to prove it, because even today in rural areas, where the institutions are suffering from many physical deficiencies, the contribution of a committed teacher is the only reason with which the institutions are living and enjoying the appreciation of the society.

> *It is uncontroversial to state that a committed Teacher can contribute significantly leading the institution to achieve its objectives inspite of odd conditions.*

The factors conducive to making the teacher contribute consciously to his profession have also been analysed by different scholars. The factors such as the family conditions, the financial conditions and the qualifications including the institution's management have been identified in this regard. Proper remedial measures were also suggested to rectify the defects for creating a healthy environment to the teacher. In spite of all these efforts, the institutions are not functioning properly. The standards are deteriorating day-by-day. The management of the institutions, is still in a Questionable state. No doubt the Centre and the State Governments are contributing their mite, perhaps, more by way of (a) financial assistance to these institutions, and (b) determining the curriculum prescriptively at school level under the Education Act, and suggestively at other levels, by precedents and expediency. But the results are not commensurate at any stage in terms of their inputs like men and material. Why are they not producing good results?

> *The material conditions of the Teacher have been improved satisfactorily. But the output is not that satisfactory.*

So, if one critically analyses the factors contributing to the successful functioning of educational institutions, one may certainly come to a conclusion that the lack of consciously committed teachers is the main reason for not producing the good students.

> *Teacher and his conscious commitment must be, therefore, analysed in detail in these changing circumstances.*

Even if all facilities other than this in-put are available in an institution, it may not lead to much success. Thus failure to have teachers with highest morale should be avoided without fail. A teacher with highest morale is the need of the hour.

So, what factors are contributing to enhance the morale of the teacher should be thoroughly analysed, since the teacher is the only major factor and also an important intermediary agency between the other factors and the students. His existence in terms of his materialistic and non-materialistic aspects must be analysed properly. His contribution in terms of academic and non-academic aspects is quite significant.

> *So, in order to identify the inability of the institutions for not producing good students, a critical analysis of the teacher and his morale is essential.*

No research has been conducted so far extensively to analyse the teacher's morale and identify the factors contributing to it. Providing all facilities in the absence of a committed teacher, to an educational institution will be an unsuccessful venture. The production of a good out-put exclusively depends upon the morale of the worker concerned, as in any production organisation.

The man before the machine should contribute consciously with professional commitment for getting optimal production. Whether it is a production unit or in a classroom situation, the person in-charge must work consciously with commitment. Otherwise the very purpose of the system will be defeated. So, it is essential to study the factors contributing for obtaining good production in an organisation. Besides, a close relationship exists between a production organisation and an educational institution from their functional point of view with certain analogies in so far as it relates to the morale of the concerned functionaries. So, it is better to have an understanding of the worker and his morale in an industry too, which thus provides an analogical situation corresponding to the one in an educational institution.

An Analogical Situation in the World of Production

Thus in Industrial concerns also, the worker's morale has received much attention as a crucial input, in order to increase the industrial out-put, Industrial research in the recent years has shown that job satisfaction is quite essential in the worker, if the increase is to be obtained properly. One question here is whether job-satisfaction leads to morale or morale leads to job-satisfaction. In all studies to understand the motivation of people at work, the following factors are considered as integral parts of work motivation:

a) Attitudes
b) Job satisfaction
c) Morale
d) Their interrelationship

We may try to understand the relationship of all the related factors herein, depicted in, Figure No.1.

We may see from it that men at work with their competence (skill and knowledge) and attitudes, perform their job through interaction with the work environment. The outcome of a person's performance, if satisfactory, generates adequate work motivation for him, develops high morale in the work group, and results in individual's job satisfaction. A series of effective performances, would further strengthen motivation, boost up the morale, and consequently increase job satisfaction and thus develop favourable attitude towards the work environment.

Ideally, management should learn the attitudes of employees through supervisors. In the medium and large sized companies, however, management at times does not trust the reports it obtains from supervisors, and it turns to other methods, such as Grievance Cell, Suggestion Box, Complaint Book etc. Personnel Officers are appointed to look after the welfare of workers. More direct methods would be Interviews and the Questionnaires. Thus, morale seems to have been recognised as one of the crucial factors to be reckoned with, in the world of production too.

Based upon certain studies in this regard two sets of factors are tabulated hereunder:

FIGURE–1

Schematic Relationship of Attitudes. Job Satisfaction , Morale, Motivation and Performance.

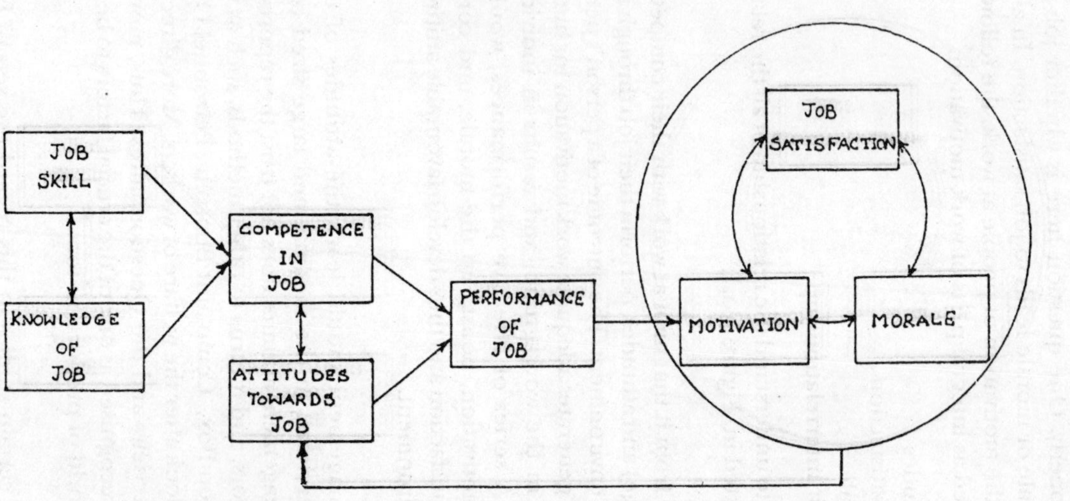

Note : 1. Job Skill, knowledge of Job and Competence in it promote not only better out-put but also improved attitudes, improved performance, more Job satisfaction, higher motivation and greater morale.

2. The diagram shows the interrelations of the Eight Factors pertaining to the Industrial Morale.

Factors Relating to Job Satisfaction and Dissatisfaction

Factors in Job Satisfaction	*Factors in Job Dissatisfaction*
Motivators/Satisfiers/ Intrinsic /Job content	Extrinsic/Job context/ Hygiene/Dissatisfiers
Achievement	Salary
Recognition	Working conditions
Work itself	Relations with co-employees
Responsibility	Relations with subordinates
Advancement	Company Policies and practices
Psychological growth	Job security, status, personal life

According to the above, satisfiers (or motivators, etc) which contributed to the feelings of satisfaction had little to contribute to dissatisfied feeling. Similarly dissatisfiers (or hygienes, etc.) contributed more to dissatisfaction than to satisfaction.

One interesting feature of the above analysis is that satisfiers not only enable a person to feel satisfied but they induce him to produce and perform more in his job. Dissatisfiers (or hygienes) do not seem to have that much potency to contribute to job behaviour.

There are many factors which interact in a complex pattern to contribute to job satisfaction. Some of the factors which are considered to be more important herein are:

1. Personal Factors

Sex, number of dependents, age, time on job, intelligence, education, personality—exclusive of intelligence.

2. Factors Inherent in the Job

Type of work, skill required, occupational status, geography, size of plant.

3. Factors Controllable by Management

Salary, security, opportunity for advancement, co-workers, responsibility, working conditions, supervision, downward flow of information.

The above analysis reveals the importance of certain crucial factors concerning with worker's performance in the world of production. Though Education (the world of knowledge) differs from this world of production in certain aspects such as the intangible nature of our product in Education unlike that of the industry, yet there are some similarities between these two worlds, in matters of psychological concern, which include 'Morale' and need a consideration for raising the 'Out-put' in these two worlds.

Thus, the teacher occupies a key position in the world of knowledge, like the worker in the world of production. These two functionaries work at the grass-root level, contributing to the society from their varied functions. Unless they are satisfied well and highly motivated, it would be difficult to obtain their valuable in-put for the required out-put to the society. While the Teacher promotes the learning of the future citizens, the worker in a production organisation helps in producing wealth for us. Both these products are essential to the society. Let us now try to study in this investigation. before we proceed further in it, the status of the Teacher who is a key figure in the world of knowledge in order to appreciate the importance of his input.

Status of the teacher in India

Teaching in an Educational Institutions is taken up, generally with the aim of promoting learning in the pupils. There are also the non-student youth who are the non starters of learning in a school. So, compulsory Education is provided by the State in order to universalise Education for bringing all children of the school age to the school. So the teacher has a pivotal place in society for educating all the youngsters who are the future citizens, in view of the fact that an enlightened citizenry is one major requirement in any modern state.

In ancient times too education was required, but mainly to promote culture in the society, by transmitting and developing it. Though the conditions of the society differed a lot in the ancient and the modern periods, yet education figured prominently in these two periods, by making the Teacher a key figure, in the educational systems in these two periods.

Teacher was regarded as a holy person in ancient India; he was compared to a God; no doubt, ancient Indian literature regarded the two parents as well as the Teacher as Gods for the child.

That is why it is said
that mother is to be treated as a Goddess
that father is to be treated as a God
that Teacher is to be treated as a God.

Besides, the Teacher is to be treated as a combination of the Trinity as well as the supreme ONE as stated in the following sanskrit verse (Transliterated in English):

Gurur Brahmá Gurur Visṇu,
Gururdevo- Maheśwaraḥ,
Guru Sakshath Paraṃ Brahma,
Thasmai Śri Gurave Namaḥ.

Meaning

Teacher is the Creator;
He is the Protector;
He is the Lord that destroys the World,
He is actually the God supreme;
Let me, therefore offer my salutation to Him.

Manu, the ancient Indian sage:

"A teacher is the image of Brahma, a father is the image of Prajapati, and a mother is the image of the Earth".

Thus, teacher was regarded as the most perfect Being in those days. So, in ancient India teaching was considered to be a holy duty. Teachers were expected to devote their lives to the cause of Education with a missionary spirit of self sacrifice and the society laid down the principle that both the public and the State should help the learned teachers and the educational institutions very liberally.

The relationship between the teacher and his pupils was regarded as filial in character. He was regarded as the spiritual and intellectual father of his students. It was the function of the teacher to bring the students from darkness of ignorance to the light of knowledge. The teacher was also compared to a lamp which would continue to burn by lighting the other lamps to burn.

In earlier periods, teacher enjoyed enormous respect and high status. There are five major reasons for this:

Firstly, he was the 'Guru'; Secondly, he performed complicated rituals and for learning these rituals, the student had to rely completely on the teacher. Thirdly, the student resides at the 'Ashram; i.e., the residence of the teacher. Fourthly, there was a close and intimate relation between the teacher and the student. Fifthly, a teacher had a few students to teach and guide.

Various meanings were attributed to the word teacher according to the functions he performs. They are *Upadhyaya, Acharya* and *Guru.*

An '*Upadhyaya*' was one who taught only a portion of the Vedas and demands reasonable remuneration from the students.

An '*Acharya*' taught the Vedas after having the ceremony of '*Upanayana*'. An 'Acharya' was ten times more venerable than an 'Upadhyaya'. He demands no remuneration.

A 'Guru' was one who having performed all rites delivered instructions in the Vedas. He knows little subject and demands more money from the students.

Besides, in ancient India, the Hindu culture developed two terms called 'Vidya' and 'Avidya', and enjoined on teachers to provide them to the youth that approach them. 'Vidya' means the knowledge with a spiritual aim in order to clarify what a human being is as a microcosm of the universe in contrast to its macrocosm, while the term 'Avidya' was used to indicate knowledge without any such aim by pertaining it to Nature and the external objects. Thus two types of education flourished in those days (spiritual and secular). Furthermore teachers were regarded as God-fathers to the youth that sought education from them. Their role was a totalitarian nature to strive for their spiritual as well as physical welfare, by acting as a friend, guide and philosopher to them.

In the medieval ages also, more or less the same concept continued. But there was a change in the attitude of the people towards functions of a Teacher under the influence of the Muslim rulers.

In the modern age the functioning of a teacher is regarded as transmitting the knowledge contained in the texts to the students. Apart from his academic work, other activities of para-academic and non-academic nature, were also entrusted to him.

We may also note one more development in the Modern period in India. After the introduction of English Education by Lord Macaulay, the old system of *Guru-Shishya* (disciple) relationship has gradually deteriorated and just the functional aspect to *Guru* remained. There is a vast change in curriculum and new subjects have been introduced. Due to the influence of the modern science and technology, the teacher's role has changed a lot. With the change in our value-system too, the commercial value in Education has increased with the result, that the teacher lost his venerated status of the Ancient period.

After the dawn of Independence, our educationists have thoroughly defined the role of a teacher and restored his importance once again in the new educational set up. Kothari Commissioin has stated that the destiny of the nation is shaped within the four walls of the class-room. Hence the teacher is considered to be the Nation builder and moulder of the personalities of children. He is responsible for shaping the character of the students and protecting the democracy. So, the importance of the teacher even in this new era is multidimensional.

Being an ideal inspirer of the student, he is the up-holder of the values and norms of our secular and democratic state. He himself is a democratic leader and he should guard the child in all aspects and bring him up in order to be a useful citizen of the country.

In addition, many media developed in the Modern period ranging from the printed textbook to several audio-visual aids of a varied nature including the T.V. with the result that the teacher's role has become one of co-ordinating, motivating, and supplementing the pupils' knowledge. In the olden days, such media had their conspicuous absence with the result that the Teacher's role was quite a different one. Besides, it is not easy for each and every learner to seek the benefit of knowledge through these media. There will be many gaps in the knowledge which these media convey to children. They have also increased the cost of Education. They have some evil influence too on the children, for they are let loose for use outside the school too. Consequently, a commercial outlook with a lot of negetive impact from them due to the violence and sex to which these media expose them corroding their value-system. How can the Teacher keep up his Morale to be able to cope up with such media which have found their way in educating the young? The role of a Teacher has thus become different and also most problematic in the Modern period, unlike that of his counterpart in the olden days. Yet the impact of the Teacher hasn't become ineffective unless he is negative in his approach and neglectful in his work, with abundant apathy to his duty of causing learning through developing thinking in the Learner.

Importance of Teacher

Besides, the Teacher's role becomes very crucial, in the education of a child whose social horizon has ceased to be confined to the impact, merely from home, parents, and the ancillary smaller group in his neighbourhood, even since he joins the primary school. It should be therefore played very effectively to channelize the socialization process which has already commenced in the child at this stage. Hence the crucial nature of that role. But still the Mass media like T.V. have not freed the child even at this pre-school stage. Besides, the child's horizon has become widened after this pre-school stage, with a lot of increasing social impact which also has become a growing phenomenon when he joins the school at the age of 5 or 6. Therefore the Teacher's role becomes most important, even from the primary Stage of Education and continues to be so till the plus 2 stage is completed, as the pupil at these stages lives first as a child and next as an adolescent. These two stages in the growth of an individual thereofre warrant a proper protective care from the Teacher in order to enable the individual to become an effective citizen in the present day society where a lot of change has taken place resulting in its high modernization. Therefore "A teacher affects enternity; he can never tell where his influence stops," so observed the historian-philosopher, Henry Adams.

For many teachers this is earnestly to be hoped; for others, it may be a despairing development. It seems to be reasonable to assume that good teachers *i.e.,* those who are skillful in developing in the pupil an understanding of the world in which he lives, and stimulating in him an intellectual appetite, patience, sympathetic understanding and sincere feelings for others—may pave the way for an enlightened and productive society. Poor teaching would seem to be a significant contributor of its unfortunate share to the perpetuation of ignorance, misunderstanding and intellectual and cultural stagnation.

The 'goodness' of an educational programme is determined to a large extent by the teaching. The identification of a qualified and able teacher, therefore, constitutes one of the most important factors in all educational concerns. Obtaining capable teachers is a matter of intrinsic interest and obligation to every educational institution. If competent teachers can be obtained, the likelihood of attaining desirable educational outcomes will be substantial. On the other hand, although schools may have excellent material resources in the form of equipments, buildings and text books and although curriculum may be appropriately adapted to the community needs, if the teachers are misfits or are indifferent to their responsibilities, the whole programme is likely to be ineffective and largely wasted. "In the age which is dawning, the school master will find, perhaps to his surprise, that he is the most important person in the world" (*Garforth*, 1962).

The key stone in an educational edifice is doubtless the teacher. A true teacher is rich without money. His wealth is to be reckoned not in terms of bank balances but in the bounteous lore and loyalty he has evoked in his pupils. He is an emperor whose empire is carved in the grateful minds of his pupils, which no power on earth can shake, no atom bomb can destroy. Expert opinion has at last established beyond all doubt, that the quality of education is commensurate with the ability, skill and zeal of the teacher. Through him a nation's culture flows from one generation to another.

Through him more readily than through any other medium, the aspirations of a society can be focused with a lot of persuasion upon the young. He stands at a point of growth where the energies of children are released into new creative possibilities.

The successful running of any educational system depends mainly upon four factors—the teacher, the pupil, the curriculum and the teaching facilities and equipment. Of these, the teacher is the most important one and is the pivot on whom the entire educational structure rests. The other three factors influence his teaching. The noble duty of transforming young children into useful citizens rests on his sincere and sustained effort. So, teaching happens to be the most useful of all nation-building activities. In building up a new world order, the schools must have influence on the community; and the teachers should have the freedom to discuss and to seek truth and understanding for setting up educational patterns according to the needs of the changing world order. In fact, the teacher is the heart of the school and hence the truism 'as is the teacher, so is the school'.

Teacher's Functions

In the present day society where there is a heavy explosion in knowledge and rapid social change, the teacher is required to perform multifarious functions. "He has to socialize, judge, select and classify the students, present equality of opportunity, impart training in democracy or indoctrinate the pupils or make them sensitive to the needs and expectations of the modernizing society of the present and future" (*Anand, et al,* 1983).

The duties and functions of a teacher can be categorised as follows; Planning, Educating, Organising, Supervising, Guiding, Recording, Evaluating and Maintaining good relations. Before proceeding with actual teaching work, he should plan the curriculum as a whole and divide the syllabus into monthly and weekly units. He should also plan the use of Audio-visual Aids, plan the time-table and also plan all the para-academic activities.

Teaching is his first and foremost duty. It is his duty to have a thorough knowledge of the subject he teaches. A teacher has to organise various curricular and co-curricular activities. He has to organise the school plant, library work of the pupils and instructional work.

A teacher has to supervise the work of his pupils. He should ensure regular attendance and regular work of theirs and detect irregularities in the same. He has to check their practical work, written work and supervised study. He has to maintain discipline and order in the school.

The teacher has to guide the students in a number of matters. He has to guide them in their studies. He shall have to recognise the personality, strengths and weaknesses of his pupils and adjust his own attitude and behaviour to them. He has to give guidance to the backward and slow learners. He has to guide and adopt remedial measures for the delinquent, abnormal and maladjusted children. He should also recognize the needs of the gifted pupils and cater to them. In brief, educational, vocational and personal guidance is an essential part of the teacher's duty.

The teacher has to keep record of the work of his pupils and of their day-to-day participation in activities. He has to maintain their admission and attendance particulars. He has to help the school office in maintaining certain school records.

A teacher is expected not only to educate, but also to evaluate the achievement of his pupils from time to time, diagnose weaknesses and spotlight brightness. For this purpose, he has to conduct house tests, score the papers, tabulate marks, determine policies of promotion and prepare results.

Thus, the teacher's role is most crucial at the school stage. Unless and until his morale is high, he can't be motivated well for playing this role effectively. Unless a teacher is equipped with sound morale he can't treat his pupils impartially. A teacher has to function without any prejudice in his profession. Having sound morale is the basis for any teacher to be able to work without fear or favour. All the other factors that contribute to the successful functioning of an educational institution exclusively rest on the sound morale of the teacher for their proper utilisation. Let us now study what is Morale and something about it, in order to be able to carry on this Investigation on Teacher's Morale in an effective manner.

Morale

Every human being needs morale, if he/she is to live and work happily in a society. His individual and personal needs should be satisfied, in order to provide satisfaction to him; but this is done within the parameters of a society. Hence, while his needs are unlimited, his resources that help him to satisfy them within a society are limited. His living in a society enjoins on him certain values on his part. We can call them as 'Moral' values or 'Social' values. For example, one can't eat, without sharing it with, or at least offering it to, others before him, thereby connoting a social value in him. Thus, a teacher who works in the school, works not only to earn his livelihood, but also to serve the society through his profession. So, a certain amount of selflessness, sacrifice, and service mindedness are essential on his part, under the so-called 'Moral' (social) values referred to above. Let us therefore assume tentatively that a human being's morale is concerned with his value system.

While his individual and personal needs give rise to certain 'individual' or 'personal' values; the needs of his existence in a society call for certain 'social' or 'Moral' values on his part. Thus, his value-system needs a balance between these two types of values in him. Without doing so, the Individual and the Society can't perform their functions. Thus, their performance of a functional nature is based upon a value-system which centres round his 'Morale'. It means that the two types of values—personal and social values should be balanced.

The value system prevalent in a group or society thus determines the level of Morale in its members, which in its turn affects the quality of their performance. As already noted, motivation and attitudes are found to have a lot of interrelationships with Morale. We also find that Morale was at its highest ebb in Ancient India, which was promoted by the then culture of her people with plain living and high thinking as one of its characteristics. That culture helped people to become spiritual-minded, dutiful, respectful to elders, most contented, and well motivated in the duties enjoined on them. Value-system also was then quite different from the present value system. People believed in absolute values. Morale was thus high among the people. Naturally Teacher Morale too was high. The Gurus had much voice in the running of their Gurukulas. We can't dream of it under the existing system wherein we have certain subsystems such as those of curriculum, examinations and certification, that have been highly centralized. Thus, there was a lot of decentralization in the olden days. Furthermore, religion became, then the basis of the society and influenced all its secular activities such as medicine, engineering, teaching, etc. which were at their zenith. Teacher morale was naturally very high in those days. It was therefore no wonder that Teacher was regarded as equal to God in the then society.

Gradually all those conditions have changed after the dawn of the Modern period. People's beliefs changed. A secular and material outlook has developed. Reasoning also developed. The old system had more of superstition and dogma which gave place to Reasoning. More than all these, a materialistic outlook has developed while old spiritualistic outlook has became out-dated. Value system too changed a lot. The old absolute values have gone into oblivion; new pragmatic values with a commercial outlook and political tinge have developed. Normally morale of the olden days would deteriorate with such an outlook. Thus, what was regarded as moral in the old society changed a lot, giving rise to problem of Ethics in the modern society where the ethical considerations are given less importance.

Teacher Morale

But teachers are entrusted with society's most valuable asset, the children and they have the responsibility of moulding character and citizenship. The future of democratic education and consequently the future of our democracy depends upon the teacher's success in his profession. It is determined largely by his morale. As the morale of a teacher is indispensable for the successful implementation of educational programme, it is essential to study the factors that affect the teacher morale.

The morale has come to be regarded as a prime requirement for effective organisation in industry as well as in education. Joseph Tiffin (1952) believes that "there is no substitute for morale in an army, in a school and in an industrial plant".

The productivity of a man is determined very largely by the way he feels about his job and other employees with whom he works and by his attitude towards the company that employes him, and these are the things considered for the whole working force which determines the morale of an industrial plant. Hence, it can be pointed out that industrial morale is related to the work-output. Much of the work on morale is done in industry but during the past few years many important educational problems have been attributed to the morale. Besides, the educational research that exists, on morale is fragmentary and static in character. The school administrators knew about the qualities of good teachers but they do not know whether such qualities are born in them or can be developed.

The morale of teachers is difficult to define like the efficiency of a teacher. It is difficult to measure objectively. It can be sensed, and defined. Even though it is illusive, there is proof of it. It can be measured in a number of ways. Industry relates it to the amount of work done in a prescribed time. Management, community organisations and others use an individual's contribution to the group as yard stick.

A better understanding of morale can be had by having a critical probe into some of the definitions given with reference to Morale.

Morale is defined by Little and Onions (1933) as, "A condition, conduct or behaviour with regard to confidence and discipline".

Floyd Honse (1947) defined Morale as, "A measure of will or tendency to act".

Emery Stoops and Lowell Ogdon (1957) defined Morale as, "That glue of intense loyalty, which makes an ordinary working group really great".

Alexander Leighten (1947) defined Morale as, "The capacity of a group of people to pull together persistently and consistently in pursuit of a common purpose".

American Association of School Administration (1955), defined Morale as, "A disposition on the part of persons engaged in an enterprise to behave in ways which contribute to the purpose for which the enterprise exists".

Willard Spalding (1946), defined Morale as, "One of those intangibles of the spirit which is essential if any group is to put forth its best co-operative effort".

For Edward Munson (1946), "Morale is a term which should be used to express the measure of determination to succeed in the purpose for which the individual is trained".

Redefer (1957), defined Morale as, "Teaching rate of Teachers".

The definitions given by Leighten, A.A.S.A. and Spalding considered 'Morale' as a capacity of group of people to pull together for a common purpose, individual's contribution to any enterprise, any group to put forth its best co-operative effort. All these definitions regarded Morale, as a group understanding to put forth its co-operative efforts. This approach may be understood as co-operative or group approach of morale.

Oxford Dictionary and Munson considered Morale as behaviour with confidence, determination to succeed in the purpose for which the individual is trained, while Redefer referred to Morale as the rate of work or an individual efficiency. Redefer considered Teacher Morale, for convenience more than for definitive purpose as the teaching rate of teachers, which implies an economy of effort and an economy of time. So, teacher morale can be understood to mean a morale related to the individual. In the present study of Teacher Morale, the definition referred to above as 'the teaching rate of teachers' has been considered as a workable definition. If the definition 'Teaching rate of teachers' is further analysed—'rate' means 'standard' that means the standard or the efficiency of teaching. Thus, the teacher morale in this study is referred to as the teaching efficiency of the teachers. The moral objective of the teacher is effective teaching to shape his wards entrusted to him by the society. A large number of factors such as physical, intellectual, social, moral, economic etc., affect the teaching rate or the efficiency of teachers. To some extent Teacher's environment too affects his morale.

Thus, Teacher morale may be regarded not only as the behaviour of an individual teacher but also as the work environment provided to him in the school; the latter pertains to the group behaviour mostly at the institutional level that would influence his individual behaviour, and consequently his professional efficiency. The same thing holds good more or less for worker too in any production organization.

Having thus realized what is Teacher morale, let us now study the significance of the problem on hand which pertains to Teacher morale and also the title of the problem. Afterwards we may perhaps state the problem cogently, (b) the objectives of the proposed investigation on this problem, (c) the hypothetical assumptions formulated in this study, and also (d) the limitations under which this study is taken up.

Significance of the Problem

The foregoing discussion on Morale and Teacher morale has prompted me to take up this investigation to study the factors contributing to Teacher morale in Secondary Schools. The problem is one of Primary importance from social as well as educational points of view, for it pertains to Teacher effectiveness which appears as a mirage as well as the need of the hour in the present-day society.

In view of the discussion referred to above on Morale and Teacher morale, we may probably assume that Teacher morale is an important factor which would, in fact, determine Teacher effectiveness. In all human societies, the teacher occupies a pivotal position, for, he moulds the destiny of the future citizens by educating them. Naturally, his role in shaping their destiny is very significant. We are also aware that the Kothari Commission has stated that the destiny of the nation is shaped within the four walls of the class-room. Hence the teacher is considered to be the nation-builder and the moulder of the personalities of children. He is responsible for shaping character of the students and protecting the democracy. So, the importance of the teacher even in this new era is multi-dimensional. Thus, the problem on hand is very significant not only for the Teacher, but also for the society.

It may not be out of place, if a reference is made again to the foregoing discussion made by us on Morale and Teacher morale, wherein we have assumed that Morale involves mainly the non-intellectual part of human personality which relates to certain aspects of social behaviour such as sincerity, interest, motivation, commitment etc. The intellectual part of human personality pertains to aspects of human abilities and skills, while the non-intellectual part of it involves aspirations, and appreciations which go a long way in raising the individual's motivation level.

Again, the above discussion on Morale and Teacher morale would show that it centred round a psychological factor pertaining to two major factors. Firstly, morale is manifest in the individual, influencing his whole personality. So, personality is one major factor that contributes to Teacher morale. Secondly, it is manifest in his group behaviour too, which provides him an Environment either conducive or not conducive to a high morale. So, in this problem, we should deal with certain factors of a psychological nature contributing to Teacher-morale.

When we ponder over the academic deficiencies in our educational system coupled with a moral decline, we find the Teacher afflicted with an unhealthy environment resulting in the deterioration of his morale. A teacher with highest morale and professional commitment is the need of the hour. As has been already stated above, the standards of morale as well as learning in educational institutions have been deteriorating day-by-day due to certain factors like value-crisis, increase of materialistic interests, etc., in the present-day society.

A committed teacher is subjected to lot of criticism in the present-day society for various reasons. So, keeping up high morale has become a problem for the present-day Teacher. Morale is governed by so many factors of academic, administrative, sociological, economic, political and social importance. These factors can't be controlled by any individual properly except through fear. So, it can't be said that if at all one wants to keep up a high morale, one shouldn't be subservient to the other factors which are having their share in moulding the individual's morale. So, we study not only the factors responsible for deterioration of morale, (economic, sociological, and administrative factors), but also those conducive to its enhancement. Thus, both the negative and positive factors should be identified.

But one thing should be noted here. The problem of Teacher-morale is quite different from the problem of educational deterioration. The former is a human problem the latter being a non-human problem of organizational and administrative nature. Both may be interlinked as all human institutions and organizations rest ultimately on the human phenomenon and the individual's motivation as well as morale. So, ultimately, it is the human problem that controls the whole phenomenon of Educational deterioration. While we can set right the non-human problems, easily and within a given time, by taking certain steps with certain educational materials and innovations, in the case of human problems like the one on hand, a developmental activity of long term nature would be required with a sustained and continuous programme of remediation. So, the problem on hand is more a problem of motivation and commitment than possession of mere amenities.

Moreover if a Teacher is inefficient, it is not because he can't or does not teach well. If a teacher is unpopular, it is not that he does not want to do what he is expected to do. If a teacher is cynical or, indifferent, it is not because he is too above his students or colleagues. If a teacher is inefficient, unpopular or cynical and indifferent, it is because his heart is not involved his work. His heart is divorced from his head. While the head is working for earning bread and butter, the heart is not co-operating but playing truant like the so-called 'naughty' boys. So, there is an imbalance in the teacher's mind.

The imbalance is the result of non-cooperation of head and heart. The palestineans' example of the war between the different parts of the body and the stomach, is worth remembering here. So, the balance between the mind and heart works wonders, *i.e.,* man must be intelligent, hard-working, and should also be understanding others' feelings, particularly in the case of a teacher as he is entrusted with improving the children's affective domain. By co-ordinating the intellectual task with the teaching work, he can be a popular teacher and can be admired by the pupils and society at large. As he is the Nation builder the society must attend to the needs of the teacher.

What therefore emrges from the above, is that the teacher morale is a peculiar type of problem. Verily, it is not the problem of Teacher alone in the present-day society; it is a problem of the whole present-day society. It didn't exist in the olden societies in the pre-modern periods, in the manner it exists in the modern societies. It is more a problem of the value system in the society unless the social value is strengthened and vitalized in the individual, we can't have the necessary pre-requisite for Morale. So, it requires a turn, rather a cultural and philosophical revolution, from the present individual-based materialistic values to the social values. This calls for, therefore, a long term action- oriented remediation. Apart from it, a realization of the distinctiveness and the unique responsibility of the Teaching profession may be considered as an additional requisite, for effectivising the Teacher morale. But it should be noted simultaneously that it is the society which supplies the necessary man-power, to this profession too. So, a good training programme also for this profession becomes one positive factor which will go a long way for building up Teacher-morale.

We may also note here, based on the above discussion, that teacher morale is manifest in a social setting of not only his professional duties, but also his life in the society through his family and citizenship. For that matter, every individual's morale is manifest so. Hence it is manifest in the case of Teacher in the course of his interaction with several groups such as pupils, colleagues, superior authorities of his profession, parents of his pupils, visitors to his place of work etc. It helps him to develop certain friendly relations with them, through this interaction for the efficient performance of his duties in the Institution with his pupils to promote their learning. The class work of his teaching schedule, and the various other aspects of his professional duties present several situations for him, for his confrontation, in the course of the above interaction which would not only develop his morale but also manifest it. Most of these situations pertain to academic, para-academic, non-academic activities of his professional domain.

Two major factors seem to affect his morale. They are his personality and his environment. Interaction is only between them. Morale gives a style to it. In fact, human life results in development, as a product of these two factors. Teacher is no exception to it. As an educated person, he must have some potential for adaptation too. Morale in him rests therefore on it.

Based on a study of the above significance of the problem, the investigator has made an endeavour in the course of his investigation to build up his tools of investigation reflecting all the above aspects of the problem highlighted in this discussion.

Need for the Present Investigation

The present system of Education has certain defects due to which Teachers stress too much on imparting of knowledge, that too from an examination point of view only, to the utter neglect of the other aspects pertaining to emotional and social development for cultivating the morale in the budding youth through Education. Consequently, the intellectual side of Education has received too much importance. The social and emotional aspects have become therefore neglected. Textbooks which are the main reading material for the pupils, and the methods of Teaching followed in the class work of the school which are still under the old memoriter system lead to too much of cramming on the part of the pupils. Too much premium on Examinations also makes the learners more interested in learning to write answers to questions. The present examinations mostly test the memory only, rather than the other intellectual abilities. So, they are essay type guestions and of other types which require inventive type of answering rather than the selective type of answering, with the result that learners essentially resort to recitation, mostly unintelligent and mechanical in its nature. No doubt, objective type questions that involve the selective type of answering are also given, but in the present system wherein the Examination subsystem is in too much dominant position over the other subsystems in the existing Educational system, they are answered most mechanically, not only by guessing, but also by malpractices like copying through different methods. Hence their positive value for objective assessment is lost by the learners who are constrained to use most of their time in and outside the schools for learning what should be written to answer, rather than how to answer the questions in the examinations. It is therefore no wonder that the only class room methods under such a set-up would be individualized recitation by the Teacher before the pupils, who naturally become only passive audience with lot of restlessness in the classroom. That is why pupils feel free to let off their pent-up energies when each of their classes comes to a close.

Under such a set-up of Teaching and Learning, one natural tendency would be the resultant latency of Teacher morale and its consequential channelization towards better results in Examinations by means other than the fair means. Consequently, teacher's professional commitment is restricted to getting examination-results only. Yet, many schools fare badly as they are ill- equipped and ill-staffed. Added, we have a very low percentage of passes at the S.S.C. level. When compared to the other levels, these results are very low, revealing only an educational malaise from pupils' sociological point of view.

Besides, the present-day Teacher is afflicted with too much of commercial out-look , due to the dominance of values which are nothing but political and economic, to the neglect of human values.

Naturally, more instruction classes in school become diverted to examination subjects, with a view to spending more time in the school for preparation of pupils for Examinations. Thus, the class-work in schools seems to be taken up more from examination point of view than any other point of view. Then, where is the Teacher-morale in the present set -up?

Let us make here a further consideration of a few more problems affecting the present Education set-up, which seem to have eclipsed the Teacher-morale as stated above. Every human personality needs some morale which will be distinct from the one in the other living beings. The former is based upon the self-consciousness in the human personality, while the latter has purely an instinctive basis. However, the morale in all the living beings helps them for self-preservation and self-propagation on some instinctive basis. In the case of human beings there is an additional faculty which is the discriminating power endowed only to human beings and not to other living beings. A prominent psychologist has therefore preferred a term 'drive' to the term 'instincts' in the case of human beings, as they are modifiable in them while they are not so in the case of other living beings. So, all human beings need a higher morale than the other living beings; this should be based upon their discriminating power; otherwise, they appear as less moral than the latter, as the instinctive base which makes the latter more moral is modified in the former by their discriminative faculty. So, the former should develop their morale most consciously and deliberately through education. The story of the development of the human personality is therefore a story of constant interaction between self (the inner reality) and environment (the outer reality). Thus, every human being has a potential for developing morale which is manifest in a process of interaction in the society. In this process the human personality also grows. So, the individual's personality participates in this interaction giving scope for a higher morale in the human beings. To some extent the values prevalent in the society, influence this morale as already discussed by us in the related section on morale.

Thus while education should enable the human beings to develop this morale, unfortunately the conditions in the present social set-up as well as in the educational set-up have eclipsed the Teacher-

Morale, with the result that the Teacher-Morale, has come to a low ebb and we have the dearth of teachers with commitment in the present educational institutions. To some extent the transformation of values in the present social set-up from the absolute values to pragmatic values and also from the higher values (social values) to the personal values (individual values) is also responsible for the above decline of the Teacher-Morale. Thus, as already stated above the present educational set-up in our country, does not enable the teacher to manifest his morale, with the result that the higher aims of education are not fulfilled well in the present system.

We all know that education has higher aims like the social aim, the cultural aim and the economic aim. The only aim fulfilled is to acquire a certification of the passable superficial attainments in certain academic subjects. Perhaps even the aim of acquiring a higher knowledge is not fulfilled by the present educational system under the various factors discussed above in this section. Naturally the results the pupils acquire in examinations are an out-come of their mechanical responses in the examinations system. In such a background of learning with examination–mindedness and cramming, we are not sure of the extent to which the teacher contributes to these results except superficially. Hence the need for a study of Teacher-morale in the present educational set-up, in order to identify and analyse the factors that contribute to it. It may also help the authorities that be, to channelise their educational policies in a broader perspective in order to foster the necessary commitment in the Teacher.

In the industrial concerns too, priorities are given, as already stated in this chapter, to the development of the worker's morale and motivation for increasing his productivity. Hence the need for this study.

Statement of the Problem

The foregoing discussion in all the previous sections of this chapter showed the importance of Teacher morale for Teacher effectiveness which is necessary for providing qualitative education in the society. We have assumed in the above discussion the following:

a) Morale was very high in Ancient India, thanks for a very high morale in the then Teacher as well as in the society.
b) Morale in the Society as well as in the Teacher have reduced, particularly in the Modern period.
c) Teacher effectiveness too is lowered in the present-day educational institutions, due to several factors.
d) Teacher morale determines Teacher effectiveness.
e) Unfortunately Teacher morale has become beclouded in the present Educational set-up of our country, duly supported by the present value system of a Modernized society.

Based on the above assumptions in the foregoing discussion, the investigator feels it desirable to take up the problem on hand for studying the factors contributing to Teacher morale in Secondary Schools. So after discussing, the significance of this problem, the need for this investigation, it would be probably in fitness of things, if this problem is stated clearly in some reasonable perspective, in order that it is given a proper title and then studied with a suitable strategy of research.

As already stated, Teacher morale is reducing due to several factors. Consequently, standards of education are also reduced. A part of responsibility for this deterioration, rests on the Teacher. His personality is thus one major factor responsible for this deterioration. As already discussed morale is a psychological and sociological issue dependent on certain factors. It is a comprehensive system with certain contributory subsystems. So, it would be better to study the contributory factors that would promote Teacher morale.

We may therefore reasonably assume that among all the academic, para-academic and non-academic factors contributing to the successful functioning of an Educational system, Teacher morale may be regarded as a pivotal force. So, for strengthening it, it is better to study the factors promoting it and their contribution in order to keep up the academic standards. With this object in view, the researcher has taken up the problem on hand with the following title:

"A Study of the Factors Contributing to the Teacher Morale in Secondary Schools"

The working hypothesis of this study is that Teacher morale is influenced by two types of factors namely Teacher Factor and Environmental Factors. Since morale is a psychological concept, it is one of the assumptions of the investigator that majority of the teachers are having high morale. The overall measure of teacher Factor and Environmental Factors is treated as reflecting Teacher-morale in this investigation.

As for the title, the above title is a simplified, direct, brief, significant, logical and clearcut statement which would indicate the problem on hand, with some reasonable appellation. As already stated, this problem raises a psychological and sociological issue, which pertains to Morale. For every functionary in the society, there should be job-satisfaction. His work-efficiency thus rests on his motivation and attitudes. His work styles therefore contribute to it. Ultimately, it is his morale that would help him to maintain a reasonably high level of work-efficiency.

Morale is influenced by certain factors like personality and Environment, as already discussed above. In other words, it involves a system from psychological point of view, and becomes manifest, merely from a sociological point of view, with reasonable contributions from all its subsystems. It is proposed to study in this investigation these factors contributing to Teacher Morale.

A study of these factors might help us to follow up this investigation in order to suggest certain steps for increase of Teacher morale. Hence the present title of the problem.

Besides, keeping in view all these assumptions of an exalted nature on this problem the investigator has worked out also certain objectives of this study in some detail. They have been formulated mainly to direct this study. Certain technical terms are used in this study. The investigator gives hereunder operational definitions of the same.

Operational Definitions of the Title of the Study

The problem taken up in this investigation is studied with the following title with a view to focus the attention of the investigator mainly on certain aspects of this subject; "A study of the factors contributing to the teacher morale in secondary Schools."

1. Study

The term 'Study' is used in this investigation, in order to indicate the process by which the investigator will be able to identify and analyse the factors assumed for the purpose of this investigation.

2. Factors

The term 'Factors' includes the two dimensions, formulated for the purpose of this study; one of them comprises the two major factors *i.e.,* Teacher Factor and Environmental Factors. It includes also the variables selected in the sample.

3. Teacher Morale

The term 'Morale' used in this study, to indicate the conscious commitment of the teacher to his profession in order to promote effectiveness of teaching and thereby provide qualitative education in the society.

4. Secondary Schools

The term 'Secondary Schools' is used in this study to include high schools functioning in Andhra Pradesh with classes VI to X to impart education at two different stages (a) Upper Primary, and (b) Secondary.

5. Secondary School Teachers

This term is used to indicate teachers handling the classes VI to X in Upper Primary and Secondary Stages of Education *i.e.,* Secondary Grade Teachers and B.Ed., Assistants.

Thus, the selected problem has been titled as shown above in a simplified manner with the above terminology for the purpose of the above investigation which is taken up with certain objectives and hypothetical assumptions for studying the phenomena of Teacher morale, with the selected sample on the basis of the foregoing discussion in this chapter on 'Morale', its meaning, importance and implications.

Objectives

The General objective of the present investigation is to study the factors contributing to Teacher Morale among the Secondary School Teachers. Based on the foregoing discussion in this chapter, the investigator assumed that there are two major factors that affect the Teacher Morale.

They are (a) the Teacher Factor and (b) the Environmental Factors.

The investigation has been designed with the following specific objectives, with reference to the above general objective:

1. To identify the distribution of morale in the Teacher Population.
2. To find out whether the teachers manifest their morale equally in Teacher Factor and Environmental Factors.
3. To identify whether the morale scores in Teacher Factor and Environmental Factors are equal in each of the subsamples.
4. To identify the influence of the variables selected under this study on Teacher Morale.
5. To identify whether all the areas included under the Teacher Factor manifest Teacher Morale equally.
6. To identify whether all the areas included under the environmental Factors manifest Teacher Morale equally.
7. To find out whether the morale components (areas) of Teacher Factor and the morale components of Environmental Factors have any relationship.
8. To study the teachers' responses item-wise under the Teacher Factor and the Environmental Factors, and thereby identify the items and their areas falling in each of the points within the 3 pt scale.

Hypotheses

According to John Best, "Hypothesis is a shrewed guess or inference that is formulated and provisionally adopted to explain observed facts or conditions and to guide further investigation."

According to Carter, V.Good, " A hypothesis is an informed guess or inference, with a reasonable chance of being right, formulated and tentatively adopted to explain observed facts or conditions and to guide in further investigation. A hypothesis serves as a powerful beacon that lights the way for the research worker."

The following tentative hypotheses are formulated to study the present problem of investigation:

1. Teacher Morale is distributed in any given group as per the pattern of Normal Probability Distribution.
2. Morale in terms of Teacher Factor does not necessarily differ from the one in terms of Environmental Factors.
3. Morale scores under the Teacher Factor do not differ from those under the Environmental Factors, in any of the subsamples.
4. All the areas included in the Teacher Factor and Environmental Factors reveal the Teacher Morale, equally.
5. The impact of the several variables selected in this investigation would be the same on Teacher Morale.
6. Teacher-Morale which would be surveyed in this investigation, would be revealed consistently item wise also.
7. Morale components (areas) of the two constituent factors of Teacher Morale would be related positively.

It is proposed to design the tools of this survey with the help of the above hypothetical as assumptions, in relation to the objectives of this study.

Limitations of the Study

The researcher confined the investigation to a study of the factors contributing to the Teacher Morale in Secondary Schools. The researcher delimited the investigation to the study of two major factors, namely 'Teacher Factor' and 'Environmental Factors' which contribute to the Teacher Morale. These two major factors are further subdivided with identical factors as six sub factors; they are presented hereunder:

Teacher Factor

1. Personality Factor

2. Professional Aspirations
3. Professional Skills
   (a) Academic Proficiency
   (b) Teaching Ability
   (c) Organising Skills
   (d) Linguistic Proficiency.

Environmental Factors

1. School Facilities
2. School Administration
3. Educational Administration
4. Environmental Impact
   (a) Family
   (b) Community
   (c) Value System.

In this study, the investigator has used a sample of 630 teachers belonging to different grades with different qualifications. The sample was identified by stratifications into different variables like Age, Sex, Qualification etc. Some of the limitations of the study are mentioned hereunder:

1. Certain factors like marital status, religion, income, family size and the other aspects of private life are not taken into account in the present study, due to time-constraint.
2. The researcher limited the study only to the Secondary School Teachers, handling the classes VI to X working under different educational managements in the Krishna District of Andhra Pradesh.
3. The area of investigation is also limited to one district i.e., Krishna District only because of certain administrative conveniences to the investigator. Moreover this is one of the few districts in Andhra Pradesh with high rate of educational growth.

A map of Andhra Pradesh showing the area under Investigation is given in Figure No.2.

FIGURE—2

Map of Andhra Pradesh showing the area under investigation

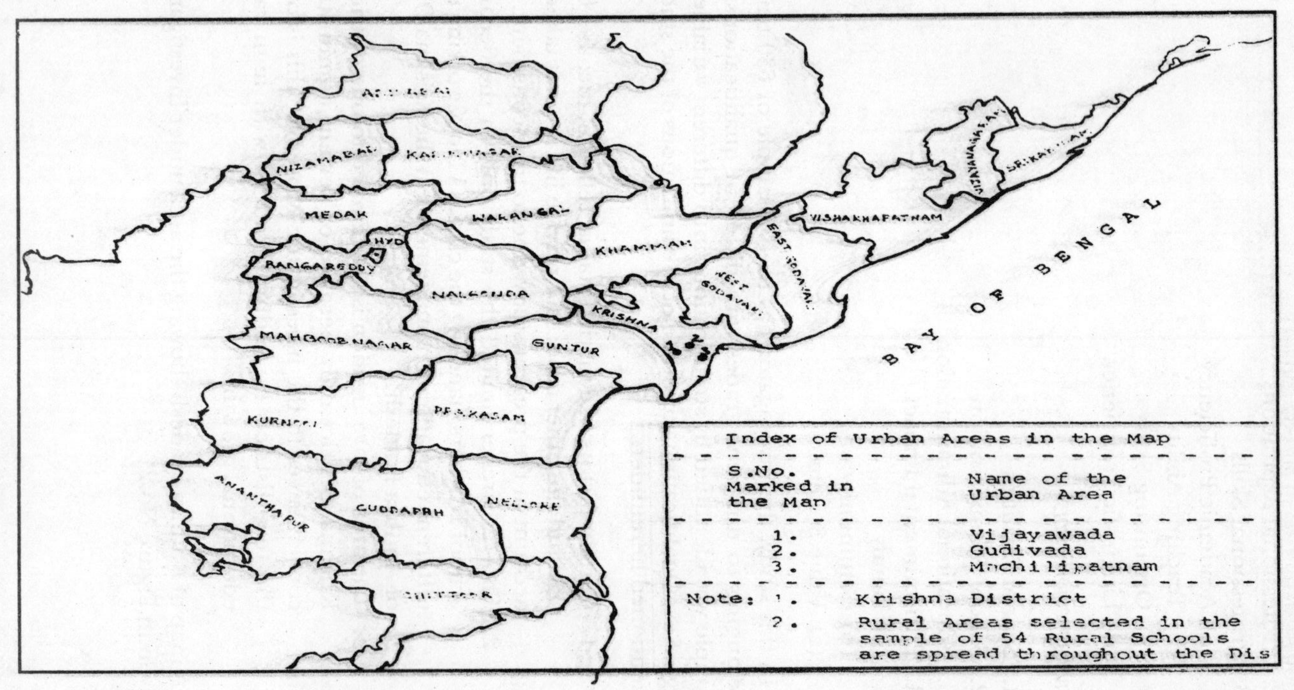

2

REVIEW OF RELATED LITERATURE

In the introductory chapter, the researcher made a thorough discussion of the problem on hand, in its various perspectives. After having discussed so, the researcher set apart this chapter for a detailed discussion of the previous investigations done on the allied subjects.

Good, Barr and Scates state thus:

> *"The competent physician must keep abreast of the latest discoveries in the field of medicine... obviously the careful student of education, the research worker and investigator... should become familiar with the location and use of sources of educational information."*

Study of the related literature implies locating, reading and evaluating reports of research as well as reports of casual observation and opinion that are related to the individual's planned research project.

In the words of Borg, R.W.,

> *The literature in any field forms the foundation upon which all future work will be built. The author further observes that if we fail to build this foundation of knowledge provided by the review of the literature, our work is likely to be shallow and will often duplicate work that has already been done better by some one else.*

A review of the related literature gives the scholar an understanding of the previous work that has been done. It develops in the investigator an insight he needs to convert his tentative research problem to a specific and concise one. It helps the research possibilities that have been overlooked. It provides the researcher, with an opportunity for understanding the methods, measures, subjects and approaches employed by other research workers. This in turn will lead to significant improvement of his research design.

Much of the work in the field of Morale has been done specifically in industry. The field of Education has shown much interest in morale as it relates to job satisfaction in teaching, but this interest has resulted more in the voicing of opinions than in attempts to do research on the problem adequately. It is a serious criticism of the educational profession that this vital problem has been attacked hardly at all in the field of education, particularly in Andhra Pradesh. However, there are a few limited investigations in different parts of the world and in India that have been made by school workers and these are summarised briefly here with.

Hocking, W.E. (1918) in his study of 'Morale and its Enemies' reports a number of factors which can be applied to school conditions. He states that morale will be enhanced by:

(a) Proper time in which to accomplish work,
(b) good physical conditions,
(c) confidence in one's skill and ability,
(d) respect and co-operation from the community,
(e) elimination of friction, and
(f) appeals to the imagination and ambition.

Dorsey, S.M. (1930) in the study of "promoting friendliness in school relationships" reports that morale will be improved by:

(a) fair teacher's load assignments,
(b) good physical surroundings,
(c) some supervision,
(d) Proper salary tenure and retirement provisions,
(e) sabbatical years,
(f) sick leave, and
(g) full credit given for all participation and contribution.

Fosdick, S.J. (1939) in his report to the National Retail Dry Goods Association Reports that morale will be improved by:

(a) credit for work done,
(b) interest in work,
(c) fair pay,
(d) understanding and appreciation,
(e) counsel on personal problems,
(f) promotion on merit,
(g) good physical working conditions, and
(h) job security.

Rorer, J.A. (1942) believes that good morale is a desirable bye-product of successful supervision rather than a major aim or purpose. There are many things which are known to build up the morale of teachers such as:

(a) better preparation,
(b) working on co-operative projects,
(c) adequate salary schedule,
(d) tenure protection,
(e) confidence in the worthwhileness of teaching,
(f) recognition of every day effort,
(g) school and community friendships,
(h) community support,
(i) affiliation with teachers organisations.

American Association of School Administrators (1944) reports the following factors for the enhancement of morale:

(a) mutual support from other staff members,
(b) effective organisation of teachers,
(c) community leadership in projects for human betterment, and
(d) worthy objectives.

Barr and others (1944) based on various studies summarise the following factors which are essential for maintenance of morale. They emphasised health as a prime requisite for morale. The other factors include:

(a) community respect,
(b) desirable social life,
(c) comfortable living conditions,

(d) minimising interference with private life,
(e) sound orientation of new staff members,
(f) invitation in policy making,
(g) confidence and security in administration by means of consistent policy.
(h) selection, appointment and promotion on merit,
(i) adequate salary schedule,
(j) reasonable security tenure,
(k) retirement provision or annuity plans,
(l) mental and physical health,
(m) fair policy of sick leave, reasonable ease of security, sabbasticals for travel or study.

Baehr, M.E. and Renck, R. (1950) in their study, "The Definition and Measurement of Employee Morale" report five primary factors for morale. They used a combination of item and category analysis, and the factors are:

(a) organisation and management,
(b) immediate supervision,
(c) material rewards,
(d) fellow employees, and
(e) job satisfaction

Hill, C.M. and Morrisett, L.N. (1951–52) in a survey of the Pasadena city schools reported the following factors which effect the morale:

(a) Physical working conditions,
(b) belongingness and participation,
(c) supervisory relationships,
(d) policies and practices,
(e) pay,
(f) communications.

Multiple choice questions were prepared covering a number of items in each area. By using IBM cards and tabular procedures, numerous impersonal comparisons were made.

Braem, W. (1957) in his study, reports that some psychological bases for morale can be found in such factors as:

(a) justice,
(b) recognition,
(c) leadership,
(d) achievement,
(e) security,
(f) mental health, and
(g) physical fitness.

Hunter, E.C. (1955) studied, "Attitudes and Professional relationships of teachers—A study of Teacher Morale." The study was conducted in the New Orleans Public Schools. He reported the following factors for the enhancement of the morale:

(a) proper school discipline,
(b) adequate supplies and equipment,
(c) proper teaching load,
(d) financial security,
(e) recognition and reward for exceptional services,
(f) evaluation of proper worth,
(g) promotion and advancement on merit only.

Wiles, K. (1955) in a survey of over 1,000 students in his graduate discussion groups found that the following were the most frequently listed factors for job satisfaction:

(a) security and comfortable living,
(b) pleasant working conditions,
(c) fair treatment,
(d) a sense of belongingness,
(e) a sense of achievement and growth,
(f) recognition of contribution,
(g) participation in deciding policy,
(h) opportunity to maintain self-respect.

Mathis, C. (1959) studied "The Relationship between salary policies and Teacher Morale". In constructing the inventory, the researcher has taken five attitude areas:

(a) self attitudes about the self, in relation to the role played in the school system;

(b) school attitudes about the immediate aspects of the school situation such as working conditions equipment and the physical plant;
(c) community attitudes about the community, in which the school is located;
(d) administration attitudes about the way, the school is administered and attitudes about the people who administered.
(e) policy attitudes, concerning the policies and policy making functions related to the school system.

Multiple choice questions were prepared covering a number of items in each area. Fifty statements were finally selected under each area consisting of 10 items. He administered the inventory in 10 sub-urban schools. Altogether he collected 614 inventories. The analysis revealed that:

(1) No significant difference in morale level was found between schools grouped on the basis of type of salary schedule;
(2) A significant difference in level of morale was found between the 10 schools involved in the sample, as measured by the attitude inventory;
(3) No significant differences in indication of morale level were found between areas of the attitude inventory.

Suchr, J.H. (1962) in his 'Study of Morale in Education' constructed as instrument, of the incomplete sentences type. One hundred items were taken and submitted to 67 teachers of various parts of the country for choice of items most suitable. From their selection 40 items were broadly classified as:

(a) community respect,
(b) professional organisation,
(c) teacher assignments,
(d) good working conditions,
(e) channels of communication,
(f) policy,
(g) confidence in school administration,
(h) personal problems,
(i) relations with principal,
(j) team work among teachers,
(k) relations with pupils,
(l) teacher welfare,

(m) fair salary, and
(n) fringe benefits.

The following conclusions were reached by him as a result of this study:

(1) Childhood background of teachers;
(2) Personality differences;
(3) Cause and effect relationships;
(4) Communication;
(5) Teacher motivation;
(6) Human relations;
(7) Recognition of teaching profession;
(8) Mental health.

These were found to be most important factors for the enhancement of the teacher morale.

William, C.M. and Wingo, G.M. (1962) in their book 'Psychology and Teaching' have listed the following factors for choosing teaching profession:

(1) Independence
(2) Social acceptance
(3) Interest in children
(4) Liked by children
(5) Liking for teaching
(6) Command in subject matter
(7) Security in job
(8) Vanguard of change.

Richardson, R.C. (Jr.) and Blocker, C.E. (1963) made a study of 'Faculty Morale' by using the factor-analytic technique. A differential Morale Attitude Inventory was constructed. In the inventory twelve areas were hypothesised:

(1) Communication,
(2) Confidence in administration
(3) Relations with immediate supervisor
(4) Relations with fellow employees
(5) Relations with students
(6) Status and recognition
(7) Identification with the institution

(8) Professional growth and advancement
(9) Adequacy of salary
(10) Adequacy of fringe benefits
(11) Work environment and
(12) Work load.

Eighty five items were taken and submitted to ten judges for assigning the statements to the hypothesised categories. Eleven statements were eliminated and seventy four were combined in an attitude inventory and administered to sixty six faculty members of a Mid-Western Junior College. The twelve categories of the inventory were subjected to a principal axis factor analysis. After varimax rotations four factors were tentatively identified:

1. Supervision,
2. Self-integration,
3. Institutional environment and
4. Employment rewards.

Jayamma, M.S. (1962) undertook a study to construct and standardise an inventory for predicting teacher efficiency of primary school teachers particularly for use in Karnataka State. The investigator prepared a questionnaire consisting of two parts—65 items in part 'A' and 35 items in part 'B' The variables studied were:

(1) Professional knowledge and skill,
(2) Acquaintance with the principles of psychology,
(3) Class Management, School organisation and Educational Administration,
(4) Relationship with others, and
(5) Individual quailties of humour, patience and sympathy.

The sample consisted of five hundred teachers drawn from sixty institutions. The Chi-square test was used to find the significance of the items. Biserial 'r' and the indices of difficulty value of the items were calculated. The five sub-tests were correlated with the whole test. The order of the sub-tests, showed that the first area was professional skill and interest, which was the best measure of efficiency. The other observations were:

(i) A teacher's professional success was in no way influenced by sex or the locality of work; and

(ii) Training, experience and qualifications could add to the professional success.

Shamusuddin, (1968) in his study on 'Teaching as a Career' has listed the following factors influencing the choice of school teaching as a career under two major headings—'External' and 'Internal':

External: (1) Suggestions by parents and well-wishers;
(2) Family circumstances;
(3) Fringe benefits;
(4) Ease of the job.

Internal (1) Natural liking for teaching profession,
(2) Betterment in studies.

Debnath, H.N. (1971) in his study reported some determinants of teaching efficiency. Two hundred and twenty six Headmasters selected by Stratified Random sampling served as the sample of the study. The variables studied here were: Age, Experience, Academic achievement and Training. A questionnaire and an evaluation sheet for observation of the lesson were developed in order to study the effectiveness of the lesson. Both Quantitative and Qualitative methods were used for data collection. The important correlates of teaching efficiency, as found in the study were: knowledge of the subject matter, sincerity in teaching, mastery of the method of teaching, academic qualifications, mode of exposition, sympathetic attitude towards students, discipline, student's participation, proper use of aids and appliances in teaching and the art of questioning. Analysis of data gathered through questionnaires revealed that professional training, intelligence, interest in teaching, friendliness, democratic behaviour, ability to judge reactions of others, and possession of all round information were related to teaching efficiency. The findings through actual class-room observations revealed that age, experience, academic achievement and professional training were the significant determinants of teaching efficiency.

National Council of Educational Research and Training (1971) undertook a survey to determine the extent of the teachers' acceptance of the role in which they find themselves. The objectives of the survey were:

(1) to know how teachers reacted to various issues related to their professional life and efficiency, and
(2) to study as to how the above reactions were related to the factors like Management, Area, Sex, Age, Experience, Academic and Professional Qualifications, Marital Status etc.

It was hypothesised that the attitudes of teachers towards the profession are not affected by management, area in which the school is situated, tenure of service, sex, marital status, age, experience, academic qualifications and professional qualifications. The sample consisted of 6,558 teachers. The final scale consisted of thirty four statements. Major findings of the study were:

(1) The attitude of teachers differed significantly under different managements.
(2) The tenure of service did not affect the attitude of teachers.
(3) The attitude of male and female teachers differed significantly.
(4) Marital status did not influence the attitude of teachers towards the profession.
(5) Younger teachers showed more positive attitude towards the profession than older teachers.
(6) Experience and positive attitude were inversely proportionate.
(7) Teachers with lower educational qualifications were having more positive attitude towards the profession than the teachers with higher educational qualifications.
(8) The attitudes of trained and untrained teachers did not differ significantly on negative items.
(9) Training appeared to be a contributing factor in the development apparent positive attitudes.

Pandey, G.S. (1973) studied, "Teachers adjustment in relation to professional efficiency". An adjustment inventory to measure the adjustment in six areas (*viz.,*) Health, Home, Social, Economic, Institutional and Ethical was constructed. To measure professional efficiency, a five-point rating scale was constructed to rate the knowledge of the subject, understanding of pupils, knowledge of methodology, expression, class management, use of teaching devices, organisation of co-curricular activities, voice and speech, health and physique, initiative and resourcefulness. The sample consisted of teachers drawn from thirty three higher secondary schools located in Uttar Pradesh. The findings revealed the following:

(1) The correlation studies of male and female teachers indicated positive relationship between all the five elements of adjustment. The strength of relationship showed that each element contributed something towards others in the process of adjustment.
(2) The cross validity indices of male and female teachers indicated that the regression equations with their assigned weights withstood the test of cross validation.

Nair, S.R. (1974) made a study to find out the impact of certain sociological factors like family background, caste, religion and sex on the teaching ability of teachers. A total of 200 secondary school teachers from Trichur district of Kerala were selected as sample. Particulars about their socio-economic status, age, etc., were collected in person. The teaching ability was evaluated by their Head Masters and pupils, using an evaluation sheet and a pupil's rating scale, respectively. The data were analysed using critical ratio and correlation. The findings revealed that:

(1) Teacher's parental socio-economic conditions had a negative influence on teaching ability.
(2) The private school teachers in general were found to have better teaching ability than Government school teachers.
(3) Sex was not found to be affecting teaching ability.
(4) The locality of the schools had no significant influence on teaching ability.
(5) A positive relationship existed between age and teaching ability.
(6) Caste and religion were not found to be affecting teaching ability.

The purpose of Chaya's (1974) study was to investigate certain psychological characteristics of an effective teacher and to compare them with those of an ineffective teacher. The investigation considered the following six characteristics.

(1) Personality Adjustment
(2) Attitude towards teaching
(3) Interest in Teaching
(4) Emotional Stability
(5) Extroversion *Vs.* Introversion and
(6) Authoritarianism.

From twenty schools of Kanpur, 100 ineffective and 80 effective teachers were selected. The teachers were categorised as effective or ineffective based on the High School Board Examination results for three years. The Sexena's Personality Adjustment Inventory was used to measure personality adjustment of teachers. A Thurstone type scale constructed by the investigator was used to measure attitude towards teaching. The Sub-test III of the test developed by Shah was used to measure interest in teaching. The Hindi version of the Maudsley Personality Inventory was used to measure emotional stability and Exroversion *Vs.* Introversion. The Raina's F–scale was used to measure authoritarianism.

The major findings of the study were

(1) Effective teachers had significantly better personality adjustment and more favourable attitudes towards teaching than ineffective teachers.
(2) Effective teachers did not show significantly more interest in teaching than ineffective teachers.
(3) Effective teachers were significantly more emotionally stable than ineffective teachers.
(4) Effective teachers were not more extrovert than ineffective teachers.
(5) Ineffective teachers were more authoritarian than effective teachers.
(6) Age and Sex of a teacher had a significant relationship with the effectiveness of teaching.
(7) Rurality or urbanity and marital status of a teacher had no significant relationship with the effectiveness of teaching.

Pillai, J.K.'s (1974) study on 'Organisational Climate—Teacher Morale and School Quality' was planned to determine the extent to which the organisational climate of schools and faculty morale in the school were related to the quality of schools. The sample consisted of 190 secondary schools, selected from Tamil Nadu State. The tools administered were:

(1) the organisational climate Description Questionnaire of Horpin and Croft
(2) the Bentley and Rempell's Purdue Teacher Opinionnaire

(3) an Inventory Scale prepared by the investigator to assess the innovative ability of the school, and
(4) a questionnaire for demographic data and pupil performance data. Pearson product-moment correlation was used to analyse the data.

The major findings of the study were as follows

(1) Performance of pupils was significantly better in open and autonomous climate schools than in schools of other climate types.
(2) Performance of pupils in high morale school was superior to that of the average morale schools which in turn was better than the low morale schools.
(3) The ability of the school to introduce innovation in educational practices was higher in high morale schools than the average or low morale schools.
(4) Higher the faculty morale, quicker and better was the school introducing newer practices.
(5) Both climate and morale were positively and highly related to both criteria, namely, pupil performance and innovative ability of schools.
(6) Curricular issues, school facilities and services, community support of education, rapport among teachers, teacher salary, satisfaction with teaching, teacher rapport with principal, community pressures, teacher status and teacher load were found to contribute to pupils performance in schools.
(7) The innovative ability of the school was significantly related to the three climates (viz.,) esprit, thrust and disengagement.
(8) The four morale dimensions namely, school facilities and services, curricular issues teacher salary and community pressures were found to influence the innovative ability of the schools.
(9) There was a high correlation between climate and morale.

Sharma, M.L. (1974) investigated into the "Organisational climate of secondary schools of Rajasthan". To collect the necessary data, a sample of 1,066 secondary schools spread over twenty seven districts were taken.

The tools used for the study were

(1) the Halpin and Croft's OCDQ
(2) the Halpin and Winer's LBDQ, and
(3) simple five-point scales to measure 'teacher satisfaction', 'principal effectiveness' and 'school effectiveness'. Factor analysis was used to identify the basic factors underlying organisational climate. Chi-square test and multiple regression equation technique were also used in the analysis of data. In addition to identifying the eight dimensions of organisational climate given by Halpin, some new dimensions, namely, psychological hindrance, Alienation controls and Humanised thrust were also found out. The results of the study were in consonance with the findings of Halpin and Croft. With respect to the Principal's behaviour significant positive correlations were found between
   (i) faculty age and 'Dis-engagement',
   (ii) faculty size and disengagement,
   (iii) teacher satisfaction and school climate,
   (iv) Head Master effectiveness and school climate,
   (v) leadership behaviour of the principal and school climate,
   (vi) esprit, controls and humanised thrust,
   (vii) school academic achievement index and humanised thrust, and
   (viii) school climate and teacher satisfaction, Headmaster effectiveness and school effectiveness.

Chhabra, N. (1975) undertook a study of 'Certain social psychological variables relating to teachers morale at secondary and college levels' with the following objectives in view.

(1) To make a comparative survey of a sample of secondary and college teachers of Meerut district relating to variables like morale, teachers adjustment, study habits and values, and
(2) to explore differences on the above variables relating to sex, length of teaching experience and level of academic attainment.

The sample comprised of 410 teachers. The tools used in the study were:

(1) the purdue Teachers Morale Inventory (Indian adaptation),
(2) the Bell's Adjustment Inventory (Adult form),
(3) an adaptation of the Jain's study Habits Inventory, and

(4) the Kulshresta's study of values. The statistics used include computation of means, standard deviations and coefficients of correlation.

Some of the major findings were

(1) Female teachers possessed higher morale than male teachers
(2) Level of academic attainment had no bearing on teacher's morale.
(3) There was a positive and significant correlation between morale and study habits, morale and adjustment.
(4) There was a negative relationship between morale and economic values of male teachers
(5) As far as morale and political values were concerned, the relationship was positive with respect to male teachers and it was absent in case of female teachers.
(6) Positive relationship existed between morale and study habits.
(7) The teaching adjustment had no relationship with their professional experience.
(8) Length of teaching experience did not show significant relationship with study habits.
(9) Male teachers placed prime importance to aesthetic values and social values, whereas female teachers gave this place to religious values.
(10) It was found that the Principal's interest in teachers and their problems, lack of co-operation among teachers, inter departmental and intra-departmental conflicts, contacts with students, salary policies, regularity of payment, feeling of economic security, prestige and status given to teaching profession and teacher-taught ratio were some of the factors affecting teacher morale.

Franklin, I. (1975) studied the "Organisational Climate and Teacher Morale in Colleges of Education in Gujarat". Three standaradized instruments, the OCDQ (Halpin and Croft), the LBDQ (Halpin and Winer) and the PTO (Bensley) were used, besides a self-devised questionnaire on 'effectiveness of teacher education programme'. A proforma on personal data was also developed by the investigator to collect further data. Other data gathering techniques employed were participant and non-participant observation and interview. The data were collected from a sample of 35 colleges. The statistical measures employed were; contingency coefficient, coefficient of correlation by product-moment method, analysis of variance and 't' test.

Some of the major findings of the study were

(1) The openness of climate in contrast to closedness of the climate did not lead to high or low effectiveness of the teacher education programme.
(2) There was no significant difference, in morale of teacher educators with an urban background and those with rural background.
(3) Morale of teacher educators was not significantly related to the number of years of teaching experience of the teacher educators.

The major objective of Singh, S.K.'s (1976) study was to examine the relationship between some personality variables and teaching effectiveness. The sample consisted of ten superior, ten average and ten inferior student-teachers out of 164 student-teachers of 1972-73 batch of Tilakdhari Teachers Training College, Jaunpur, Uttar Pradesh. The instruments used in the study were:

(1) the Thematic Apperception Test, and
(2) a Rating Scale to measure the teaching stimulus of the teacher by the observer which included fifty characteristics relevant to the teaching effectiveness in the areas, such as
   (a) knowledge of the subject,
   (b) communicability,
   (c) sincerity,
   (d) ability to stimulate,
   (e) intelligence,
   (f) responsibility,
   (g) honesty,
   (h) emotional balance,
   (i) punctuality,
   (j) appearance,
   (k) resourcefulness,
   (l) judgement and reasoning,
   (m) sense of dedication,
   (n) helpfulness, and
   (o) ability to organise.

The major findings were as follows

(1) Prominent needs of inferior teachers were succourance, deference and play.
(2) The most prominent needs of superior teachers were achievement counteraction and aggression.
(3) The organisation pattern of superior teachers was generally logical and that of inferior teachers was emotional.
(4) The superior teachers used more literary language than average and inferior teachers.

Samron Pengru (1976) studied 'Organisational Climate and Teacher Morale in Secondary Schools in Central Zone of Thailand. Sixty secondary schools were selected randomly from the total of 105 schools in the city of Bangkok and round about provinces. The data were collected with the help of three tools developed by the investigator (*viz.,*) tool on organisational climate, tool on teacher morale, and tool on leadership behaviour. The study showed the following:

(1) In the central zone of Thailand, majority of Schools belonged to the intermediate climate type and the least belonged to the closed climate type. The open climate schools constituted thirty per cent of the total number of schools.
(2) Open climate schools had higher mean scores on dimensions of Esprit, Intimacy, and Communication.
(3) Of the total sampled schools, thirty seven per cent had high teacher morale, thirty three per cent had average teacher morale and thirty per cent schools had low teacher morale.

Dekhtanwala, P.B. (1977) studied "Teacher Morale in secondary Schools of Gujarat" in the year, 1977.

The important objectives of the study were

(1) to construct and standardise a teacher morale inventory to measure morale of the secondary school teachers of Gujarat State, ·
(2) to study the morale of teachers in schools of Gujart in relation to various regions, area, types of schools, size and achievement of schools, and

(3) to subject the results of the developed inventory to factor analysis. The teacher morale inventory was standardized.

The sample comprised of 1,220 secondary teachers. Means, Standard deviations and 't' values were found out. The data were subjected to factor analysis by the principle axis method.

The major findings of the study were

(1) Teachers of South Gujarat region possessed highest morale whereas Kutch-Saurashtra manifested lowest morale.
(2) There was significant relationship between teacher morale and achievement of students, but no significant relationship was found in relation to size of the schools, types of the schools and area of the schools.
(3) No significant relationship was found between teachers morale and teachers experience.
(4) Through factor analysis, thirteen factors were extracted. They were teacher characteristics and leadership behaviour, teacher feelings towards teaching profession, teacher cheerfulness, group cohesiveness, rationality and efficiency towards the teaching profession, leadership behaviour and teaching profession, leadership behaviour and teaching efficiency, satisfaction with the school climate, school climate and teacher work load, feelings towards the institution, community support, teacher zeal and extra effort, satisfaction towards the job and attitude towards the job.

In this study on 'Institutional Climate as a factor of Staff Morale', Mehta, A.V. (1977) formulated the following objectives:

(1) To develop two research instruments to identify, describe and evaluate institutional climate and teacher morale of the sampled colleges.
(2) To find out whether perceptions of different dimensions of institutional climate by principals and teachers differ significantly.
(3) To inquire into possible effects, some institutional and some teacher variables, leave on institutional climate.
(4) To determine whether any significant relationship exists between

(a) Climate and teacher morale in general and

(b) Dimensions of institutional climate and factors of teacher morale in particular.

(5) To find out the relationship between types of institutional climate and student control ideology. The stratified sample consisted of 122 colleges. The tools used were:

(1) Institutional Climate Description Questionnaire (ICDQ), and

(2) The College Teacher Morale Opinionnaire (CTMO) and

(3) Student Control Ideology (SCI). Standard procedures were used to analyse the data. The statistical techniques used were the 't' test, 'F' test, Chi-square and Regression Equation.

The major findings of the study were as follows

(1) About half the number of colleges were found to manifest closed climate.

(2) The two negative behaviours of principals were 'aloofness' and 'consideration'.

(3) Marked variations existed between different faculties of colleges of Gujarat University in general.

(4) The teachers belonged to the 'Average Morale' category.

(5) Faculty wise variations were significant but size of the colleges and location did not significantly relate to morale of teachers.

(6) Teacher Morale and Institutional climate were related at 0.01 level.

(7) Significant faculty wise differences were found in mean perceptions of teachers on custodial and humanistic control ideology.

(8) Positive and significant inter-relationships existed among institutional climate, teacher morale and student control ideology of the teachers of affiliated colleges.

Mahatma, C.M.'s (1980) study on "class room Ethos and their Relationship with Teacher Behaviour Characteristics and Teacher Morale, was planned to determine the nature and characteristics of ideal class rooms and its relationship with the teacher's class room behaviour. The sample consisted of 1,234 boys and 480 girls selected from schools belonging to five districts of Bikaner and Jodhpur ranges.

The major objectives of the study were

(i) to make a survey of classroom ethos as perceived by the tenth grade students of Bikaner and Jodhpur ranges of Rajasthan,
(ii) to identify the characteristic patterns, ALP themes and educativeness of tenth grade actual and ideal class-room,
(iii) to identify the actual and ideal ethos patterns of Hindi, Social Studies, Mathematics and General Science subjects.
(iv) to predict the educative life of different classrooms of tenth grade in the light of educational ethos.

The major findings of the study were

(i) Classrooms were generally characterized as personally-supportive milieu, less interactive and less democratic in the real teaching-learning situations.
(ii) Students desired more autonomy for decision making and interpersonal cooperation or support for effective group actions.
(iii) The classrooms of mathematics were generally characterized as co-operative supportive milieu inter-personally. The classrooms were oriented to the desired accomplishment of group tasks and the clarification of personal experience.
(iv) The authenticity aspect of tenth grade actual classrooms was significantly related to autocratic democratic, harsh-kindly, evading-reasonable etc., characteristic s of the teacher's classroom behaviour.

Jain, B.'s (1982) study was to investigate the relationship between the teachers' attitudes towards profession and their morale and classroom behaviour patterns of teachers. The sample of the study consisted of 100 trained graduate teachers teaching mathematics in class VIII of government higher secondary schools of Delhi.

The objectives of the study were to find out the relationships between

(i) the teachers' attitude towards profession and the classroom behaviour patterns of teachers,
(ii) the teachers' morale and the classroom behaviour patterns of teachers,
(iii) the teacher's values and the classroom behaviour patterns of teachers,

(iv) the teachers' attitude towards profession and the teachers' morale,

(v) the teachers' morale and the teachers' values, and

(vi) the teachers' values and the teachers' attitude towards profession, and to predict the classroom behaviour patterns of teachers through the teachers' attitude towards their profession, the teachers' morale and the teachers' values taken in combination.

The findings of the study were

(i) Male teachers devoted more time in asking questions than female teachers.

(ii) Pupils interacted differently in the classes of married, unmarried or deserted teachers.

(iii) Teachers with a positive attitude towards child centered practices, educational process, pupils and teachers devoted more time to asking questions in the classroom while guiding the more content-oriented part of the class discussions.

(iv) Teachers with a positive attitude towards teaching profession, classroom teaching, child centred practices and educational process reacted to ideas and feelings of pupils and frequently created an emotional climate in the classroom.

(v) Pupils interacted more in the classes of teachers having a positive attitude towards teaching profession, pupils and teachers.

(vi) There was significant Positive relationship between teachers' status and teachers' questions.

(vii) Teachers who had full freedom to discuss controversial issues in the classroom, asked more questions.

(viii) Pupils interacted more in the classes of the teachers who enjoyed rapport with the principal.

(ix) Pupils interacted less in the classes of teachers having political and religious values.

(x) Sex was not significantly related to any dimension of the teacher's morale.

(xi) There was significant positive relationship between the age of teacher and the religious value.

(xii) Married, unmarried and deserted teachers differed with respect to theoretical value.

(xiii) The interference of the community in educational programmes was not favoured by teachers.

Sharma, R.C., (1984) undertook a study of the prospective teachers' Teaching aptitude, intellectual level and morality.

The objectives of the study were

(1) to find out aptitude, intellectual level and morality of prospective teachers,
(2) to compare these factors between male and female teachers and
(3) to compare teachers of different disciplines in relation to these factors.

The sample of the study included 412 Student teachers who were studying in ten Teachers' colleges of three universities in Rajasthan. The teaching Aptitude Test, Group Mental Ability Test and self-made Teachers Morality Test were used for data collection.

The findings were

(1) About 75% of Student teachers were below average in aptitude and intellectual ability
(2) An insignificant difference was found in teaching aptitude abilities sex-wise and discipline wise comparison
(3) A positive correlation was found between teaching aptitude, intellectual level and morality of prospective teachers.

Panda, U.N. (1985) studied the "Management, Organisational Climate and Teachers Morale in Orissa Schools".

The major objectives of the studies were

(1) to explore the problems faced both by the Government and Private High Schools
(2) to study the nature of problems which have been responsible for creating various difficulties, hardships, handicaps, and hurdles for those schools
(3) to make a comparative study of the problems of the Government and Private High Schools, and

(4) to suggest possible remedial measures for the improvement of the existing conditions.

The tools used for data collection were questionnaires for the headmasters, teachers and members of the managing committee. The sample included the schools chosen from two coastal districts. *viz* Puri and Balaspur.

The sample respondents were 100 headmasters, 200 teachers and 100 managing committee members.

The findings of the study were

(1) The Government Schools had better physical facilities in comparison with those of private Schools.
(2) Both Private and Government Schools were lacking in library facility.
(3) The results of S.S.C. Examination for private schools were better than those of Government Schools.
(4) The Headmasters of Governments Schools were not satisfied with the Government management, whereas the Private School Head masters were somewhat satisfied with their management system.
(5) The teachers were not satisfied with their present salary and other financial incentives.

Puranik, S.D.'s (1985) study was to examine the relationship of maturity of pupils on the one hand and organisational climate and morale of teachers on the other.

The sample of the study included 70 schools, 2,634 students and 712 teachers in the primary Schools of Bangalore city.

This study was conducted to find out

(1) the levels of social maturity of male and female students separately
(2) the levels of Social maturity of students under the influence of selected independent variables
(3) the relationship between social maturity of students on the one hand and organisational climate and morale of teachers on the other

(4) morale of male and female teachers separately, and
(5) morale of teachers under different variables.

The major findings of the study were

(1) the social maturity level of female students was higher than that of male students.
(2) In the development of social maturity, autonomous climate, private managements of unaided schools and urban location of schools were found to be most conducive factors
(3) the morale of female teachers was higher than that of male teachers
(4) the controlled organizational climate, Government management and urban locality were conducive to develop the morale of teachers
(5) No effect of morale of teachers of both sexes was noticed on the development of social maturity of even under the influence of organizational climates, school organizations and localities.

Pandey, Saroj (1985) undertook a study of the relationship between the leadership behaviour of principals, organisational climate of schools and Teacher morale.

The objectives of this study are

(1) To find out the relationship between the leadership behaviour of Principals and the organizational climate of Schools.
(2) To investigate the relationship between the leadership behaviour of principals and Teacher morale.
(3) To investigate the relationship between organisational climate and teacher morale.

The sample in this study included 34 secondary schools drawn from a population of 138 secondary schools of Allahabad district, through the stratified random sampling technique. A total of 404 teachers of these schools participated in this study.

The major findings were

(1) no significant difference was found between the relationship behaviours of rural and urban principals.

(2) Rural Schools were more open than those in urban area.
(3) Teacher morale was positively and significantly related to the initiating structure and consideration dimensions of leadership and controls, production emphasis and humanized thrust dimensions of organizational climate
(4) Chi-square value was found significant at 0.05 level between high *vs* Low teacher morale and open *vs* closed climate.

In Educational India of November, 1976, the importance of a code of conduct was emphasized under the Editorial, in the name of Mr. R.C. Wadhera, Sainik School, Chittoorgarh. Probably, Teacher-Morale would grow in schools when such code is implemented in them.

Prahallada, N.N. (1977) in his study on Moral and Spiritual Education in Teacher-Education (reported in Educational India of March, 1977) stated that we can not have a great nation with men of low character. Probably Teachers with a high morale alone would be able to produce men of high character.

Sexena, K. (1988) studied the 'professional Factors influencing Teacher Morale' in the colleges of Garhard University during 1988. The sample comprised of 15 Teachers working in the affiliated colleges of Garhard University in U.P.

The findings of this study were

(1) Teachers' rapport with principal leads to high morale.
(2) 'Teachers' rapport with other teachers does not affect teachers' morale.
(3) Teachers' personal satisfaction with teaching does not affect teachers' morale.
(4) Teachers' morale is affected by teachers' status.
(5) Teachers' work-load affects teachers' morale.

The following are thus the factors of Teacher-Morale studied in the Investigation.

1. Relations with principal
2. Relations with other teachers
3. Job satisfaction

4. Salary
5. Work Load.

Sundararajan, S. and Ashrafullah, A.M. (1990) made a study on 'Job satisfaction of the Harijan Welfare School Teachers in Tamil Nadu', during May, 1990.

The major findings of this study were

(1) Women Teachers have better job satisfaction than Men Teachers.
(2) Teachers with a Teaching Experience of above ten years have better job satisfaction than those with Teaching Experience only upto ten years.
(3) Teachers with a monthly salary upto Rs. 1500 have better job satisfaction than those with a monthly salary exceeding Rs. 1500.
(4) Graduate Teachers have better job satisfaction than the Post-graduate Teachers.
(5) Teachers who are above 40 years of age have better job satisfaction than those who come below that age.

"The Job Satisfaction Questionnaire" (J.S.Q) standardised by Kumar and Mutha (1985) was used in this study. It consists of 29 items. Two point scale was adopted. Three schools were selected in South Arcot district for this study and all their 159 teachers were included in the sample.

Sundararajan, S. and Vivekanandam, R. (1990) studied on job satisfaction of teachers working in some selected higher secondary schools in the city of Madras, during September, '90.

Random sampling technique was used in the selection of the sample, which consisted of 350 Graduate and Post-graduate Teachers. 'The Teachers' job satisfaction inventory' constructed and standardized by Jaya Lakshmi Indiresan was used. It has 30 items. 5 point. scale was adopted.

The findings of this study are

(1) The variable of Management has had some impact on Job-satisfaction; corporation school teachers stood first; and Govt.

school teachers stood next; the other group from Matriculation schools stood last.

(2) The variable of sex has not manifested any significant difference in respect of job satisfaction.

(3) There is no significant difference between Post-graduate and Graduate Teachers in respect of job satisfaction.

Mehta, P.M. (1993) studied the 'Teacher Morale as Determinant of Teacher Perception of Supervisory Behaviour' in two elementary schools and two High Schools of New York City in 1992.

In this study, the object of the investigator was to explore the relationship between teachers' morale and their perceptions of supervisory behaviour. He took up an operational definition for the term Teacher Morale and stated that "Morale is vague term and has several definitions. However for the purpose of this study he took teacher Morale as a teacher's sense of belonging and loyalty to the school and his satisfaction with the work environment. Similarly, he gave an operational definition of the term 'supervisory behaviour' by stating that this term does not imply the actual administrative and supervisory behaviour of a supervisor: rather this represents his behaviour as perceived by the teachers whose instruction he is helping to improve. He took up for his sample the schools referred to above with a total No. of 100 teachers randomly selected. He developed a Questionnaire consisting of eight items in order to measure the level of Teacher Morale. He also develcped another questionnaire to collect the data on the teacher's perceptions of the supervisory behaviour. He identified from his study the teachers in the high and low morale groups who differed significantly on 18 of the 30 items (60%) in their perception of the supervisory behaviour. He thereby inferred the morale is one of the determining factors in a teacher's image of his supervisory behaviour. He also found from his study that low morale teachers reported that occassionally their supervisor was willing to make changes, did little things to make the group members happy, acted without consulting the group and tried out his new ideas with the group. But the teachers agreed that he seldom ruled with an iron hand.

The Research Bulletin of Maharashtra S.C.E.R.T. (1993) for March, 1993 reported a study on character development among children of 4–8 years. The children belonged to the age group of 4–8 years. They were selected from four different schools of Nagpur City. It was reported in this study that "Parents showed great concern for scholastic achievement of their wards rather than character building." It was also reported that "with the advancement of age children are found to be less honest". The investigator observed also that "today teaching morals and values in the school system is facing one of the most delicate problems". While "on one hand the nation is passing through the stage of moral conflict, on the other, it is a general feeling that schools are ineffective in promoting moral conduct. The growing importance of competition and lack of concern on the part of teachers and Parents towards the healthy growth of character for various reasons can be partly responsible for the chaos in society."

Savadamuthu, T. (1994) studied the "Teacher Morale and Student Morale at Secondary Level" in Dindigul Anna District of Tamil Nadu. He believed that the functional aspect of educational environment was determined by the morale of the teachers and students. He formulated certain hypotheses and selected normative Survey as his Research Strategy. He collected data from 200 teachers and 1200 students. He developed two tools one-to measure the Teacher Morale and another to measure Student Morale.

The findings of this study are

(1) The level of morale of teachers is high.
(2) The morale of Women Teachers is higher than that of Men Teachers.
(3) The morale of Rural School Teachers is higher than that of Urban School Teachers.
(4) The morale of Government and Private School Teachers was the same.
(5) There is no significant relationship between the Teaching Experience of the Teachers and their Morale.
(6) There is no significant association between the qualification of the Teachers and their Morale.
(7) There is significant relationship between the morale of teachers and that of their students.

An Educational Project was taken up in 1986 in Zambia for teachers in Rural areas by the concerned Ministry, with an object of Promoting Teacher Effectiveness, as reported by UNESCO in their publication 'Education For All' during November, 1994. This publication was issued by UNESCO, as a "Data Base" for "Certain Innovative Basic Education Projects in Developing Countries". It is heartening to note here that "Self-help" which is a characteristic feature of "Morale" was taken up as one Goal in an Innovative Basic Education project taken up by a developing country in Africa in 1986. One of the object in the project is said to be "to strengthen the professional and material capacity of schools... for self-help through school based teachers and agricultural resource centres".

Mishra, A.N and Jaya Mishra, (1993) Education faculty members of Kurukshetra University studied "Leadership Behaviour of the Heads of Secondary Schools". They took 10 schools selecting 5 teachers from each of them, according to the method of random sampling.

The results of this study are:

(1) The academic heads require their abilities to be improved for betterment of their institutions and students.
(2) No academic leader was found to have very high and very low leadership qualities.
(3) As many as 90% of the academic leaders possessed leadership qualities ranging from average to above average—obviously not encouraging.

Thus, different investigators took different factors basing on the problem of their study. In order to arrive at factors for the present study, it is necessary to have a critical understanding of the various aspects studied by the previous investigators on Morale.

The first and the foremost investigation in this connection was done by foreign educationalists on industrial morale.

Hocking, while studying Morale and its Enemies, stated the areas such as proper time in which to accomplish work, good physical conditions, confidence in one's skill and ability, respect and co-operation from the community, elimination of friction and appeals to the imagination and ambition.

Fosdick in his work quoted the areas such as credit for work done, interest in work, fair pay, understanding and appreciation, counsel on personal problems, promotion on merit basis, good physical working conditions and job satisfaction.

Baehr and Ranck pointed out in their report that five primary factors for morale. They are organisation and management, immediate supervision, material rewards, fellow employees and job satisfaction.

The investigations conducted by Hocking, Fosdick and Baehr and Ranck were related to industrial morale. They studied various aspects of morale and all the factors are practically applicable to school situation with reference to teacher morale.

Few more investigations were conducted with reference to teacher morale. Dorsey may be the earliest, who discussed some of the aspects for the improvement of Teacher Morale like fair teacher load assignments, good physical surroundings, sane supervision, proper salary tenure, retirement provisions, sick leave and credit for participation and contribution. John Rorer also studied the 'Factors that effect the morale of the teachers'. He introduced nine factors. They were better preparation, working on co-operative projects, adequate salary schedule, tenure, protection, confidence in the worthwhileness of teaching, recognition of every day effort, school and community friendship, community support and affiliation with teacher organisations.

While discussing staff relations in school administration, American Association of School Administrators (AASA) discussed the morale of teachers wherein it was pointed out that to build up morale such factors like mutual support from other staff members, effective organisation of teachers, community leadership in projects for human betterment and worthy objectives were essential. But Barr and others, Hill and Morrisett in their comprehensive survey summarised the following factors for morale improvement. They were relations with supervisor, policy, fair pay, physical working conditions. In addition to these, Barr and others included confidence in administration, community respect, relations with co-workers, leadership, Professional growth and advancement, adequacy of fringe benefits, mental and physical health and then private life. Hill and Morrisett, touched the factors such as communication and identification with institution, which were not listed by Barr and others.

Probably, the first comprehensive and practical investigation in this field was done by william Braem and he cited justice, recognition, leadership, stimulating contacts, achievement, security, mental health and physical fitness as factors for Morale. But Elwood Hunter in his investigation conducted at New Orleans public schools pointed out the following factors for morale building. They were proper school discipline, adequate equipment, proper teaching load, financial security, recognition and reward for exceptional services, evaluation of proper work and promotion and advancement of merit.

Kimball Wiles in a survey found the factors such as security and comfortable living, pleasant working conditions, fair treatment, a sense of belonging, a sense of achievement and growth, recognition and contribution, participation in deciding policy and opportunity to maintain self-respect were important to job satisfaction.

Claude Mathis in his study of 'Teacher Morale' with reference to salary schedule' cited, self, school, community, administration and policy were significant factors for morale.

John Suchr in his study of 'Teacher Morale' broadly classified the areas in the following manner, Community respect, professional organisation, teacher assignments, good working conditions, channels of communication, policy, confidence in school administration, personal problems, relations with principal, team work among teachers, relations with pupils, teacher welfare, fair salary and fringe benefits.

Richardson and Blocker in their study of Faculty Morale included the following areas: communication, confidence in administration, relations with immediate supervisor, relations with fellow employees, relations with students, status and recognition, identification with institution, professional growth and advancement, adequacy of salary, adequacy of fringe benefits, work environment and work load.

William and Wingo listed the following factors for choosing teaching profession: Independence, social acceptance, interest in children, liking by children, liking for teaching, command in subject matter, security in job and vanguard of change.

After thus going through the different foreign studies, journals and publications for the purpose of identifying the related literature in this chapter, the investigator finds that most of the above investigations by foreigners were conducted on the nature, importance, and measurement of morale along with some other aspects. Factors contributing positively, or negatively for cultivating morale among the teachers were included directly or indirectly in these studies.

It is also evident that some of the scholars studied the factors related to supervision of schools namely, A.S. Barr, J.A. Rorer and K.Wiles. Researchers like S.M.Dorsey, E.C.Hunter and C.Mathis studied the factors related to promoting of good relationships and attitudes among school teachers.

Probably, the first comprehensive and systematic investigation in India on 'Teacher Morale' was done by Dekhtawala and he studied the factors that affect teacher morale through the factor analytic method. The factors were: Teacher characteristics and leadership, attitude towards profession, cheerfulness, group cohesiveness, efficiency, school climate, work load, community support feelings towards institution, job satisfaction and attitude towards the job.

Now, as for the studies by the Indian scholars, we find that studies made by Jayamma. Shamusuddin, Debnath Pandey, Nair, Chaya, Sharma and Singh were not directly related to Teacher Morale. However, the aspects studied by them are related to Teacher Morale.

Pillai in his study identified the areas such as school facilities, community support, rapport among teachers, rapport with principal, community relations, work load and status which influence faculty morale.

Chhabra in his study summarised the following factors which affect Teacher Morale:

(1) principal's interest in teachers problems,
(2) lack of co-operation among teachers,
(3) lack of contact with students,
(4) salary policies,
(5) security and status.

Franklin in his study on the "Organisational Climate and Teacher Morale in Colleges of Education" included the following areas:

(1) belongingness,
(2) policy, and
(3) physical working conditions.

Samron Pengru studied the "Organisational climate and Teacher Morale in Secondary Schools of Thailand". The following two factors were inclued:

(1) Communication, and
(2) Physical working conditions.

Mehta found that factors such as: Relations with superiors, co-workers, others and pupils and physical working conditions were essential for better institutional climate, which would in turn affect teacher morale.

Mahatma in his study identified the factors such as ideal class-rooms, interpersonal relationships, co-operation, guidance to students, characteristics of the teachers which influence the morale of the teacher.

Jain in his study on the "Class-room behaviour patterns of Teachers in relation to their attitude towards profession, morale and values" revealed the following areas:

(1) professional attitudes,
(2) class room behavioural patterns,
(3) child-centred activities,

(4) teaching skills,
(5) rapport with principal, and
(6) community participation.

Sharma studied the factors in his investigation such as intellectual traits, teaching aptitude, and moral values.

Panda in his investigation conducted at Orissa Schools pointed out factors such as : physical facilities, library facilities, salary position and financial incentives.

Puranik in his study "on the relationship of Social maturity of pupils with organisational climate and Teachers morale in the Primary Schools of Bangalore city" incited factors such as maturity level of pupils, organisational climates of school localities.

Pandey, Saroj, studied the "Leadership Behaviour of the Principal, Organisational Climate and Teacher Morale". The following two factors were included:

(1) Organisational climate of schools, and
(2) Leadership behaviour of principals.

Wadhera emphasized the importance of a Code of Conduct, in his study on this subject during the year 1976.

Prahallada, in his study on Moral and Spiritual Education in Teacher Education during the year 1977, laid stress on moral behaviour and the importance of men with character.

Sexena found in his study during 1988 that factors such as: rapport with principal, rapport with pupils, personal satisfaction with teaching, teacher's salary and work-load would affect teacher morale.

Sundararajan and Ashrafullah in their study during the year 1990 identified the factors such as salary level, experience of teachers, age, sex of the teacher which influence the job satisfaction of the teachers.

Sundararajan and R. Vivekanandan found in their study during 1990 that Teacher Morale varied with reference to the management of the school and that it was not affected by sex and qualifications.

Mehta, P.M. found in his study that factors such as supervisory behaviour, sense of belongingness, loyalty to the school, satisfaction with work environment would affect teacher morale.

During 1993, the S.C.E.R.T. of Maharashtra reported a study on character development in children of 4-8 years, showing that parents manifested a greater concern for scholastic achievement than for character development.

In 1994 Savadamuthu, T. found by his studies on Teacher Morale and Student Morale that the variables of sex and rurality, had some significant impact on Teacher Morale, while the other variables—Management, Experience and Qualifications did not affect it.

The review made in the above paras on the related researches by foreigners as well as Indians has revealed the following with reference to the Investigation on hand:

(a) Most of these researchers studied, along with Teacher-Morale, some other related phenomena too, such as Teacher's attitude, their class-room behaviour patterns, their aptitude for teaching etc.
(b) Probably, that is why no effort could be made in most of them, to make a concerted study of the crucial factors having a bearing on Teacher-Morale, by way of synthesizing them; consequently, no action could be taken to identify the crucial factors that affect the Teacher Morale and the extent to which they affect it.
(c) The present investigation is therefore focused, merely, on the Teacher–Morale; its objectives therefore do not include any other related phenomena as included in the previous investigations.

Considering the above, the investigator chose two major factors, that cover most of the factors which have been highlighted in the previous investigations, and which influence Teacher Morale; namely, 'Teacher Factor' and 'Environmental Factors', as they may have a direct influence on the standard of teaching. Thus, an attempt is made in this investigation to adopt a synthesizing approach to the above two major factors which might facilitate a concerted study of the several constituent factors that affect the Teacher-Morale. Hence the above two major synthesized factors (Teacher Factor and Environmental Factors) have been identified in this investigation as suggested hereunder.

The teaching efficiency of the teacher depends upon his personality factors, professional aspirations, professional skills that pertain to Academic Proficiency, Teaching Ability, and other skills like maintaining proper relationships with pupils, organisation of curricular and co-curricular activities, language ability etc. Keeping these factors in view, the researcher included the following six sub-factors under the first major factor *i.e.*, 'Teacher Factor'.

1. Personality Factors
2. Professional Aspirations
3. Professional skills:
   (a) Academic Proficiency
   (b) Teaching Ability
   (c) Organising Skills
   (d) Linguistic Proficiency.

Furthermore, the morale of the teacher depends not only upon Teacher Factor but also on the Environmental Factors namely (a) the physical facilities like library and laboratory etc. (b) working conditions of the Teachers, (c) Administration of the school, (d) Family and (e) Community support etc. Keeping in view these factors, the present researcher included the following sub-factors under the second major factor, namely, Environmental Factors.

1. School Facilities
2. School Administration
3. Educational Administration
4. Environmental impact:
   (a) Family
   (b) Community
   (c) Value System.

The present investigation is therefore proposed to study the above factors, duly synthesized under the two related major factors. We may also assume from the review made in this chapter on the previous related researches, that no research has been taken up by any of the previous investigators, covering comprehensively the Teacher Factor, and the other factors included in the present investigation. Besides, the present researcher has not concentrated much, on the factors already studied in the previous investigations. He rather included some more which were left out by the previous researchers as in the case of the sub-factors such as those under Teacher Factor, and Environmental Factors.

In addition, none of the previous studies could highlight the impact of some of the factors such as the size of the class handled by Teacher. Hence the present investigator chose to include it in this investigation under the variables.

Moreover, sex seems to haven't had a consistent impact in the previous investigations. For example in a study made by N.C.E.R.T. it was found that the attitudes of male and female teachers differed significantly. But in a study made by Pandey, G.S., a positive relationship was found between the scores of male and female teachers. In another study by Nair, S.R., it was found that sex has not affected Teaching Ability. In the study by Chaya, sex was found to be one of the factors having significant relationship with effectiveness of Teaching. Thus, sex of the teacher is one major variable whose impact was found to be different in different studies.

Based on these observations and the theoretical studies of the problem in relation to Teacher-Morale, the investigator has chosen to investigate the impact of this major variable of sex, as well as that of class size on the Teacher-Morale in the sample in order to identify whether Teacher Morale would differ on the basis of these variables.

Thus, the study of the related literature in the field helped the present investigator to a large extent in designing his investigation on the problem selected or him, as already stated above. Besides, the opinions expressed in the previous related literature on Teacher Morale, as reviewed in this chapter helped the investigator in preparing his plan of action. Keeping in view these researchers and opinions, the investigator formulated his theoretical constructs and selected the method of research, the sample of the study, selection and construction of the tools of investigation, collection of data, administration, scoring, analysis and interpretation of results.

In this way, the study made in this chapter on the related literature includes:

(a) the studies made by foreigners as well as indians,
(b) research studies as well as theoretical studies indicative of the observations made by certain writers in some eminent journals etc.,
(c) the studies made on allied problems also, pertaining to morale in general.

These studies helped in the present investigation, to take up, in addition a suitable operational definition of the term 'Teacher Morale'. The investigator hopes that these studies are comprehensive enough covering the latest studies also.

The studies referred to above have yielded findings of two types: (1) those pertaining to certain variables like sex, experience and (2) those pertaining to certain factors of Teacher Morale. In the first type, variables like sex seem to have given rise to certain conflicting findings in the related literature under review. In second type of findings, factors such as the following seem to show some positive impact on Teacher Morale.

(1) Physical conditions in the school.
(2) Incentives such as favourable service conditions to the staff.
(3) Preparatory activities for better teaching.
(4) Human relations in the school.

Some studies seem to have focused upon factors like job-satisfaction, in order to yield some data regarding conditions conducive to it. Thus, various studies have been made on this subject as well as its allied subjects.

However, very few studies have been made directly on Teacher Morale as already stated earlier. The investigator made use all these studies in his endeavours under the present investigation, not only in matters like method of research, designing and developing his tools, etc., but also in comparing his findings with the findings of earlier studies.

3

METHODOLOGY

In the process of any investigation, methodology has a pivotal position and helps the investigator to draw the required conclusions in order to achieve the objectives of the study. So, the success of research depends upon the method, the researcher employs, the sample he selects and the tool he constructs for the collection of the data. To carry out any type of research investigation, data are gathered with which the hypothesis may be tested. A great variety of methods and procedures have been developed to aid in the collection of data. Tools of many kinds are employed as distinct ways of describing and qualifying the data. Each is particularly appropriate for certain sources of data, yielding information of the kind and in the form that would be most effectively used.

The investigator makes an attempt in this chapter to describe the method in investigation, selection of the sample, selection of the tools of investigation, construction of tools, and their administration and scoring.

Method of Study

When we discuss the methodology of the present study in this chapter, we use the term 'methodology' to connote two relevant terms *viz* the 'procedure' and the 'method' which would be appropriate for adoption in this study. But it is not infrequent to find these terms used "interchangeably to research literature. It is because both the terms are generally understood to connote tools and techniques adopted in research study". Research investigations in any field of knowledge can be of different types (e. g. historical, normative survey, experimental, case clinical.) but they all involve "more or less the same steps of procedure" like selection, formulation and definition of the problem, survey of the related information, collection, analysis, and interpretation of new data and reporting of the work done which "are steps of procedure common to all types of methods of research. Hence it can be held that steps of procedure in Educational research" like the above "are an element common to all educational investigations while methods of research in education are broad distinguishing features of different researchers".

Besides, "while historical studies describe and interpret what existed in the past", there are other kinds of investigations which study, describe and interpret what exists at present." The latter are concerned with conditions or relationships that exist, practices that prevail, beliefs, points of view or attitudes that are held, processes that are going on, effects that are being felt, or trends that are developing. The literature of such investigations includes expressions like the "descriptive survey, normative, status or trend." The terms 'survey and status suggest' the gathering of evidences relating to certain current conditions. The term 'normative' may be taken to imply the determination of the actual existing conditions. The term 'normative survey' is generally used for the type of research like the one on hand wherein it is proposed to survey certain beliefs of a population through certain sampling procedures, regarding an aspect like the morale in certain conditions applicable to Teachers' behaviour in educational institutions and identify their variations with reference to its constituent factors and the subsamples of the selected part of population.

The other methods such as experimental, case-clinical methods are not relevant in the present study. Hence it is not proposed to discuss them here.

As for the method adopted in this study, we may call it survey research, which is "a method for collecting and analysing data obtained from a large number of respondents representing a specific population collected through highly structured and detailed questionnaire or interviews."

Such studies of the survey type collect three types of information.

(i) 'of what exists' by studying and analysing important aspects of the present situation

(ii) 'of what we want' by clarifying the goals and objectives, possibly through a study of the conditions existing elsewhere or what the experts consider to be desirable, and

(iii) 'of how to get there' through discovering the possible means of achieving the goals on the basis of the experiences of others or the opinions of experts.

Some of the above studies like the one on hand lean more heavily upon the human element. In the present case, the human element of school population i.e., Secondary School Teachers becomes the object of our survey. As already stated above, we employ the survey method, herein to study the beliefs or points of view held by Secondary School Teachers, on the problem on hand.

The following are some of the characteristics of the Survey Method of Research:

1. It gathers data from a relatively large number of cases.
2. It is essentially cross-sectional, mostly of the 'what exists' type.
3. It is concerned not with the characteristics of individuals but with generalized statistics of the whole population or a sample thereof.
4. It is an important type of research involving clearly defined problems and definite objectives. It requires an imaginative planning, a careful analysis and interpretation of the data and a logical and skillful reporting of the findings.
5. It does not aspire to develop an organized body of scientific laws but provides information useful to the solution of local problems. It may, however, provide data to form the basis of research of a more fundamental nature.
6. Descriptions may be either verbal or expressed in mathematical symbols.
7. The great range of phenomena forming the subject of educational surveys may be classified as:
   a) physical conditions related to learning (building, furniture and libraries, etc.).
   b) Behavioural conditions related to learning (behaviour of pupils, teachers and parents, etc.).

c) The results of learning or the pupils' ability to learn (achievement or basic skills, information or attitudes).

8. It fits appropriately into the total research scheme of the stages in exploring a large field of investigation. It may (a) serve as a reconnaissance or getting acquainted stage of research in entering a new area, or (b) represent a specific interest in current conditions within a field that has long since been explored and developed by research.

Tools of Research in Normative Surveys

Inquiry forms are some of the major tools of research employed in the above studies. They are as follows:

1. Questionnaire
2. Schedule
3. Checklist
4. Rating Scale
5. Score card
6. Opinionnaire or Attitude Scale.

Out of the above six inquiry forms, the opinionnaire form is adopted in the present investigation. In this form, we ask the selected respondents to check the statements given to them in a list with which they are in agreement, and indicate the degree of their agreement or disagreement on certain aspects of educational phenomena like the Morale as in the problem on hand. Usually the Likert scaling Technique is adopted in this tool to provide scaling for the degree of agreement or disagreement. In this technique, we usually adopt a five point scale or occasionally a three-point scale. There are some limitations for opinionnaires, e.g. no basis for equal spacing of the degrees of agreement or disagreement, dubious value in equality of 'forness' or 'againstness' of the responses, etc. However, until more precise measures are developed, the "opinionnaires remain the best devices for the purpose of measuring... beliefs in social research, as they determine the direction and intensity of a person's feelings for or against some belief or practice and are also used to measure any changes in opinions which may result from factors introduced purposely or occurring independently." Thus, the opinionnaire form was adopted for this investigation, and two tools were designed accordingly, in this form of opinionnaire for carrying out the necessary inquiring on the problem selected for this study.

Stages in the Preparation of Tools of Study

Three stages were involved in preparation of Tools and their finalization:

In the first stage, the investigator had informal discussion with various experienced teachers and Head Masters about the statements included in the opinionnaire; later also he consulted the experts in the field. The first stage enabled the investigator to have a clear idea of the areas in this study and helped in the construction of opinionnaire.

The second stage, included the pre-testing of the opinionnaire which the investigator prepared with 170 items based on the discussions and administered to a selected sample. This sample consisted of ninety teachers of 15 different types of secondary schools in Krishna District. The pre-testing data of 170 statements in the opinionnaire were subjected to statistical treatment by applying the chi-square test and eliminated ten (10) items out of these 170 items. This pre-testing helped the investigator to finalize the opinionnaire.

The final tool thus consists of 160 items on a three point scale of Likert type to collect the opinions of teachers. Under each item, included in opinionnaire, the three alternative responses (*viz*) Agreed, Neutral Opinion, Disagreed are given and the subjects were asked to draw a circle one of those with which they concur.

Type of the Research Method Adopted

In the light of the over-view of the related literature, the investigator fixed up the design of the study. The problem for the present investigation is "A study of the Factors contributing to the Teacher morale in Secondary Schools".

The problem involves a study of the opinions expressed by the subjects involved in the research to provide exact information about the factors which are contributing to the promotion of Teacher morale. As such the present piece of research falls under the Normative survey type of research, referred to above.

Sample for the Study

This study was confined in Krishna District only, as already stated in the Chapter No. 1. The investigator has selected the following sample for the study, with certain considerations of Sampling Theory discussed separately under the section 'Administration' (of the Tools). As already proposed above, the study was confined to one district i.e., Krishna District.

In Krishna District, there are 203 rural schools and 79 urban schools. For the present study the investigator has taken up only 54 rural schools and 46 urban schools by applying the method of stratified random sampling.

From urban area the investigator has selected 46 schools, out of which 5 are under Government, 12 under municipal, 28 under private aided and 1 under Zilla Praja Parishad managements.

From rural area 54 schools were selected, out of which 5 are under government, 39 under Zilla Praja Parishad, and 10 under private aided managements.

The required data were collected from the above schools. For each school 7 staff members were selected on an average. Of these 4 are males and 3 are female. So the total sample was 630 teachers drawn from 100 schools i.e., 46 urban, and 54 rural schools.

Variables of the Study

In the selection of the sample for this study, the following eight variables were selected.

1) Age	:	Between 26–30/ Between 31–40/ Between 41–50/ Above 50 years.
2) sex	:	Male /Female.

3) Qualification	:	under Graduate /Graduate / Post-graduate.
4) Designation	:	Secondary Grade Teachers / B.Ed., Teachers / Head Masters.
5) Experience	:	Below 5 years / Between 6 and 10 years/ Between 11 and 15 years / Above 15 years.
6) Management	:	Government Schools/Local Body Schools/ Private Schools.
7) Location of the school	:	Urban / Rural.
8) Size of the Class	:	50 or more students in the section / 30-49 students in the Section / Below 30 Students.

For the purpose of the present investigation, the teachers working in high schools were selected. In the State of Andhra Pradesh, most of the high schools are with VI to X classes. So, the sample of teachers selected for this study includes teachers working in high schools (Secondary Schools) in Krishna District. Let us now study in detail regarding the variables of sample in this study.

The investigator has noted that certain variables like age, sex, qualifications, experience etc. of teachers have been selected in the previous studies on this problem already reviewed in chapter No. II. According to John, W. Best and James V. Kahn, 'Variables' are certain conditions or characteristics in the sample. Each Variable stratifies the sample into some sub-samples with reference to these conditions.

According to the above writers, a variable is an attribute such as sex, which may have an impact on a phenomenon like Teacher Morale. An investigator manipulates or controls these attributes, with reference to their probable impact on this phenomenon, by selecting the related variables. The following seven variables of the present investigation have been selected in the previous studies also which showed certain findings with reference to these variables manifesting their impact on the phenomenon studied here in.

S.No.	Variable
1.	Age
2.	Sex
3.	Qualifications
4.	Designation
5.	Experience
6.	Management
7.	Location of the School

For example, age has shown certain impact in these studies, in the case of sex, its impact was not found in certain studies, while it has found in others. In this way, the present investigator has made certain assumptions, in regard to certain variables, while stating his hypotheses in chapter No:1.

Thus, one object of selecting the variables is to study the phenomenon in question in depth, from different aspects, by selecting them appropriate to the problem on hand. The present investigator has accordingly selected eight variables. While the variable pertaining to class-size has not been selected in any of the previous studies, the other seven variables have been selected in them with certain findings on the same. One assumption in regard to class-size is that generally teachers handling large-size classes meet certain problems of effective teaching, which is an aspect of Teacher Morale, when compared to teachers handling small size classes.

Further more, the present investigator has stratified each of above eight variables, (abstracted here-under for ready reference) in order to identify certain sub-samples with reference to these variables.

Sl. No.	Variable	Number of Stratifications
1.	Age	4
2.	Sex	2
3.	Qualifications	3
4.	Designation	3
5.	Experience	4
6.	Management	3
7.	Location of the School	2
8.	Size of the class	3
	Total	24

The stratifications under the variables of age, experience and size of class are fixed relatively arbitrarily, for the convenience of the investigation in order to stratify the sample in a reasonable way. Their number under each of these three variables is not the least when compared to their number under the other five variables. Under the latter variables, the sample is stratified according to each variable. For example under sex, the no. of sub-samples is 2; under qualifications, it is 3 in view of the nature of the sample selected for the present study from the secondary school teacher population.

Similar is the stratification under the other variables like Designation, Management and Location of the School.

The investigator has thus selected certain variables of sample for designing the above sub-samples, in order to identify certain significant categories of teachers, so that we may be able to find certain manifestations of Teacher Morale at least in some of these categories if not in all.

Every variable as a phenomenon has some significance for it. For example in certain physical phenomena some variables like the mass of the matter, its weight etc. have some significance in order to cause certain changes in the phenomenon on account of the changes in a variable. Even in the social phenomena, Variables such as sex may cause some significant changes in certain social phenomena. There might be thus some relationship between phenomenon and variable in order to facilitate a scientific study to find out whether variations on account of variable in the sample will cause changes in the related phenomenon in the concerned sub-samples.

Teacher-morale is a complex social phenomenon prevalent in a group, affecting the teacher performance. Teachers employed in an institution generally manifest their morale in accordance with the institutional objectives for which they are employed. Besides, every teacher works in a group.

After the institutionalization of education, teaching has been organised in certain classes, wherein pupils of more or less equal standards, with reference to their age, attainments in the prescribed course of the subjects, and other related aspects of the pupil-achievement, have been graded and organised as groups, each of them being with an optimal size, say, 30 to 40. For certain administrative reasons the size of the class has been raised up to 60.

In this way the phenomenon of teaçhing has been institutionalized as a social phenomenon presenting a lot of interaction in groups. In view of the linkage between the Teacher-morale and groups of peers as well as pupils and interaction with other groups like colleagues, administrative superiors, the Head Masters, the management, inspecting officers etc, (we may add parents also in these groups), the study of the related phenomenon in any research activity may be based upon certain assumptions with reference to the variables selected in the study.

Based upon the knowledge acquired regarding the variables and sampling, the investigator has selected seven usual variables which are selected generally in investigations of the teacher phenomena. In this study he selected in addition to the above seven variables one more variable *i.e.,* the size of the class, which may be one of the significant factors pertaining to Teacher morale.

As already discussed above, the size of the class is mostly weighted, as an administrative convenience in almost in many educational institutions under the State control with reference to the finances available to the school. Usually the size of the class is 50–60 particularly in Urban areas. Under the Government Educational Rules obtaining in Andhra Pradesh, a class may be bifurcated into an extra section if the strength of the class exceeds 60; this requirement is prescribed and adopted mostly for the purpose of Governmental assistance in the case of private aided secondary schools.

Thus the size of the class in almost many secondary schools is very high particularly in urban areas, some times due to paucity of funds in many secondary schools, under municipalities and also in the case of private managements. A section of the class may thus have a strength of more than 60, some times ranging up 100 to 150, but these are all exceptions. Besides, there are some secondary schools particularly in remote rural areas mostly under the Zilla Praja Parishat Managements where the class size is not so high. In some cases it is below 30. Therefore in the present investigation the variable pertaining to the size of the class has been included in view of its probable impact on Teacher morale by classifying this variable into three categories as shown hereunder.

	Total No.	
1. 50 or more students in the section	285	45%
2. 30-49 students in the section	252	40%
3. Below 30 students in the section	93	15%
	630	

Categories 1 and 3 are almost exceptions while category No. 2 is the usual phenomenon in the school system in general. However in view of the increasing urbanization most of the urban schools come into category No.1, while very few of these urban schools come into category No.2. In the case of category No. 3 they are in the rural area and are very few in their number.

Thus the investigator has selected a total number of eight variables which may serve as some extrinsic factors of the sample (quite different and separate from the intrinsic factors of the Teacher morale under the two major factors), in order to identify and analyse some of those factors which have greater relationship with the Teacher morale.

Tools of Research Adopted in the Present Study

For the purpose of the investigation, the researcher has adopted the opinionnaire developed on the Likert method of summated ratings for testing the hypotheses and collection of data.

In order to collect the data for making a study of the factors contributing to teacher morale, the researcher has constructed a opinionnaire with 170 statements.

The opinionnaire was divided into two parts, grouping all the identical statements under one part. Each part was treated as separate tool. So, the first part (Tool—I) was named as *Teacher Factor* and the Second part (Tool—II) was named as *Environmental Factors.*

For convenience sake the two tools, *viz,* Teacher Factor Tool and Environmental Factors Tools were got printed in the same booklet, and administered for the collection of data.

In the opinionnaire, the first page is set apart for name and address of the respondent and an appeal was also made to the respondents to express their opinions freely and frankly. In the second page variable particulars were given. They were asked to draw a circle around the appropriate alternative with which they agree most from among the three alternatives, viz., Agree/ Neutral opinion/ Disagree.

Description of the Tools of Investigation

A detailed discussion on the preparation and administration of the above mentioned tools is made in the following paras.

The problem under this study is concerned with certain factors which affect Teacher-Morale. As already stated the investigator identified two major factors pertaining to personality of the teacher i.e., Teacher Factor and Environmental Factors. Each of them is related to social situations which a teacher comes across in and outside the school.

While identifying the above two factors and their constituent sub-factors, bearing on the problem on hand, the investigator referred to the previous studies on the problem. He selected the various areas to be included in the Tools of Investigation As they Didn't Receive much Focus in the previous Investigations and are at the same time very important in Teacher-Morale.

These areas are as follows:

Teacher Factor

1. Personality Factors
2. Professional Aspirations
3. Professional Skills:
   (a) Academic Proficiency,
   (b) Teaching Ability,
   (c) Organising Skills,
   (d) Linguistic Proficiency.

Environmental Factors

1. School Facilities
2. School Administration
3. Educational Administration
4. Environmental impact:
   (a) Family,
   (b) Community,
   (c) Value system.

All the above factors and sub-factors may be treated as extrinsic in their nature, as they are external to the Teacher. The investigator selected also some intrinsic factors which are internal to the sample obtained for the study: they are the eight variables.

The opinionnaire is prepared separately in two different tools one for each of the above two major factors. Each of the tools has thus six areas of study. So, we have total No. of 12 areas of study in the tools of Investigation.

With a view to obtaining an insight into the various factors included in the above 12 areas of study, under this investigation into the factors determining Teacher-Morale, it is proposed to discuss these factors, area-wise hereunder:

Tool –I : Teacher Factor

Any activity taken up by an individual living in society is more or less a reflection of an interaction between the individual's personality and his or her environment. This interaction is a process which thus involves two major constituents i.e., Personality and Environment. It is apparent in every society. Teacher-performance to is a similar interaction occurring in a society. Teacher-Factor deals with the personality of the Teacher, which is one factor involved in this interaction, of Teacher performances.

The first factor of the Interaction referred to above i.e., the Teacher-performance comprises certain sub-factors such as Personality Factors, Professional Aspirations and Professional Skills of the Teacher. Let us therefore study the Teacher Factor, under three sections pertaining to these three aspects.

Before dealing with the above three aspects, it is pertinent to note that the Teacher Factor is a base for the interaction referred to above. Naturally, it is a major factor in this interaction process. 'Environment' is another major factor for the interaction. Thus these two major factors interact with each other giving rise to the Teacher-Morale which is the theme of this study.

In some stages of the interaction referred to above, Teacher's Personality under goes a lot of change by acquiescing in and adjusting to, the other factor. At the other stages, we find some adaptation in it with an impact on the Environmental Factors. Consequently, the latter too undergoes changes. In fact human civilization itself is a product of such an interaction between Human Personality and the Environment. It, necessarily, involves cultural aspects of man's behaviour. These cultural aspects manifest through his beliefs and interests, which should be channelized constructively by them. Naturally, human civilization is an evolutionary outcome which has undergone a lot of change, particularly during the Modern period. Furthermore, it bears an ample evidence of interaction between Human Personality and Environment. Besides, Human Personality cannot be static. Similarly, the Environment can't be static. Both undergo a change constantly and continuously.

Morale is therefore the way in which Human Personality acts and reacts with the Environment. We find in Environment not only the social forces that act on the Human Personality but also the Nature which manifests in some physical phenomena surrounding the Human Personality.

In view of the above, the Teacher Factor comprises the Human Personality, while the Environmental factors comprise the social forces as well as the physical phenomena referred to above. Naturally, Teacher-Factor furnishes the necessary motive-force, for its Interaction with the Environment. So, it can't but serve as a base on which Environment works out with its forces. Let us now study its sub-factors already enumerated above.

The investigator constructed the Teacher Factor opinionnaire with 85 items under six areas. The distribution of the items included under the different areas of this tool are presented in Table No.1.

TABLE—1

Table showing the distribution of items –Teacher Factor Tool.

Sl. no.	Area No.	Name of the Area	No. of items included
1.	1	Personality factors	27
2.	2	Professional Aspirations	25
3.	3	Professional Skills:	
4.		(a) Academic Proficiency	8
5.		(b) Teaching Ability	9
6.		(c) Organising Skills	8
7.		(d) Linguistic Proficiency	8
		Total	85

With a view to have an insight into the various factors included under different areas in Teacher Factor Tool, to study the factors contributing to Teacher-Morale in Secondary Schools and the items formulated and set forth under each area, the investigator made an area-wise discussion in the following paragraphs. Each area was analysed followed by the items.

Area–1: Personality Factors

Personality Factors refer to a psychological phenomenon. These are described under the pre-tryout Tool—I, in 27 statements which depict certain situations of Teacher behaviour dependent upon certain personal traits of the Teacher. All teachers may not manifest them uniformly. Teacher-behaviour in terms of these twenty seven (27) statements therefore varies a lot. it, however, reflects Teacher - Morale.

According to Allport, personality is a dynamic organisation within the individual; it comprises a psycho—physical system that determines his adjustment to his environment. According to J.P. Gilford, individual's personality is a unique pattern of traits. The teacher stimulates the students with his own personality traits like domination, submissiveness, conversational etiquette etc., which influence the pupils in various situations. As seen above, personality is also the adjustment and accommodating nature of the person which is a factor that stimulates his morale. Coming to the other factor of personality namely the intro-version *Vs* extro-version, the agreeableness, the conscientiousness, emotional, stability, sociability and culture, they play the main role under personality factors and the percentage of those traits is in direct proportion to the morale.

Basing on the above the investigator has given twenty seven items under the Personality Factors, which enrich the morale of the teacher. They come under different dimensions like motivational, adjustment, emotional, democratic, cordial relationships, dutifulness etc.

Besides, personality is more or less a stable and enduring organisation of an individual's character, temperament, intellect and physique, which determine his unique adjustment to the environment.

Personality of the teacher affects his morale. The teacher maintains good relations with his pupils, in order to prepare them for a worthy life in the democratic society. He maintains impartiality in assessing the pupils' academic achievement. He tolerates the errors of theirs and at the same time endeavours to correct them.

Punctuality in performing the academic and non- academic duties, promotes morale. His behaviour should be exemplary to his pupils. It should stimulate their love. He must keep the welfare of his pupils as his principal obligation. In the teaching-learning process the teacher has to give freedom for the pupils to exchange ideas, and encourage their original ideas. He must act as a friend, philosopher and guide to his pupils. All these factors contribute to enhance the morale of the teacher.

Maintaining emotional balance with the students, colleagues, Head Master and other superiors will help him to develop his morale. The democratic nature of the teacher in the class room management enhances his morale. He must be co-operative, respectful, resourceful, constructive in advice and helpful to his colleagues and pupils. On the basis of these qualities which a teacher requires for his success in the profession he can afford to maintain good cordial relations with the fellow teachers which would help the promotion of a higher morale. We have given here under the statements included in the pre-tryout opinionnaire, under this area, covering the above aspects.

1. I motivate my pupils to learn well.
2. I discourage them to think independently.
3. I encourage their original ideas.
4. I exchange my ideas with them.
5. I enjoy the co-operation from my pupils.
6. I encourage them to make their own decisions in class room management.
7. I guide them to cultivate good habits.
8. I tolerate the errors in their behavioural changes (Intellectual and moral) in order to develop them constructively.
9. I maintain cordial relations with them.
10. I act as a loco-parent for them.
11. I act as a friend, guide and philosopher to them.
12. I am impartial in assessing their academic work.
13. I maintain emotional balance with them.
14. I tend to be easy going.
15. My colleagues give respect to my ideas.
16. I maintain cordial relations with my colleagues.
17. I am undemocratic in class-room management.
18. The size of the class has no impact on my teaching.
19. I find no monotony in my routine class work.
20. I take my classes punctually.
21. I am conscientious in performing my duties.
22. I attend the Daily Assembly in my school.
23. I take part in additional duties such as polling census work etc, willingly.
24. I welcome suggestions on my academic activities.
25. I enjoy the freedom of expression in my profession.
26. I discourage malpractices in examinations.
27. I do so paying scant attention to the results.

Area —2: Professional Aspirations

Aspirations of an individual motivate him towards a greater effort, while his Personality Factors give him some enriched goals to be pursue by him. A teacher needs them in order to develop a higher morale.

Professional Aspirations therefore contribute a lot in promotion of Teacher-Morale. They would be useful not only to the individual but also to the society at large. They require a lot of dedication and devotion on the part of the Teacher; otherwise, Professional Aspirations become routine, and mechanical. So, when compared to other professions; teaching is a more responsible profession than all other professions. Bad teaching affects the whole Nation, while bad performance in certain professions like Law, Medicine, Engineering etc, affects primarily the individuals concerned only. Thus, teaching profession is responsible for the actions of the past, the present and the future. But the other professions are responsible in general, for the actions of the present only. So, professional Aspirations supply a powerful force under the Teacher Factor.

Teaching Profession, requires expert knowledge and specialised skills, acquired and maintained through rigorous and continuing study and their application in the services of humanity.

We may also say the teaching profession reflects high degree of excellence, repertory of teaching skills and practical wisdom on one hand and a well-integrated value system on the other hand and both oriented towards altrustic service.

As John Adams said, the verb of teaching governs two accusatives—the 'subject' and 'pupils'. Hence the teacher must acquire, before attempting to teach, a thorough knowledge about the pupils, i.e., the child psychology and also the subject, its methodology and content. He thus becomes aware of the objectives of teaching, the principles of learning, psychological principles governing the behaviour of the child the ways and means of providing general and vocational guidance, the pupils, individual differences, need for using their leisure time for their academic development, need to be in touch with the latest developments in the subjects of his specialization. All these come under the area of Professional Aspirations of a teacher.

The teacher should apply the subject of Educational psychology in identifying the weakness and strengths of students. To achieve these aspirations one may have to attend refresher courses, seminars and publish articles which may help him to develop (a) a sense of confidence, and (b) also his Teaching Abilities.

The following are the twenty five (25) statements, formulated under this sub-factor, based on these considerations.

28. I make myself available to my pupils out of the school hours also, for heir guidance.
29. I give them educational as well as vocational guidance.
30. I discourage creativeness among them.
31. I develop logical reasoning in them through my class work.
32. I adapt my teaching to the needs of individual differences among them.
33. I co-operate with my colleagues for our mutual constructive guidance.
34. I discuss with my colleagues on academic matters.
35. I conduct private tuitions to supplement my income.
36. I take decisions for the proper management of the classes.
37. I conduct the school programmes in such a way as to serve the needs of the local community.
38. I use my professional security for the benefit of my pupils.
39. In view of the security of my job, I work without fear or favour.
40. I use the opportunities available to improve my academic qualifications.
41. I keep in touch with the latest developments in the methods of teaching my subjects.
42. I read books and journals for my professional growth.
43. I strive for my professional growth by participating in the in-service programmes willingly.
44. I secure professional growth by undertaking action research.
45. I see the T.V. News -Bulletins regularly.
46. I use general knowledge in teaching, wherever it is applicable.
47. I am very much benefited with the subject of psychological foundations of education in my class-room teaching.

48. I grade the questions in school examinations in terms of their difficulty level.
49. I use the pupils' responses in examinations, to give them remedial instruction.
50. I love to work in professional organisations.
51. I enjoy my professional status.
52. I am personally interested in the teaching profession.

Area –3 : Professional Skills

(a) Academic Proficiency,
(b) Teaching Ability,
(c) Organising Skills, and
(d) Linguistic Proficiency.

Teacher is a learner for ever. He not only causes learning but also learns continuously. In fact, every human being is endowed with a potential for learning throughout his life. One should therefore cultivate the skills of learning; in other words doing so is a habit formation or an attitude towards life. B.F. Skinner states that learning occurs through conditioning, which is reinforced through Education, after a skill is learnt by the organism. By a number of trials and by elimination of errors, one gets proficiency in a skill.

Teacher is only a guide to help in the acquisition of certain basic skills. In order to provide this guidance effectively, he should develop certain skills which are professional in their nature; these are, in addition to the Personality Factors and Professional Aspirations described above.

Professional Skills involve certain abilities in the teacher. The investigator has identified, in the course of his study on this problem four fundamental skills pertinent to teaching. They are mentioned above. Of course, Academic proficiency is one that indicates a mastery in the subject taught by him. In the proverbial statement, "the teacher teaches John Latin". Latin refers to the subject taught by him and without the necessary proficiency in that subject, he can't teach it effectively. Now-a-days, knowledge is exploded most intensively and rapidly. This explosion has much impact on every subject. Besides, many media convey the exploded knowledge. Teaching alone can fill up the gaps in it. So, necessarily, teacher should have much Academic proficiency.

Proficiency in the subject will not hold good in order to make one a good teacher. He must have the communicative skills too. These are involved in the term 'Teaching Ability'. These do not include a mere ability to communicate; they necessarily comprise a verbal skill too, in order to, explain the communicated content clearly. The term 'Communicative Skills' is not therefore comprehensive without these two components of the content as well as the verbal skill.

That 'a teacher is born and not made', is an old adage. We have a few 'born teachers' who have the necessary potential for communicative skills with the above components. But we need many teachers to do the job. So, they should be 'made'. Besides, in the modern age, due to the vast expansion of research methods, the technology of teaching has become a technique and skill. The modern equipment like A.V.Aids, Video and Audio tapes, Overhead projectors have lessened the burden of the teacher. The language laboratories are also contributing a lot to teach languages in a systematic way, taking the linguistic aspects into consideration. So, in a way, the teacher has to be thorough with the modern teaching techniques like Micro-teaching, Team -teaching and Programmed learning. He should also be able to prepare the lesson plans, and for using the aids mentioned above.

In addition to 'Teaching Ability', the teacher needs Organising Skills which would be helpful to him to organize his instructional activities in the class for promotion of effective learning by the pupils in the class.

Finally, the teacher needs Linguistic Proficiency as language becomes an effective tool for the verbal explanation resorted to by him in his instructional activities. So, in addition to mastery over the subject which is involved in 'Academic Proficiency', command over the language is also essential for a teacher in order to be able to explain the communicable content clearly and comprehensively.

Let us now consider each of these four skills separately with reference to the statements included in the Opinionnaire under it.

Area–3 (a) : Academic Proficiency

This is the most pivotal area with which the teacher flourishes well, and this is the chief requisite also for one to be an effective teacher. He is a good teacher who can answer his pupils's doubts in a logical and rational way. For this he should have an abundant knowledge in his subject and should always be up-to-dating his knowledge and utilise his leisure time meaningfully and also be attending the seminars and workshops conducted by the Department and the other agencies. The investigator has given eight (8) items in this area which deal with the subject under this head as focused above.

53. I clarify the doubts of my pupils in my subjects.
54. I work hard to acquire an up-to-date knowledge in my school subjects.
55. I strive to enrich my knowledge of the content in the subjects I teach.
56. I evince keen interest in attending the library.
57. I am satisfied with the library accommodation in my school.
58. I utilise my leisure time for writing articles on education.
59. I use my leisure time to prepare instructional materials regularly.
60. I participate in the academic meetings held by Education Department and others.

Area–3 (b) : Teaching Ability

Pedagogy has been developed during the Modern period, in order to train the Teacher. Teacher-Training for Primary and Secondary Education has become indispensable. In many countries the pre-service Teacher Training is a must for teaching at these levels of School Education. In recent years in-service Teacher-Training has been developed. The chief object of all this Training is to promote the Teaching Ability. Let us consider the following nine (9) items included in the Opinionnaire under this skill.

61. I encourage pupils to acquire practical knowledge.
62. I prepare my daily lesson-plans before going to classes.
63. I use suitable teaching aids in my classes.
64. I prepare new models of teaching aids every year.
65. I don't teach my subjects systematically.

66. I adopt new teaching methods like team teaching, group discussion etc.
67. I plan my teaching procedures regularly in large size classes.
68. I use electrical gadgets and T.V. in the classroom teaching.
69. I use Community Resources for enriching my classroom instruction.

Area–3 (c) : Organising Skills

Organization of skills plays the key role in teaching process. The effectiveness of it gives good satisfaction to the teacher which in turn develops high morale in him. The organisation part is multi-dimensional. It carries many perceptual values. The business man always modernises these skills in order to attract the consumer.

The Gestalt group of psychologists also give importance to perceptual groupings in order to give solution to problems. So, it occupies an important place in learning. For this, the teacher has to prepare an year plan, providing for the activities of the science clubs, exhibitions, educational tours, national functions, cultural activities, social service camps, competitions in sports and games, dramas and songs to improve one's own histrionic talents etc. So much so, the proper organisation of these events will certainly improve the teachers' morale. Eight (8) items have been framed in this section.

70. I take up experimental projects to improve my teaching teachniques, procedures, and methods.
71. I participate in the subject club activities.
72. I participate in the Science fairs/ Science Exhibitions.
73. I participate in the organisation of student councils.
74. I discourage my pupils to participate in Dramatic clubs.
75. I take active part in Intramural competitions.
76. I involve myself actively in the Annual Day Celebrations of my school.
77. I participate in the social service camps.

Area–3 (d) : Linguistic Proficiency

Language is the main Tool of Education. We have thus a language as the medium of instruction. Pronunciation being one main

Linguistic aspect, one has to acquire an intelligible pronunciation, while expressing one's ideas to others. Whatever be the status of the language namely the regional, the national and the link language, unless the teacher is thorough with rules and regulations of that language and uses simple, intelligible sentences, there will be communication gaps between the two parties: (pupil and teachers). The stress pattern, the pauses, the intonation and accent play the main role. A teacher should essentially be bilingual in the present day society. He has to give the regional equivalence for the second language. In this respect many suggestions have been given by the educationists like Palmer, Hornby, Thorndike, and a host of others. It is better one may refer to their works in teaching English as a foreign language, Doing so might be helpful to the teachers for better communication. Satisfaction in this respect certainly develops one's morale. The investigator has given seven (7) statements under this area to have a view of the subject.

78. I make my pronunciation intelligible to all the students in the class.
79. I use simple language, appropriate to the class level.
80. I don't like to use simple sentences in my language.
81. I use colloquial style in my classes.
82. I speak in the classes with reasonable pauses, intonation and accent.
83. I observe the necessary modulations while explaining the lesson.
84. I always learn to use correct language while communicating to the students.

Tool–II : Environmental Factors

In addition to the Teacher Factor, factors in and outside the school environment where he works *i.e.,* Environmental Factors influence the morale of the teacher. The success of teaching mainly depends upon the physical facilities, working conditions and academic facilities available in the school. Here we may perhaps refer to the process involved in the teacher performance, which process takes place between the Teacher Factor ánd the Environmental Factors. We have discussed so far the Teacher Factor which is one of the two major components in this process. The other component comprises the Environmental Factors, which include: (a) the School Facilities available to the Teacher, (b) the School Administration system, (c) the Educational Administration system, and (d) the Environmental impact through Family, Community and Value system. We have discussed so far the constituents of the Teacher Factor such as Teacher's Personality, his Professional Aspirations and his Professional Skills. Teacher Morale is assumed to be an outcome of the interaction between (a) these constituents of Teacher Factor on one hand, and (b) the components of the Environmental Factors on the other hand. Let us discuss now briefly these components of Environmental Factors described in Tool—II.

As already stated, each statement in the opinionnaire reveals a situation wherein the teacher performance takes place in the course of discharging his educational tasks. So, all the situations given in the opinionnaire under the two tools pertain to one of the constituents of the major factor described above.

The morale of a teacher depends upon the interaction between the Teacher Factor and his Environmental Factors, as already assumed in this investigation. We have already discussed the Teacher Factor with reference to the various statements included in Tool—I. We shall now study the Environmental Factors that come into play through an interaction with the Teacher Factor. A teacher's environment comprises: (a) the locality in which he lives, (b) the school in which he works, (c) the administrative system of Education in general and of the School in particular wherein he is employed, (d) his family, (e) his community, and (f) the value system prevalent in his group.

Adequate accommodation, equipment, proper teaching aids, library and laboratory facilities also exercise considerable influence on the standard of teaching. The human relations that exist among the school personnel like his pupils, parents, Head Master and other teaching staff and non-teaching staff also determine his morale. Good working conditions such as considering the employee's seniority, sanctioning increments every year, leave facilities, and providing academic requirements and the necessary infra-structure improve the efficiency of the teacher to a large extent in any school system. At the same time these facilities induce the morale of the teachers. The work-load of the teacher also influences his morale. The administrators' democratic approach in the allocation of the work to the teachers and in all administrative affairs of the school, and providing guidance to all staff in academic and administrative affairs would help the teacher in developing his morale. Another important factor i.e., family, also contributes a lot in promoting the morale of the teacher. The encouragement given by family members in developing favourable attitudes towards teaching profession, and their support fcr professional development etc, would help the teacher to promote his morale. Non-interference of the teachers in local politics, non-politicization of the school issues, following the higher values in dealing with the caste and religious groups would help the teacher in promoting his morale.

The investigator constructed the Environmental Factors opinionnaire with 86 items under six areas. The distribution of the items included under the different areas of this tool is indicated in Table—2.

TABLE—2

Table showing the Distribution of items –Environmental Factors Tool.

Sl. No.	Area No.	Name of the Area	No. of items included
1.	1	School Facilities	17
2.	2	School Administration	26
3.	3	Educational Administration	16
	4	Environmental Impact:	
4.		(a) Family	6
5.		(b) Community	11
6.		(c) Value system	10
		Total	86

With a view to have an insight into the various factors included under different areas in Environmental Factors Tool, and to study the factors contributing to Teacher Morale in Secondary Schools, the investigator made area wise discussion in the following paragraphs. Each area was analysed according to the items given under each.

Let us now deal with each of the six sub-factors included in these Environmental Factors, in detail.

Area–1: School Facilities

The school in which a Teacher works provides a major environment for him. His morale is influenced mostly by this Environmental Factor, for, it is concerned with the facilities offered to him for his work. These facilities pertain firstly to location of the school in healthy surroundings. A school located in unhealthy surroundings like those of drunkards, or other distracting factors, or a polluted area, naturally affects the teacher's morale adversely. The other facilities include physical facilities like accommodation provided to the school. These range from drinking water facilities to the building and its sanitary conditions. Naturally, class-room has a greater impact, for, it is here the instructional activities are mostly carried on. Library and reading room are an important facility. Laboratory is another important facility that affects the learning in sciences. Play facilities provide a recreational atmosphere in the school. Seventeen (17) statements are given in this area of the pre-tryout tool covering most of the above aspects. They are as follows:

85. My school is located in healthy surroundings.
86. My school has adequate and suitable physical facilities.
87. My school is having drinking water facilities.
88. My school has adequate sanitary facilities.
89. My school has adequate garden facility.
90. My school authorities maintain the sanitary facilities with proper cleanliness.
91. A Committee of pupils and Staff assists the School Administration to maintain the sanitary facilities in my school.
92. My class room is decorated with photos of national and international leaders.
93. My class room is ventilated well.
94. My school library has out-dated and unsuitable books.
95. Books are stocked in good and attractive book-shelves at my school library.
96. There is no qualified librarian in my school.
97. My school has separate reading room with all the required facilities for reading comfortably.
98. My school Laboratory has adequate accommodation.

99. It is convenient to conduct all the Science Classes: Demonstration Classes and Experiments in my school laboratory.
100. My school play-ground is adequate to conduct a variety of sports and games.
101. My school has adequate games and sports material.

Area–2: School Administration

One of the major Environmental Factor that affects the Teacher's Morale pertains to the way in which school is organised and administered. The Head Master is the key figure in this area. Next to Head Master, another important functional group that affects the Teacher's morale is that of his colleagues on the teaching and the non-teaching staff in the school. He must have good and positive relations with Head Master as well as this functional group, if his morale is to be positively high. There is one more functional group comprising the school pupils. The way in which the school is organised and administered raises its tone and affects the interpersonal relations maintained in it. Twenty-six (26) statements are included in this area in the pre-try out tool covering these aspects. They are as follows:

102. I follow the suggestions given by the Head Master and other authorities.
103. I support my school authorities constructively.
104. I involve myself actively in the preparation of institutional plan.
105. My work-load is optimal *i.e.,* neither too heavy nor too light.
106. I treat some of the assignments given by my school Head Master and the other superiors as useless for improving my academic work.
107. I often accept these assignments to win the favour of my superiors.
108. My academic talent is properly recognised in my school.
109. There is team-spirit among my school staff.
110. My school Head-Master receives good co-operation from his office staff.
111. The office staff co-operates with all the teaching staff in their academic, para-academic and non-academic activities.
112. I co-operate with my school non-teaching staff in their work.

113. My school Head-Master maintains friendly relations with all the staff-members.
114. He does not confer any undue favour on any one of the staff-members.
115. He gives proper recognition to the good work done by them.
116. He is democratic in his school administration.
117. He adopts a humanitarian approach to his staff.
118. His supervision provides constructive guidance to the school staff and pupils.
119. His guidance is available to all the staff, without any exception.
120. He guides them to prevent their errors.
121. He pardons them for their errors and also helps them to rectify them.
122. He takes action against them whenever their errors result in moral turpitude among the pupils.
123. He guides us to understand the importance of avoiding such errors.
124. We respect him for his moral stature.
125. My School Managing Body keeps in touch with all the school activities.
126. They strive to satisfy the felt needs of my school periodically.
127. My school assists all the Teacher-Welfare Activities.

Area–3 : Educational Administration

This system pertains to the State control over the Education imparted within its territory. The State issues certain rules to see that the education imparted in the Educational Institutions of its area would be excellent. These rules provide also for utilization of state grant-in-aid by the institutions that receive it. States provides for inspection too. In addition, State regulates the matters relating to the services of teachers. State lays down its educational policy, for the guidance of the public under its existing educational policies, primary and secondary education may be organised by local bodies, Government and Private agencies; in the case of higher education, it may be organized by two types of agencies only—Government and Private agencies. Besides, under the existing educational policies, primary education is compulsory (6–11). Thus, Educational Administration controls the educational institutions and the instruction imported by them. We have given hereunder sixteen (16) statements covering the above various aspects of this area.

128. My school provides good working conditions to all its staff by
    a) Protecting their seniority.
    b) Sanctioning their normal increments every year.
    c) Granting leave as per rules.
    d) Providing the academic requirements and the necessary infra-structure for the proper functioning of the school.
129. I explain to the pupils the need for the rules and regulations issued by the State.
130. I help neither the gifted Pupils nor the slow learners in my classes.
131. I co-operate with school administration to involve the students in matters such as fixing holidays, dates of examinations etc.,
132. I help my school to satisfy all the conditions, prescribed for its recognition.
133. I co-operate with the school authorities for the smooth conduct of all the school and public examinations.
134. I co-operate with my school authorities in Admission work.
135. I follow the syllabus prescribed by the Government.
136. I discuss with the inspecting officer about the class room procedures.
137. I implement the suggestions given in the syllabus for pupil's practical activities also.
138. I don't follow the suggestions given at the annual inspection of my school.
139. I endeavour to achieve the objects of non-detention policy to evaluate and improve my pupils' learning.
140. I work hard to win distinctions such as National awards in my profession.

Area–4: Environmental Impact through–Family Community and Value System

The teacher is influenced by three major environmental forces of a general nature. Family is one of them. It is primary group organized from the olden days. It differs from the secondary groups in the society. School, and occupational group are secondary groups. Furthermore, the inter-personal relations in a family are based on blood relationships. Those in the secondary groups are not based on them.

Man lives under the influence of a large community due to his gregarious culture. This may be based on language or religion or some ethnic considerations such as Nation. A community has thus something common among its members. It is organised through the several groups that function in it. Several institutions have been set up in it, in order to institutionalize its group activities. For example, family is one primary group based on the Institution of Marriage. In this way, a community exists and influences every individual throughout his 'life', by organising and developing certain cultural relations too, among these individuals.

Human beings are also influenced in their behaviour through their value system. Values are therefore certain pre-dominant interests developed in the individuals which impel them to seek something higher than what is now available to them to satisfy their interests. Hence a behavioural pattern arises in every individual manifesting his values through attitudes and beliefs based upon a culture developed in them. Thus, we had a different value system in the olden days, with certain values which may be called Absolute Values, quite different from the values prevailing in the modern period. In this way, we find that many changes have taken place in our value system, under the influence of pragmatism.

Naturally, environment shows much impact on the individual through certain major forces like the above, affecting his morale. We have given certain statements in each of these three sub-areas under Area No.4, covering the above aspects, as shown here under:

(a) Family	:	6 statements
(b) Community	:	11 statements
(c) Value system	:	10 statements
		27 statements

Let us consider also the various aspects of these three areas, separately; before looking at the statements under each of them.

Area–4 (a) : Family

The factors outside the School Administration are Family and Community. Coming to Family, there is a lot that reflects on the personality of a person by the influence of Family.

The encouragement given by Family members to develop favourable attitude in the individual, helps him a lot in his social life. Some of these attitudes like service to fellow-beings, and love for children, may help him to acquire favourable disposition with certain congenial beliefs and interests, towards teaching profession. Besides, factors such as the following go a long way to improve the Teacher-Morale:

(a) the support from Family for his professional aspirations,
(b) the activities which the members of the Family take up to increase the socio-economic status of the Family, and
(c) their positive attitude towards his school problems. If these factors are favourable, the emotional poise of the teacher will increase and his work will not be disturbed. Thus the teacher maintains high morale with the help of his family members.

The investigator has given six (6) statements in this area in order to know the opinions of the subjects relevant to the situation.

141. My parents have helped me to develop certain favourable attitudes towards others.
142. My family members refuse to support my professional aspirations.
143. My family supports me in planning my school work.
144. I avoid projecting my family worries into my school work.
145. I think aloud with my family members about my school problems.
146. I try out my plans of innovative teaching on children.

Area–4 (b) : Community

Under this head, the investigator has given eleven (11) statements which are relevant to the situation. One must maintain good relations with community of which one is a member. His responsibility is two-fold here: One, as a teacher: and the other, as a member of the society. As a teacher it is his duty to inform the progress of his pupils to their parents. He should also have friendly relationships with them and seek the support of the community. His sincerity and committed responsibility will help him get a recognition and support from community for his professional work. So, he should endeavour to participate in their social and cultural functions, and thus develop good relations with them. These relations help him have a free and frank discussion, in order to serve the interests of both the school and the community. But no activity should be detrimental to the school activity. If such an atmosphere is maintained, the resultant Teacher Morale will be high. Besides, parent-teachers association will help him to discuss the school problems and standards of their children. Then he can receive suggestions from them and get support from the parents which will help him to promote his morale. It also helps to provide the school with useful resources like library, as well as a good campus for the school programmes, by which the parents can be attracted to the school and also involved in helping the developmental activities, of the school. Thus rapport between the teachers and parents will be established. Thereby the parents' involvement and commitment will increase which indirectly helps the institution in its improvement activities. Hence the teacher's image will enhance which would boost up his morale. The following are the eleven (11) items under this sub area, covering some of these aspects.

147. My school parent-teacher association gives its support to my school activities.
148. I inform the parents of the progress of their wards as well as their difficulties if any, from time to time.
149. My school resources are made available for the programmes of the Local community, without detriment to school activities.
150. My school participates in the social and cultural functions of the Local community.
151. My school organizes its social service programmes to serve the Local community.
152. My school receives community-support for its activities.
153. My Local community gives necessary recognition to my professional aspirations.
154. My sincerity and commitment help me to command respect from all sections of the society.

155. My school authorities deal effectively with the pressure groups who approach them in matters of admissions, conduct of examinations etc.
156. They study the demand in a realistic situation.
157. They open a dialogue with them, in a friendly atmosphere.

Area–4 (c) : Value System

The last and final sub-area of the Environmental Factors, namely the value system is the most important one. Without value system no activity will be successful. For this, the teachers' resourcefullness, intellect, and his personality traits help a lot. The teacher and the school must be above all the local politics. If the moral and social values are not maintained, there will be scope for narrowness, thus spoiling the morale of the school and the teacher, as well. For this, harmony of religions, maintaining brother-hood with the people of various castes would be quite essential. In this task, one has to face many hurdles when pressure groups shoot up either on caste basis or on religious basis disturbing the atmosphere with some vested interests of their own. If one has a low morale one will be a victim of these pressure groups and derive temporary benefits only. Probably such pressure groups should be fought, on the basis of higher values, in order to build up a social order without such narrow mindedness. Hence, it is necessary for teachers to be influenced by them in the interest of the school in order to impart Education with higher objectives for buildings up such a social order. Dealing with pressure-groups on these lines of a higher value-system might help the Teachers to develop a high morale. The following are the ten (10) items included under this sub-area, covering some of these aspects.

158. All my school personnel keep aloof from local politics.
159. My school authorities politicize the school issues.
160. They are guided mostly by social values in disposing of these issues.
161. They are guided by similar values i.e., higher values in dealing with the caste and religious groups of the community.
162. They don't allow any pressure-group of the community to pressurize the legitimate interests of their school work.
163. They deal with all these pressure-groups democratically, on a higher ethical basis.

164. They strive to keep up their school morale in spite of the problems created by these groups.
165. They manifest their belief in their behaviour that a person with low morale may get temporary pleasures with these groups, but will fall ultimately.
166. They maintain high morale even if they are tempted with money and other material benefits by these groups.
167. They caution the teachers having low morale to be careful with these groups.

Pre-Tryout

For finalising the Tool a pre-tryout was conducted on a random sample of 90 Secondary School Teachers. The Teacher Factor Tool consisted of 84 statements and Environmental Factors Tool consisted of 86 statements. The preliminary tool was put to item analysis. A hypothesis was formulated in it to the effect that reaction of the sample to each of the statements will be divided as per the pattern of normal Probability Distribution. Hence by using the related hypothesis chi-square values for each statement were calculated and tested for significance at 0.01 level. The pre-tryout study statements and the respective chi-square values are given hereunder. The list of schools adopted for the Pre-Tryout was enclosed under Appendix No. II.

Chi-square Values

These ninety (90) filled in opinionnaires were analysed and all the 170 (one hundred and seventy) items were put to chi-square (X^2) test. The equation for chi-square is given below.

$$x^2 = \sum\left[\frac{(fo - fe)^2}{fe}\right]$$

in which,

fo = frequency. of occurrence of observed or experimentally determined facts.

fe = expected frequency of occurrence on some hypothesis.

According to Garrett,'

"The chi-square test represents a useful method of comparing experimentally obtained results with those to be expected theoretically on some hypothesis".

The obtained chi-square value was checked for the degrees of freedom 2 at 0.01 level which is 9.210. The chi-square values are computed in respect of all the one hundred and seventy (170) items of the opinionnaire and the obtained values are presented in the Table—3.

TABLE—3

Table showing the chi-square values for all the 170 items of the opinionnaire.

Area No.	Item	Chi-Squre Value	Area	Item No.	Chi-square Value
1	2	3	1	2	3
Tool–I					
Area –1	1	106.81	Area–2	26	91.63
	2	110.72		27	87.18
	3	76.35		28	101.36
	4	57.66		29	43.88
	5	7.41 *		30	97.14
	6	91.94		31	66.27
	7	95.31		32	50.62
	8	40.64		33	31.24
	9	33.54		34	10.98
	10	101.72		35	50.81
	11	97.35		36	27.23
	12	102.63		37	10.05
	13	86.72		38	35.64
	14	8.62 *		39	47.21
	15	35.83		40	83.74
	16	43.46		41	103.52
	17	98.57		42	97.15
	18	92.01		43	82.03
	19	54.32		44	46.17
	20	106.52		45	25.43
	21	87.63		46	94.61
	22	89.38		47	15.36
	23	65.62		48	56.63
	24	42.13		49	62.27
	25	72.02		50	31.62

Cont..

1	2	3
	51	72.04
	52	93.83
Area-3(a)	53	82.71
	54	28.52
	55	101.25
	56	73.58
	57	46.27
	58	15.63
	59	57.36
	60	43.04
Area-3(b)	61	21.72
	62	109.18
	63	96.52
	64	71.03
	65	84.17
	66	90.25
	67	6.13 *
	68	32.36
	69	43.71
Area-3 (c)	70	102.53
	71	94.04
	72	76.58
	73	7.22 *
	74	49.19
	75	27.63
	76	39.25
	77	51.72
Area-3 (d)	78	73.85
	79	95.04
	80	111.23
	81	12.61
	82	27.37
	83	49.06
	84	88.27
Tool-II		
Area-1	85	61.99
	86	84.26
	87	51.42
	88	70.16
	89	5.34 *
	90	43.13
	91	68.25
	92	93.52
	93	8.53 *
	94	107.35
	95	65.21
	96	78.26
	97	83.19
	98	89.43
	99	51.71
	100	13.25
	101	65.07
Area-2	102	53.27
	103	6.46*
	104	71.34
	105	98.16
	106	101.42
	107	111.34
	108	86.05
	109	67.13
	110	15.52
	111	71.37
	112	53.24
	113	96.02
	114	74.13
	115	80.56
	116	103.31
	117	21.03
	118	35.26
	119	62.47
	120	86.33
	121	101.52
	122	96.71
	123	73.63
	124	52.17
	125	21.53
	126	82.07
	127	68.14
Area-3	128 a	60.32
	b	32.17
	c	25.26
	d	43.51
	129	61.78
	130	92.26
	131	54.33
	132	32.55
	133	71.03
	134	27.18
	135	89.59
	136	5.41
	137	21.53
	138	75.49
	139	53.08
	140	97.53
Area-4(a)	141	44.53
	142	105.81
	143	6.04 *
	144	58.72

Cont...

1	2	3	1	2	3
	145	37.23		157	64.31
	146	55.12	Area-4 (c)	158	93.05
Area-4 (b)	147	73.41		159	76.36
	148	107.53		160	82.61
	149	61.34		161	60.42
	150	26.07		162	21.56
	151	63.72		163	44.31
	152	70.24		164	32.06
	153	4.92 *		165	67.13
	154	84.13		166	26.81
	155	52.05		167	41.56
	156	19.52			

TABLE —4

Table showing the chi-square values in respect of the ten items fall below 9.210.

Area	Item No.	Item	Chi-square value
Tool–I			
Area–1	5	I enjoy the co-operation from my pupils	7.41
Area–1	14	I tend to be easy going	8.62
" 3 (b)	67	I plan my teaching procedures regularly in large size classes	6.13
" 3 (c)	73	I participate in the organisation of student councils	7.22
Tool–II			
Area–1	89	My school has adequate garden facility	5.34
Area–1	93	My class-room is ventilated well	8.53
" 2	103	I support my school authorities constructively	6.46
" 3	136	I discuss with the inspecting officer about the class room procedures	5.41
" 4 (a)	143	My family supports me in planning my school work	6.04
" 4 (b)	153	My local community gives necessary recognition to my professional aspirations	4.92

Hence the above ten items with less chi-square values below 9.210 were deleted and the final opinionnaire was prepared with 160 items and administered successfully for obtaining the data.

TABLE –5
Table showing the finalized opinionnaire of 160 items.

Sl. No.	Area	No. of items Included in it
	Tool–I : Teacher Factor:	
1.	Personality Factors	25
2.	Professional Aspirations	25
3.	Professional Skills:	
	(a) Academic Proficiency	8
	(b) Teaching Ability	8
	(c) Organising Skills	7
	(d) Linguistic Proficiency	7
		80
	Tool –II: Environmental Factors:	
1.	School Facilities	15
2.	School Administration	25
3.	Educational Administration	15
4.	Environmental Impact:	
	(a) Family	5
	(b) Community	10
	(c) Value system	10
		80

Thus, the finalized opinionnaire consists of fifteen pages. In the first page an appeal was made to the subjects to give their free and frank opinions. Space for personal data was also provided. In the second page particulars of various variables selected under this study and instructions as to how to fill in the opinionnaire were given. Statements under Tool—I and Tool—II were given on pages third to fifteenth.

A copy of the above finalized opinionnaire was enclosed under Appendix—I.

Administration

After the Teacher morale opinionnaires were thus designed, they were administered to Seven hundred (700) secondary school teachers working in secondary schools in Krishna District of Andhra Pradesh.

In this connection, let us study briefly the sample surveys, hereunder.

William G. Cochran (1959) while discussing the advantages of the sampling method of surveys, writes:

> *"In every branch of science we lack the resources to study more than a fragment of the phenomena that might advance our knowledge".*

He analyses four principal advantages of sampling as compared with complete enumeration. They are :

(i) reduced cost,
(ii) greater speed,
(iii) greater scope, and
(iv) greater accuracy.

In the field of education, normative survey of various types are usually sample surveys. That is, they usually define and measure the properties of an accurately defined population by means of the information obtained from a sample thereof. Until recently, relatively little attention was given to the problem of how to draw a good sample. This does not matter so long as the material from which we are sampling is uniform, so that any kind of sample gives almost the same results. But in the field of education, material is usually far from uniform so that the method by which the sample is obtained becomes critical.

Sampling Problems

Almost all research studies in education may be termed sampling studies as data are usually collected from parts of whole population. The obtained facts from samples should only be considered 'estimates' of the 'true' facts. Determination of sample should be based upon the purposes of the investigation, a precise description of the population to be investigated and the sources of that population, from which samples can be selected. Is the problem restricted to a particular group or are the conclusions to be generalized to a broader population?

The determination of the size of the sample is always a difficult problem for the researcher. Of course, the sample should be 'adequate' and 'representative'. But what do these terms mean with reference to a particular research project? No definite answer can be given to this problem. The researcher should be able to give conclusions based on samples with great confidence. The number should be larger in a sample from a heterogeneous population as compared with the number in a sample from a homogeneous population. If there are several categories of data in an educational experiment, e.g., size of the school, type of school, age of pupil, sex, rural, urban etc., the number in the sample is bound to become larger.

The method of Random sampling was adopted in respect of the selection of teachers as discussed previously. In addition, the variables such as Age, Sex, Qualification, Designation, Experience, Management, Location of the School, and Size of the Class were given due consideration in the selection of the sample as already mentioned. We may therefore probably state that a modified form of random sampling, "stratified or quota sampling, sometimes called controlled sampling, a device which ensures representativeness in selecting a sample from a population composed of subgroups or strata of different sizes", has been adopted in this study.

The investigator thus selected a sample of 700 teachers, with considerations like the above, visited a number of Secondary Schools selected for the sample and administered the opinionnaire personally. In some cases in which this couldn't be done, the tools were mailed by post.

The investigator received back only six hundred and fifty (650) opinionnaires. Of these some are not filled completely and some are defective. So, the investigator eliminated them to the tune of Twenty in number and took only six hundred and thirty properly filled in opinionnaires which are fool-proof. Variable-wise details of the 630 subjects are given in the following table.

TABLE—6

Table showing the Variable-wise details of opinionnaire taken up for study.

Sl. No.	Variable	Category	Number of Subjects	Total
1.	Age	1. Between 26–30 Years	80	
		2. Between 31–40 Years	162	
		3. Between 41–50 Years	183	
		4. Above 50 years	205	= 630
2.	Sex	1. Male	360	
		2. Female	270	= 630
3.	Qualification	1. Under Graduate Teachers	60	
		2. Graduate Teachers	400	
		3. Post-graduate Teachers	170	= 630
4.	Designation	1. Secondary Grade Teachers	188	
		2. B.Ed Teachers	342	
		3. Head Masters	100	= 630
5.	Experience	1. Below 5 years	107	
		2. Between 6 and 10 years	130	
		3. Between 11 and 15 Years	170	
		4. Above 15 Years	223	= 630
6.	Management	1. Government Schools	97	
		2. Local Body Schools	312	
		3. Private Schools	221	= 630
7.	Location of the School	1. Urban	353	
		2. Rural	277	= 630
8.	Size of Class	1. 50 or more students in the section	285	
		2. 30–49 students in the section	252	
		3. Below 30 students	93	= 630

The list of institutions from where the above sample is drawn is enclosed under Appendix—IV.

Scaling

The final Tool consisted of 160 statements (80 in Tool—I and 80 in Tool–II). The investigator felt that three (3) point scaling will help the sample to respond properly to these statements. For each statement the respondents were asked to draw a circle around the appropriate alternative with which they agree most from among the three alternatives (*viz*) Agree/ Neutral Opinion/Disagree. Out of 80 statements in Tool—I there are 73 positive statements and seven (7) negative statements. In Tool—II out of the 80 statements there are 72 positive statements and eight (8) negative statements. A table given hereunder indicates the area-wise distribution of the above two types of statements.

TABLE —7

Table showing the area wise distribution of the positive and negative statements.

S.No.	Area	No. of positive items	No. of negative items with Sl. Nos	Total
Tool–I:	*Teacher Factor:*			
1.	Personality Factors	23	2(2,15)	25
2.	Professional Aspirations	23	2(28,33)	25
3.	Professional Skills:			
	(a) Academic Proficiency	8	—	8
	(b) Teaching Ability	7	1(63)	8
	(c) Organising Skills	6	1(70)	7
	(d) Linguistic Proficiency	6	1(76)	7
	Total No. of items	73	7	80
Tool–II: Environmental Factors:				
1.	School Facilities	13	2(88,90)	15
2.	School Administration	23	2 (99,100)	25
3.	Educational Administration	13	2 (123,130)	15
4.	Environmental impact:			
	(a) Family	4	1(134)	5
	(b) Community	10	—	10
	(c) Value system	9	1(149)	10
	Total No. of items	72	8	80

Scoring

Since a 3 point scale was adopted for each statement in a Tool the following scale values are arrived.

Nature of the Statement	Agreed	Neutral opinion	Disagreed
Positive Statement	3	2	1
Negative Statement	1	2	3

Addition of the scale value for items in the Tool yielded the morale score for that tool. Addition of the morale scores of Tool—I and Tool—II would give an overall Morale score. Similarly for each area sub-scores were also computed. These scores, so arrived at, were statistically analysed.

Statistical Procedures Adopted

1. From the analysis of overall Teacher morale scores the investigator verified the hypotheses formulated by him. Chi-square values were calculated. The level of significance chosen for statistical interpretation of this study is 0.01 level.
2. Similarly Teacher Factor scores distribution and Environmental Factors scores distribution were tested by applying Chi-square procedures.
3. For identifying the relationship between Teacher Factor and Environmental Factors in this sample product Moment coefficients of correlation were calculated.
4. For comparing the Teacher Factor and Environmental Factors variable wise, 'T' test was applied and the C.R. Values were tested for significance at 0.01 level.
5. Similarly for each of the areas in the two tools, C.R. Values were calculated and interpreted, variable-wise.
6. In order to identify the reasons for differences in each sub-area item mean-scores for each sub-sample were calculated and their differences were tested for significance and conclusions were drawn.
7. Since each of the areas had different/unequal number of items and in order to make a comparison, the Area-Mean-Scores of that area were averaged and named as Area-Mean. The Area-means were compared.
8. Since the Tool consisted 12 areas he correlations of each area with other areas were calculated and a correlation matrix was presented. The correlations were arranged in Rank order and patterns of interrelationships identified.

The analysis of data for testing the Hypotheses of this study is presented in the next chapter.

4

PRESENTATION AND ANALYSIS OF DATA

The subsequent steps in the process of research are generalization, analysis and interpretation of the data and formulation of conclusions and generalizations to get a meaningful picture out of the new information collected.

Organization

The mass of data collected through the use of various tools however reliable, valid and adequate it may be, is yet but raw. It needs to be systematized and organized, i.e., edited, classified and tabulated before it can serve any worthwhile purpose. The importance of proper arrangement and appropriate statistical treatment to the acquired data, has been aptly described by S.P. Sukhia (1974) as "Editing implies the checking of gathered data for accuracy, utility and completeness. Classifying refers to the dividing of the information into different categories, classes or heads for use. Tabulating denotes the recording of the classified material in accurate mathematical terms."

Tabulation of data includes marking and counting frequency tallies for different items on which information is gathered. Before tabulating, all raw data should be tested on the basis of the purpose for which they are gathered and only the useful and usable data should be tabulated. J.C. Aggarwal has also stressed the importance of proper treatment of data as "However valid, reliable and adequate the data may be, it does not serve any worthwhile purpose unless it is carefully edited, systematically classified and tabulated, scientifically analysed, intelligently interpreted and rationally concluded."

Analysis

Analysis of data means studying the tabulated material in order to determine inherent facts and meanings. It involves breaking down existing complex factors into simpler parts and putting the parts together in the new arrangements for purposes of interpretation. According to Wolfe, "The discovery of order in the phenomena of nature, not withstanding their complexity and apparent confusion is rendered possible by the process of analysis and synthesis."

"Analysis as a process enters into research in one form or the other form, from the very beginning in the selection of the problem in the determination of methods and in interpreting and drawing conclusions from data gathered" (Sukhia S.P., Mehrotra P.V., and R.N. Mehrotra).

A plan of analysis can and should be prepared in advance before the actual collecting of material. The process of analysis requires an alert, flexible and open minded planning. Caution is necessary at every step. No similarities, differences, trends and outstanding factors should go un-noticed. Larger divisions of material should be broken down into smaller units and re-arranged in new combinations to discover new factors and relationships. Data should be studied from as many angles as possible to find out new and newer facts.

Simple statistical calculations find a place in almost any research study dealing with large or even small groups of individuals, while complex statistical computations form the basis of many types of research. Most commonly used method of analysing data statistically are:

- — Calculating frequency distribution of items under study;
- — Testing data for normality of distribution—Skewness and Kurtosis;
- — Calculating percentiles and percentile ranks;

— Calculating measures of central tendency—Mean Median, and Mode and establishing norms;
— Calculating measures of dispersion—Standard Deviation, Mean Deviation, Quartile Deviation and Range;
— Calculating measures of relationship—coefficient of correlation, Reliability and Validity by the Rank Difference and Product—Moment Methods;
— Graphical presentation of data—Frequency Polygon Curve, Histogram, Cumulative Frequency Polygon and Ogive.

While analysing the data, investigators usually make use of as many of the above simple statistical devices necessary for the purpose of their study. There are other devices of statistical analysis listed below which the researchers use in experimental or complex casual comparative studies and investigations.

1. Tests of students 't' and analysis of variance for testing significance of difference between statistics especially between Means;
2. Chi-square Test for testing null hypothesis;
3. Calculation of biserial 'r' and Tetrachoric 'r' for finding out relationship between different phenomena in complex situation;
4. Calculation of partial and multiple Correlation and Bivariate and Multivariate Regression Equation for finding out casual relationship between various phenomena involved in a situation combining tests into a battery;
5. Factorial Analysis for the purpose of analysing the composition of certain phenomena.

In the present investigation, the investigator has adopted the common statistical methods as well as some of the special statistical methods for the analysis of the data.

Interpretation

"The process of interpretation is essentially one of stating what the results (findings) show? What do they mean? What is their significance? What is the answer to the original problem"? (Good, C.V., Barr, A.S. and Scates, D.E.)

The analysis and interpretation of data represent the application of deductive and inductive logic to the research process. Interpretation calls for a critical approach to all the limitations of his data-gathering and his subjective attitude. Interpretation—a most important step in the total procedure of research, is purely subjective and many errors are made at this stage. An adequate knowledge not only of techniques or research, but also of one's field of study and a capacity to do careful and critical thinking are very essential to safeguard against misinterpretation.

It is essential while interpreting the results secured after a statistical analysis of complex data to test whether the observed value of differences in statistics (Mean, Standard Deviation or 'r') are at all significant, whether they are not caused by change errors of sampling. If significant, how significant they are? For answering such questions, the statistical device used is that of calculating the probable error of the statistics in question. it takes the following forms:

1. Probable Error of the Mean
2. Probable Error of the Median
3. Probable Error of the Correlation Coefficient
4. Probable Error of the difference between two means or other measures;
5. Chi-square Test;
6. Tests of Students 't' and Analysis of Variance.

It is only after applying the suitable statistical formulae that the investigator can say at what levels of significance the results can be relied on or in other words, what the extent of the play of chance factors is in the observed results.

Analysis and Interpretation of the Data Collected Through Teacher Morale Opinionnaire

The analysis of data was done by using the statistical procedures discussed above and the hypotheses of this study were tested. It was basically, assumed that teacher morale is a psychological trait and that the distribution of this trait in the sample can be expected to be normal. In changed conditions the teaching profession was expected to show different types of distribution patterns in the sample of secondary school teachers. Since last (10) years teachers' status and working conditions, have undergone some changes. The nature of changes lies in increase of salaries, improvement in working conditions, changes in the school Administration, increase in the use of Educational Technology, Quality of syllabus, improvement in in-service training programmes, social recognition, changed relations with community and similar other qualitative changes in the teaching profession. As already described in earlier chapters combination of a variety of factors contributes to the level of morale in a particular profession and Teaching profession is no exception to this rule. With this working assumption the hypotheses of this study were chosen, selected and data analysed. The analysis of data is presented in four (4) sections.

Section—A: Analysis of the Tool-wise Data.
(Table Nos 8 to 14)

Section—B: Analysis of the Variable -wise Data.
(Table Nos 15 to 18)

Section—C : Analysis of the Area-wise Data.
(Table Nos 19 to 39)

Section—D: Analysis of the Item-wise Data.
(Table Nos 40 to 57)

Analysis of the data in the above 4 sections indicates a classification of the data in the Tables 8 to 60, on the basis of what has been indicated therein.

Section–A : Analysis of the Tool-wise Data

It shows the data pertaining to the Whole Opinionnaire and its two constituent Tools i.e., Teacher Factor Tool and Environmental Factors Tool, to indicate (a) their chi-square values and also (b) a comparison of the Mean-Scores in the constituent tools Tables 8 to 11. In addition, it presents separately a split-up of the Teacher Responses in the Whole Opinionnaire in two different Tables (Table Nos 12 and 13) in order to establish the inter-relations between the two constituent areas, a separate Table (Table No.14) is given for analysing the Tool-wise Data to indicate their coefficient of correlation.

Section–B : Analysis of the Variable -wise Data

It is quite different from Section—A and is indicative of the following data in four Tables:

(a) Comparison of the Variable-wise Data in the two constituent Tools of Teacher Morale Opinionnaire, i.e., Teacher Factor Tool and Environmental Factors Tool (Table No. 15).
(b) Variable-wise Data of the Whole Opinionnaire (Table No. 16).
(c) Variable-wise Data of its two constituent Tools i.e., Teacher Factor Tool and Environmental Factors Tool (Table No.17 and 18).

So, it gives findings pertaining to the impact of the nature of each sub-samples on the morale of the respondents.

Section –C : Analysis of the Area-wise Data

It presents Area-wise Data of the two constituent Tools of Teacher Morale, i.e., Teacher Factor Tool and Environmental Factors Tool (Table Nos 19 to 39) as well as the following aspects of the study.

(a) Area-wise Mean–Scores in each of the two constituent Tools and their Rank-Order (Table Nos. 36 and 37).
(b) Their Area-wise interrelations (coefficients of correlations) Table No. 38).
(c) Ranking of the Area-wise interrelations (coefficients of correlation) (Table No. 39) .

Section–C presents its data thus in a total No. of 21 tables.

Section–D : Analysis of the Item-wise Data

It presents Item-wise Data of the Teacher Responses in the 12 areas of the Whole Opinionnaire separately, in order to indicate Mean-Score of each item and thereby its point score in the 3 pt scale . Thus, the whole data are presented as per this classification to facilitate the drawing of inferences from them for a study of their findings.

A Break-up showing these four sections is given hereunder:

Sl. No.	Section	Name of the Section	Table Nos.	Tabal No. of Tables
1.	Section—A	Analysis of the Tool-wise Data	8 to 14	7
2.	Section—B	Analysis of the Variable-wise Data	15 to 18	4
3.	Section—C	Analysis of the Area-wise Data	19 to 39	21
4.	Section—D	Analysis of the Item-wise Data	40 to 57	18
		Skewness of Whole Tool, Tool—I and II	58 to 60	3
			Total	53

SECTION—A

Analysis of Tool-wise Data

In this section the Total tool scores, and the Sectional tool scores are analysed. Chi-square test is applied to the data by using Normal Probability Hypotheses.

TABLE—8

Table showing the Frequency Distribution of scores in the Whole Opinionnaire and their Chi-square Values.

Class Interval	f_o	f_e	$f_o - f_e$	$(f_o - f_e)^2$	$\frac{(f_o - f_e)^2}{f_e}$
Below 304	121	100.8	20.2	408.04	4.048
304–419	396	428.4	–32.4	1049.76	2.450
Above 419	113	100.8	12.2	148.84	1.476
					7.974

Chi-square = 7.974 ; for 2 d.f., P–at 0.2 level is 7.824

The mean and S.D for the sample of 630 on Whole Opinionnaire scores are 361.11 and 57.49 respectively. The data is subjected to Chi-squire test using Normal Probability Hypothesis. The Class intervals are taken as given hereunder.

< Mean–1 S.D. = 304 (361.11–57.49) ; Below 304

Mean–1 S.D to Mean +1 S.D = 304–419

> Mean + I.S.D = 419 (361.11 + 57.49) Above 419

From Table No. 8, it may be noted that the obtained Chi-Square Value is significant at 0.02 level. The Distribution of morale scores in the whole sample is normal.

TABLE —9

Table showing the Frequency Distribution of scores in the Teacher Factor Tool and their Chi-Square Values.

Class Interval	f_o	f_e	$f_o - f_e$	$(f_o - f_e)^2$	$\frac{(f_o - f_e)^2}{f_e}$
Below 156	105	100.8	4.2	17.64	0.175
156-214	419	428.4	-9.4	88.36	0.2062
Above 214	106	100.8	5.2	27.04	0.2682
					0. 6494

Chi-square = 0.6494; for 2 d.f; P–at 0.005 level is 5.991

The Mean and S.D for the sample of 630 on Teacher Factor Tool scores are 184.87 and 29.13 respectively. The data is subjected to Chi-square test using Normal Probability Hypothesis. The Class Intervals are taken as given hereunder.

< Mean–1 S.D. = 156 (184.87–29.13); Below 156

Mean–1 S.D. to Mean + 1 S.D= 156 to 214

> Mean + 1. S.D. = 214 (184.87 + 29.13) ; Above 214

From Table No. 9, it may be noted that the obtained Chi-square Value is not significant at 0.05 level; The Normal Probability Hypothesis is rejected for the Teacher Factor Tool Scores.

TABLE —10

Table Showing the Frequency Distribution of scores in the Environmental Factors Tool and their Chi-square Values.

Class Interval	f_o	f_e	$f_o - f_e$	$(f_o - f_e)^2$	$\frac{(f_o - f_e)^2}{f_e}$
Below 144	104	100.8	3.2	10.24	0.1015
144- 208	389	428.4	-39.4	1552.36	3.6236
Above 208	137	100.8	36.2	1310.44	13.0003
					16.7254

Chi-square = 16.725; for 2 d. f; P–at 0.01 level is 9.210.

The Mean and S.D for the sample of 630 on Environmental Factors Tool Scores are 176.24 and 31.76 respectively. The data is subjected to Chi-square test using Normal Probability Hypothesis. The Class Intervals are taken as given hereunder.

< Mean – 1 S.D = 156 (176.24–31.76) below 144

Mean – 1 S.D. to Mean + 1 S.D = 144–208

> Mean + 1 S.D. = 208 (176.24 + 31.76) Above 208

From Table—10, it may be noted that the obtained Chi-square Value is significant at 0.01 level. The distribution of morale scores pertaining to Environmental Factors Tool of the sample is normal.

TABLE—11

Table showing the comparison of the mean scores of Teacher Factor Tool and Environmental Factors Tool.

Name of the Tool	N	Mean	S.D	Mean Difference	C.R.
Teacher Factor	630	184.87	29.13	8.63	5.02 *
Environmental Factors	630	176.24	31.76		

In this table the C.R. Value being significant. Teacher Factor operates more than Environmental Factors in determining the perception of Teacher-morale. Evidently, as per the perception made by the sample, the Teacher Factor appears to be more significant in view of its greater mean-score.

TABLE—12

Table showing the split-up of Teacher responses as per the three point scale in Positive and Negative items of the Whole Opinionnaire.

Tool	Total No. of Statements	Total Number of Statements (Positive and Negative)	Agreement	Undecided	Disagreement
Tool - I	80	Positive—73	26	47	—
		Negative—7	6	1	—
			32	48	
Tool - II	80	Positive—72	23	49	—
		Negative—8	7	1	—
			30	50	
			62	98	

1. the above table reveals that we have about 10 per cent of the items in each of the two constituent factors of Teacher Morale, under negative items; thus, positive items have taken 90 per cent of the space in them.
2. Negative statements seem to have received more agreement from the sample than the positive statements.
3. Besides, no item received disagreement from the sample.

4. We may perhaps lean more on the other types of data like variable-wise, area-wise and item wise data than the above data (Tool wise data) in studying the morale scores.

TABLE—13

Table showing the split-up of Teacher responses as per the 3 point scale in percentages under the whole opinionnaire.

Tool	Percentage of Statements Agreement	Percentage of Statements Undecided	Percentage of Statements Disagreement
Tool—I	40	60	—
Tool—II	37.5	62.5	—
Whole Tool (Tool—I & II)	38.8	61.2	—

The data of of Table—12 converted into percentages shows that in both the tools, 60% and slightly above, of the Statements fall in the category of no opinion. This sample of teachers has not shown significant opinion on 61.2% of the statements. They have marked opinion on 37% of statements in Tool—II, and 40% of the statements from Tool—I. The sample has not disagreed with any one of the statements. This itself is one interesting trend in the sample. In addition, the sample appears to be relatively more agreed on the items of Tool—I than on Tool—II, with a slight marginal difference.

TABLE — 14

Table showing the co-efficients of correlation between the Teacher Factor Tool and Environmental Factors Tool.

Items	Correlated	Co-efficients of correlation
Tool—I	Teacher Factor	
	Vs	0.783
Tool—II	Environmental Factors	

As can be seen from the above table the relationship of Teacher Factor with Environmental Factors was found high, which would show that both these factors are interrelated positively. It means that one who has high Teacher Factor morale is likely to have a high Environmental Factors morale too.

SECTION —B

Analysis of of the Variable-wise Data

Eight variables were selected for this study as already stated. Analysis of variables for the whole Tool, Teacher Factor Tool and Environmental Factors Tool are presented below, separately.

For each subsample, means and standard deviations are calculated and mean differences tested for significance at 0.01 level by applying the 't' test. Let us see here under tables No. 15 to 18 for the above analysis of variable-wise and tool-wise data.

TABLE—15

Table showing a comparison of the variable wise data in Teacher Factor Tool and Environmental Factors Tool.

Variable and its Categories	N	Mean	S.D.	C.R.
1	2	3	4	5
Age				
1. 26-30 Years	80	T.F. 181.41	23.03	2.14
		E.F. 173.10	26.08	
2. 31-40	" 162	T.F. 179.67	31.46	2.52
		E.F. 170.65	32.91	
3. 41-50	" 183	T.F. 182.52	32.45	3.11 *
		E.F. 171.52	35.13	
4. 50 Above	" 205	T.F. 192.41	24.22	2.48
		E.F. 186.10	26.95	
Sex				
1. Male	360	T.F. 176.90	29.66	3.71 *
		E.F. 168.73	29.95	
2. Female	270	T.F. 195.49	24.63	3.79 *
		E.F. 186.27	31.28	

(Cont.)...

1	2	3	4	5
Qualification				
1. Under Graduate	60	T.F. 194.10	29.62	1.35
		E.F. 186.18	33.23	
2. Graduate	400	T.F. 180.88	30.09	4.08 *
		E.F. 171.87	32.45	
3. Post Graduate	170	T.F. 190.98	24.38	2.84 *
		E.F. 183.02	27.18	
Designation				
1. Secondary Grade	188	T.F. 190.07	26.52	3.77 *
		E.F. 179.06	29.75	
2. B.Ed. Assistant	342	T.F. 179.85	30.67	3.8 *
		E.F. 170.57	33.11	
3. Head Master	100	T.F. 192.22	24.62	0.53
		E.F. 190.35	24.66	
Experience				
1. Below 5 Yrs	107	T.F. 178.28	26.78	1.71
		E.F. 171.85	27.98	
2. 6-10	" 130	T.F. 182.77	32.00	2.49
		E.F. 172.42	34.74	
3. 11-15	" 170	T.F. 184.09	33.48	2.94 *
		E.F. 172.89	36.65	
4. Above 15	" 223	T.F. 189.83	23.44	2.86 *
		E.F. 183.13	25.85	
Management				
1. Government	97	T.F. 183.11	30.60	1.95
		E.F. 173.71	36.04	

Cont...

1	2	3	4	5
2. Local Body	312	T.F. 179.10	30.14	3.32 *
		E.F. 170.87	31.95	
3. Private	221	T.F. 193.78	24.37	3.59 *
		E.F. 184.94	27.21	
Location				
1. Urban	353	T.F. 181.16	29.28	4.29 *
		E.F. 171.25	31.96	
2. Rural	277	T.F. 189.58	28.19	2.8 *
		E.F. 182.60	30.28	
Size of Class				
1. 50 More	285	T.F. 178.40	29.68	3.87 *
		E.F. 168.46	31.71	
2 30-49	252	T.F. 188.20	29.60	2.80 *
		E.F. 180.40	32.65	
3. Below 30	93	T.F. 195.63	19.79	2.26
		E.F. 188.85	21.49	

* Significant at 0.01 level.

Tables 11 and 15 show respectively (a) a comparison of the Teacher Factor means with Environmental Factors means for the whole sample, and (b) data of the variable-wise sub samples.

1. A comparison of the toolwise data in Table—11 shows that the Teacher Factor mean is significantly higher than the Environmental Factors mean, while the eight sub-samples reveal two different types of findings from Table—15 : one, indicating equivalence of the two constituent factors of Teacher morale i.e., Teacher-Factor and Environmental Factors (in the case of 9 out of 24 categories) and the other, indicating a preference given by some categories of respondents in these subsamples for the Teacher factor (in the case of 15 categories out of 24 categories). Hence we may infer that Teacher Factor morale appears to be higher than Environmental Factors morale.

2. When the subsample wise comparison is made, in 15 out of 24 subsample categories the Teacher Factor morale is found to be higher, significantly, when compared to the Environmental Factors morale. These 15 subsample categories are distributed in all the 8 variables, vide the following details:
   a. There are reasons to believe that the higher the age, the higher is the Teacher Factor morale. But this is not found to be so significantly, in all higher age-groups; as can be seen from Table—15, there are four categories of respondents on the Age-variable; of these, only one category reveals its preference for Teacher Factor morale, while the other three categories reveal the equivalence given by them to the two constituent factors of Morale.
   b. For both Male and Female teachers the Teacher Factor morale is higher than the Environmental Factor morale.
   c. In Graduate Trained Teachers and Post-graduate Teachers the Teacher factor morale is higher than the Environmental Factor morale. However, the Under Graduate teachers' subsample didn't manifest a similar phenomenon.
   d. In Secondary Grade and B.Ed., teachers the Teacher Factor morale is higher than Environmental Factor morale. Again, here also, the other subsample i.e, he Head Masters didn't manifest the same belief.
   e. Experience wise, it seems that the higher the experience, the higher is the Teacher Factor morale.
   f. For teachers working in Local Body Schools and Private Management Schools, Teacher Factor morale is higher. Here also the other subsample i.e., those working in Government Schools didn't manifest this finding.
   g. In both Urban and Rural School teachers the Teacher Factor morale is higher than the Environmental Factor morale.
   h. Similarly, size of the class is also affecting the Teacher Factor morale. Environmental Factor morale is lower than Teacher Factor morale. But teachers handling the smallest size classes i.e., below 30 didn't share this belief of the other two subsamples and revealed the equivalence of these two factors of Morale.

TABLE—16

Table showing the variable-wise data of the whole opinionnaire.

Variable and its Categories	N	Mean	S.D.	Categories related	C.R.
1 2	3	4	5	6	7
Age					
1. 26-30 Years	80	354.51	43.32	1-2	0.61
2. 31-40 "	162	350.32	61.24	1-3	0.07
3. 41-50 "	183	354.04	64.25	1-4	4.07 *
4. 50 above "	205	378.51	48.00	2-3	0.55
				2-4	4.81 *
				3-4	4.21
Sex					
1. Male	360	345.62	55.76	1–2	8.28 *
2. Female	270	381.76	53.00		
Qualification					
1. Under Graduate	60	380.28	59.78	1-2	3.33 *
2. Graduate	400	352.75	58.98	1-3	0.73
3. Post Graduate	170	374.00	48.19	2-3	4.49 *
Designation					
1. Secondary Grade	188	369.13	52.84	1-2	3.71 *
2. B. Ed., Assistant	342	350.42	60.13	1-3	2.21
3. Head Master	100	382.57	46.96	2-3	5.63 *
Experience					
1. Below 5 Yrs	107	350.13	50.85	1-2	0.68
2. 6-10 "	130	355.19	63.26	1-3	0.96
3. 11-15 "	170	356.98	67.08	1-4	3.94 *
4. Above 15 "	223	372.97	45.68	2-3	0.24
				2-4	[illegible].81 *
				3-4	2.67
Management					
1. Govt.,	97	356.82	63.37	1-2	0.95
2. Local Body	312	349.97	58.49	1-3	3.04 *
3. Private	221	378.71	48.19	2-3	6.20 *

Cont...

1 2	3	4	5	6	7
Location					
1. Urban	353	352.42	57.35	1-2	4.37 *
2. Rural	277	372.18	55.63		
Size of Class					
1. Above 50	285	346.86	57.40	1-2	4.31 *
2. 30–49	252	368.60	59.02	1-3	7.15 *
3. Below 30	93	384.48	38.75	2-3	2.90 *

* Significant at 0.01 level

As can be seen from the above Table—16, out of 26 C.R. values for the 24 categories of subsamples, 17 C.R. Values are significant under all the eight variables; which would mean that in each of those variables, only 17 categories of respondents secured higher meanscores than the other 7 categories in the whole opinionnaire comprising the Teacher Factor morale and the Environmental Factors morale.

The above table reveals the following findings pertaining to the composite morale score under the two factors of Teacher-morale.

1. With reference to the variable 'Age', Teachers above the age of 50 years hold a comparatively higher Teacher morale.
2. In respect of the Variable Sex, female teachers hold higher morale than male teachers.
3. In terms of Educational Qualifications, Graduate Teachers hold a lower Teacher-morale than Under Graduate and Post-graduate Teachers.
4. With reference to the Designation in school system, it is evident that the Head Masters hold a high morale when compared with B.Ed Teachers. At the same time it is interesting to note that the Secondary Grade Teachers with lower Educational Qualifications hold a comparatively higher morale than B.Ed., Teachers who were more qualified. Evidently, the qualification based designation phenomenon has not much impact on morale score.

5. Teachers with more than 15 years of professional experience hold a comparatively higher morale than each of the other three subsamples in this variable.
6. Indian Teachers are working in different managements. A comparison of Teacher morale in this variable shows that teachers working in private management schools hold comparatively a higher morale than teachers working in Government Schools and schools managed by Local Bodies.
7. Location wise, Teachers working in rural areas have a better morale than teachers working in urban areas.
8. The size of the class also seems to be an influencing variable. Teachers handling small size classes have higher morale than teachers handlings large size classes and median size classes.

TABLE—17

Table showing the variable wise data of Teacher Factor Tool.

Variable and its Categories	N	Mean	S.D.	Categories related	C.R.
1 2	3	4	5	6	7
Age					
1. 26-30 Years	80	181.41	23.03	1-2	0.49
2. 31-40 "	162	179.67	31.46	1-3	0.32
3. 41-50 "	183	182.52	32.45	1-4	3.57 *
4. 50 above"	205	192.41	24.22	2-3	0.83
				2-4	4.25 *
				3-4	3.37 *
Sex					
1. Male	360	176.90	29.66	1-2	8.59 *
2. Female	270	195.49	24.63		
Qualification					
1. Under Graduate	60	194.10	29.62	1-2	3.22*
2. Graduate	400	180.88	30.09	1-3	0.73
3. Post Graduate	170	190.98	24.38	2-3	4.21 *
Designation					
1. Secondary Grade	188	190.07	26.52	1-2	4.01 *

(Cont.)...

1	2	3	4	5	6	7
2.	B.Ed., Asst.,	342	179.85	30.67	1-3	0.69
3.	Head Master	100	192.22	24.62	2-3	4.17 *
Experience						
1.	below 5 Yrs	107	178.28	26.78	1-2	1.18
2.	6-10 "	130	182.77	32.00	1-3	1.59
3.	11-15 "	170	184.09	33.48	1-4	3.82 *
4.	Above 15 "	223	189.83	23.44	2-3	0.35
					2-4	2.20
					3-4	1.91
Management						
1.	Government	97	183.11	30.60	1-2	1.13
2.	Local Body	312	179.10	30.14	1-3	3.04 *
3.	Private	221	193.78	24.37	2-3	6.21 *
Location						
1.	Urban	353	181.16	29.28	1-2	3.66 *
2.	Rural	277	189.58	28.19		
Size of Class						
1.	Above 50	285	178.40	29.68	1-2	3.82 *
2.	30-49	252	188.20	29.60	1-3	6.38 *
3.	Below 30	93	195.63	19.79	2-3	2.68 *

* Significant at 0.01 level

As can be seen from the above table out of the 26 C.R. Values 15 are significant at 0.01 level. It can be observed from the table that all the 8 variables are associated in these 15 C.R. Values.

The following are the findings from this table in Teacher Factor morale:

1. Teachers who fall within the age group above 50, hold a comparatively higher morale score.
2. Female Teachers have a higher morale than Male Teachers.
3. Under Graduate Teachers and Post-graduate Teachers have a higher morale than Graduate Teachers.
4. Head Masters and Secondary Grade Teachers have a higher Teacher Factor morale than Graduate Teachers. Evidently the Qualification based Designation hasn't much impact on the Teacher-Factor morale too.

5. Teachers with more than 15 years experience have a higher score in Teacher Factor morale, only when compared to those within 5 years experience. These two groups are at the two extremes. The other two groups which are consecutively the middle groups don't differ in their Teacher Factor morale scores from each other as well as from the above two groups at the extremes. Probably, changes in Teacher Factor morale occur among teachers only after 15 years' experience. Hence the Teacher Factor morale scores of category No. 4 (those with more than 15 years experience) don't differ from those of group Nos 2 and 3 nor do those of the latter differ from those of group number 1.

Thus, the experience variable has a very low impact and Teacher Factor morale probably grows, only by a longer experience which may be synonym for morale.

6. Teachers working in private Management Schools have a higher Teacher morale than Teachers working in Government and Local Body Schools.
7. Teachers working in rural Schools have higher Teacher Factor morale than Teachers working in Urban Schools.
8. Teachers handling small size classes have a higher Teacher Factor morale than Teachers handling large size classes.

TABLE—18

Table showing the variable wise data of Environmental Factors Tool.

Variable and its Categories	N	Mean	S.D.	Categories related	C.R.
1 2	3	4	5	6	7
Age					
1. 20-30 Years	80	173.10	26.08	1-2	0.63
2. 31-40 "	162	170.65	32.91	1-3	0.40
3. 41-50 "	183	171.52	35.13	1-4	3.75 *
4. 50 above "	205	186.10	26.95	2-3	0.24
				2-4	4.83 *
				3-4	4.85 *
Sex					
1. Male	360	168.73	29.95	1-2	7.09 *
2. Female	270	186.27	31.28		

Cont...

1	2	3	4	5	6	7
Qualification						
1.	Under Graduate	60	186.18	33.23	1-2	3.12 *
2.	Graduate	400	171.87	32.45	1-3	0.66
3.	Post Graduate	170	183.02	27.18	2-3	4.22 *
Designation						
1.	Secondary Grade	188	179.06	29.75	1-2	3.02 *
2.	B.Ed., Assistant	342	170.57	33.11	1-3	3.44 *
3.	Head Master	100	190.35	24.66	2-3	6.49 *
Experience						
1.	Below 5 Yrs	107	171.85	27.98	1-2	0.14
2.	6-10 "	130	172.42	34.74	1-3	0.27
3.	11-15 "	170	172.89	36.65	1-4	3.51 *
4.	Above 15 "	223	183.13	25.85	2-3	0.11
					2-4	3.06 *
					3-4	3.10 *
Management						
1.	Government	97	173.71	36.04	1-2	0.70
2.	Local Body	312	170.87	31.95	1-3	2.74 *
3.	Private	221	184.94	27.21	2-3	5.47 *
Location						
1.	Urban	353	171.25	31.96	1-2	4.55 *
2.	Rural	277	182.60	30.28		
Size of Class						
1.	Above 50	285	168.46	31.71	1-2	4.29 *
2.	30-49	252	180.40	32.65	1-3	7.00 *
3.	below 30	93	188.85	21.49	2-3	2.79 *

*Significant 0.01 level

As can be seen from the above table out of the 26 C.R. Values, 18 C.R. Values are significant at 0.01 level in the Environmental Factors morale, as against the 15 C.R. Values significant in the Teacher Factor morale, which would show that a larger No. of categories of respondents got a higher morale score in the Environmental Factors morale than in the Teacher Factor morale. The following are the findings from this table:

1. Teachers above the age of 50 years have a higher morale score in the Environmental Factors tool as in the case of Teacher Factor morale. There is some difference in this finding regarding this category in the highest age-group, as far as the morale scores in the two factors are concerned. In these scores of both the factors, only this category got a higher meanscore; but in the case of Teacher Factor scores, this mean score is significantly different from that of the youngest age group alone; while in the Environmental Factors scores, it is significantly different from those of all the other three categories.
2. Female Teachers have higher Environmental Factors morale than male Teachers as in the Teacher Factor.
3. Graduate Trained Teachers have lower Environmental Factors morale too than Post-graduate and Under Graduate Teachers as in the Teacher Factor.
4. Head Masters and Secondary Grade Teachers have higher Environmental Factors morale than B.Ed Teachers. There seems to be some difference between the impact of Teacher Factor morale and the Environmental Factors morale, in the case of the Head Masters and Secondary Grade Teachers, as the former group got a higher level of the morale than the latter in the Environmental Factors morale but both these groups didn't differ from each other in the Teacher Factor morale. Evidently, realization of the Environmental Factors morale is higher in the head masters, when compared to the one in the Teacher Factor morale.
5. In regard to experience the situation under the Environmental Factors seems to be quite different from the one under Teacher Factor. This is because the teachers with the highest experience differ from the other three groups in their Environmental Factors morale scores unlike in the Teacher Factor morale scores wherein they differed only from the least experienced teachers. Evidently, Environmental Factors morale has a greater impact from Experience variable, even before one acquires an experience for 15 years while the Teacher Factor morale has lesser impact from this variable, as it is operative here only after one acquires 15 years experience, which may be equated with same type of maturity.
6. Teachers working in private Management Schools have a higher Environmental Factors morale than, teachers working in

Government Schools and Local Body Schools, as in the case of Teacher Factor morale.

7. Teachers working in Rural Schools have higher Environmental Factors morale than Teachers working in Urban Schools as in the case of Teacher Factor morale.
8. Teachers handling small size classes have better Environmental Factors morale than the teachers handling large size classes, as in the case of Teacher Factor morale.

SECTION—C

Analysis of Area-wise Data

Tool—I : Teacher Factor

This Tool consists of six areas namely:

1. Personality Factors,
2. Professional Aspirations,
3. Professional Skills:
   (a) Academic Proficiency,
   (b) Teaching Ability,
   (c) Organising Skills,
   (d) Linguistic Proficiency

Under each area, scores of each subsample were calculated. Means and standard deviations for these scores of the subsample in each area were also calculated and compared for significance at 0.01 level.

TABLE —19

Table showing the data of Area (i) Personality Factors.

Variable and its	Categories	N	Mean	S.D.	Categories related	C.R.
1	2	3	4	5	6	7
Age						
1.	26-30 Years	80	59.88	8.43	1-2	1.24
2.	31-40 "	162	58.28	11.27	1-3	0.65
3.	41-50 "	183	59.05	11.52	1-4	2.65 *

Cont...

1	2	3	4	5	6	7
4.	50 above "	205	62.84	8.61	2-3	0.63
					2-4	4.27 *
					3-4	3.64 *
Sex						
1.	Male	360	55.92	10.44	1-2	14.30 *
2.	Female	270	65.89	7.05		
Qualification						
1.	Under Graduate	60	63.20	9.58	1-2	3.15 *
2.	Graduate	400	58.94	10.91	1-3	0.80
3.	Post Graduate	170	62.07	8.78	2-3	3.61 *
Designation						
1.	Secondary Grade	188	61.67	9.47	1-2	3.24 *
2.	B. Ed., Assistant	342	58.70	11.11	1-3	0.76
3.	Head Master	100	62.50	8.52	2-3	3.64 *
Experience						
1.	Below 5 Yrs.	107	58.49	10.23	1-2	0.63
2.	6-10 "	130	59.35	10.91	1-3	0.57
3.	11-15 "	170	59.25	11.82	1-4	3.27 *
4.	Above 15 "	223	62.22	8.50	2-3	0.08
					2-4	2.57
					3-4	2.78 *
Management						
1.	Government	97	59.82	11.09	1-2	1.57
2.	Local Body	312	57.82	10.64	1-3	3.07 *
3.	Private	221	63.71	8.57	2-3	7.06 *
Location						
1.	Urban	353	59.08	10.52	1-2	3.07 *
2.	Rural	277	61.61	10.05		
Size of Class						
1.	Above 50	285	57.80	10.80	1-2	4.22 *
2.	30-49	252	61.64	10.26	1-3	5.84 *
3.	Below 30	93	63.60	7.33	2-3	1.97

* Significant at 0.01 level.

As can be seen from the above table, out of a total No. of 26 C.R. Values, 15 C.R. Values are significant at 0.01 level. The following are the findings from this Table:

1. In terms of Personality Factor age seems to be an influencing variable. The Higher the age, the higher is the Personality Factor mean score as found under the analysis of variable wise and tool wise data.
2. Female teachers reveal a highly greater influence of Personality Factor on their morale than male teachers as found under the analysis of variable wise and tool wise data.
3. Under-Graduate Teachers and Post-graduate Teachers reveal a higher influence on their morale from their Personality Factor than Graduate Teachers as found under the analysis of variable wise and tool wise data.
4. Head Masters and Secondary Grade Teachers reveal a higher influence on their morale from their Personality Factor than B.Ed Teachers as found under the analysis of variable wise and tool wise data.
5. In terms of experience, there are reasons to believe that highly experienced teachers reveal a higher influence from their Personality Factor on their morale. But, the category with the most highly experienced teachers differed only from two categories out of the remaining three categories; it means; its mean-score didn't differ significantly from that of one category in the latter, which seems to show that the middle two categories of teachers with an experience range from 6 to 15 years do not differ from each other in their mean-scores. So, we may infer that morale appears to change considerably that is significantly, only after the 15 years' experience in personality factors, as in the case of Teacher Factor morale scores.
6. As far as the type of management is concerned teachers working in schools under Private Managements have a higher Personality Factor than teachers working in Government Schools and Local Body Schools.
7. Teachers working in Rural Schools reveal a greater influence on their morale from their Personality Factors, than teachers working in Urban Schools.
8. Size of the class seems to be a variable influencing the Personality Factor. However Teachers handling small size classes and median size classes, have a higher mean than the other group (Category No. 1).

TABLE—20

Table showing the data of area (2) Professional Aspirations.

Variable and its Categories		N	Mean	S.D.	Categories related	C.R.
1	2	3	4	5	6	7
Age						
1. 26-30 Years		80	58.05	9.56	1-2	0.14
2. 31-40 "		162	57.86	11.15	1-3	0.44
3. 41-50 "		183	58.66	11.50	1-4	3.20 *
4. 50 above "		205	61.98	8.68	2-3	0.65
					2-4	3.87 *
					3-4	3.18 *
Sex						
1. Male		360	58.37	11.25	1-2	3.13 *
2. Female		270	60.91	9.14		
Qualification						
1. Under Graduate		60	61.65	10.88	1-2	2.36
2. Graduate		400	58.10	10.81	1-3	0.14
3. Post Graduate		170	61.87	8.82	2-3	4.35 *
Designation						
1. Secondary Grade		188	61.64	9.79	1-2	4.41 *
2. B.Ed., Assistant		342	57.54	11.04	1-3	0.24
3. Head Master		100	61.90	8.11	1-3	4.33 *
Experience						
1. Below 5 Yrs		107	57.14	10.15	1-2	1.16
2. 6-10 "		130	58.76	11.35	1-3	1.60
3. 11-15 "		170	59.26	11.73	1-4	3.49 *
4. Above 15 "		223	61.12	8.64	2-3	0.38
					2-4	2.04
					3-4	1.73
Management						
1. Government		97	58.55	10.84	1-2	0.50
2. Local Body		312	57.91	11.22	1-3	2.81 *
3. Private		221	62.03	8.53	2-3	4.81 *

Cont..

1	2	3	4	5	6	7
Location						
1. Urban		353	58.23	10.70	1-2	3.37 *
2. Rural		277	61.01	9.96		
Size of Class						
1. Above 50		285	57.56	10.89	1-2	2.83 *
2.	30-49	252	60.18	10.58	1-3	5.89 *
3. Below 30		93	63.29	7.01	2-3	3.15 *

* Significant at 0.01 level

As can be seen from the above table, out of a total number of 26 C.R. values, 14 C.R. Values are significant at 0.01 level. The following are the findings from this table:

1. In this area of Professional Aspirations, Age seems to be an influencing variable. The higher the age, the higher are the Professional Aspirations as in the case of Personality Factors.
2. Interestingly, Female Teachers have more professional Aspirations than Male Teachers as in the case of Personality Factors.
3. Post-graduate Teachers have higher Professional Aspirations than Graduate Trained Teachers as in the case of Personality Factors. Interestingly the level of Professional Aspirations for Under-Graduate Teachers and Graduate Teachers appears to be similar.
4. Head Masters and Secondary Grade Teachers hold the same level of Professional Aspirations which is higher than that of B.Ed., teachers as in the case of Personality Factors.
5. In-experienced teachers and experienced teachers differed in the level of Professional Aspirations. Naturally, experienced teachers have a higher level of Professional Aspirations, when compared to the inexperienced teachers. However, unlike in Personality Factors, here the experienced teachers in category No. 4 of the respondents above 15 years' experience differ in their morale score of Professional Aspirations, and from that of the inexperienced teachers who belong to category No. 1 of the respondents within 5 years' experience. They do not differ from the categories No.2 and 3, which would mean that the impact of this area on Teacher morale seems to change very

imperceptibly until one acquires 15 years experience and most perceptibly, only later.

6. Teachers working in Private Management Schools have higher Professional Aspirations than teachers working in Government and Local Body Schools as in the case of Personality Factors.
7. Teachers working in Rural Schools have higher Professional Aspirations than teachers working in Urban areas as in the case of Personality Factors.
8. Size of the Class appears to be a variable influencing Professional Aspirations. Teachers handling smaller size classes have higher Professional Aspirations than the teachers handling large size classes. But, unlike in the Personality Factors, wherein the teachers, handling median size classes (category No.2) equalled those handling the small size classes in their higher morale score, here in Professional Aspirations, the three categories of respondents showed three different levels significant from one another, ranking them in order of their morale score as shown here-under:

Rank No.	*Category*
1.	Teachers handling small size classes.
2.	Teachers handling median size classes.
3.	Teachers handling large size classes.

TABLE —21

Table showing the data of area 3 (a) Academic proficiency.

Variable and its Categories	N	Mean	S.D.	Categories related	C.R.
1 2	3	4	5	6	7
Age					
1. 26-30 Years	80	16.76	2.82	1-2	0.02
2. 31-40 "	162	16.75	3.25	1-3	0.96
3. 41-50 "	183	17.16	3.63	1-4	2.23
4. 50 above "	205	17.59	2.82	2-3	1.09
				2-4	2.56
				3-4	1.30
Sex					
1. Male	360	17.03	3.26	1-2	1.04
2. Female	270	17.30	3.13		

Cont...

1	2	3	4	5	6	7
Qualification						
1.	Under Graduate	60	18.18	3.58	1-2	2.94 *
2.	Graduate	400	16.75	3.16	1-3	0.90
3.	Post Graduate	170	17.72	2.99	2-3	3.49 *
Designation						
1.	Secondary Grade	188	17.80	2.99	1-2	4.04 *
2.	B.Ed., Assistant	342	16.67	3.29	1-3	0.71
3.	Head Master	100	17.54	3.03	2-3	2.49
Experience						
1.	below 5 Yrs	107	16.60	2.81	1-2	1.16
2.	6-10 "	130	17.08	3.54	1-3	1.77
3.	11-15 "	170	17.29	3.71	1-4	2.25
4.	Above 15 "	223	17.33	2.68	2-3	0.52
					2-4	0.71
					3-4	0.11
Management						
1.	Government	97	16.92	3.24	1-2	0.32
2.	Local Body	312	16.80	3.24	1-3	2.10
3.	Private	221	17.73	3.05	2-3	3.40 *
Location						
1.	Urban	353	16.82	3.25	1-2	2.92 *
2.	Rural	277	17.56	3.10		
Size of Class						
1.	Above 50	285	16.69	3.21	1-2	2.53
2.	30-49	252	17.41	3.34	1-3	3.38 *
3.	Below 30	93	17.80	2.55	2-3	1.13

* Significant at 0.01 level

Area–3: Professional Skills

a) Academic Proficiency

The area Professional Skills is divided into four sub areas, namely:

a. Academic Proficiency,
b. Teaching Ability,

c. Organising Skills,
d. Linguistic Proficiency.

As can be seen from the above Table—21 dealing with the sub area No. (a) Academic Proficiency, out of 26 C.R. Values only 6 C.R. Values are significant at 0.01 level, which would mean a low impact of this sub area in Teacher Morale; particularly in view of a large No. of C.R. Values (as many as 20) being insignificant.

1. Significant mean differences are found only in five variables; Qualification, Designation, Type of Management, Location and Size of the Class. The other three variables have insignificant mean-differences which would mean that none of their constituent categories got a higher morale score than the other constituent categories.
2. Post-graduate Teachers and Under Graduate Teachers seem to differ from Graduate Teachers with reference to the area of Academic Proficiency. It is quite surprising to note that Under Graduate teachers have a higher Teacher–morale than Graduate Teachers even in items pertaining to Academic Proficiency which might mean that this area does not seem to influence the morale of the Under Graduate Teachers and Graduate Teachers.
3. As for the Variable 'Designation', only the Secondary Grade Teachers seem to have scored a higher mean, in their morale, than the B.Ed., Trained Teachers. This finding tallies to some extent with the situation in the case of the Qualification variable.
4. There is difference between teachers working in Local Body Management Schools and Private Management Schools. Teachers working in Private Management Schools show a higher mean in this area. But in the case of Government School Teachers, their morale score seems to be equal to that of Teachers of schools under Private Managements. Evidently this sub-area 'Academic Proficiency' doesn't affect the morale of the Government School Teachers.
5. Rural School Teachers have shown higher mean in this area than Urban School Teachers, as in the case of Personality Factors.
6. Teachers handling small size classes differ from teachers handling large size classes i.e., above 50 students in a class. But in the case of teachers handling median size classes, their mean scores are equal to those of the other two categories, probably due to a low impact of this sub area on this category of Teachers.

TABLE—22

Table showing the data of area 3 (b) Teaching Ability.

Variable and its Categories	N	Mean	S.D.	Categories related	C.R.
1 2	3	4	5	6	7
Age					
1. 26-30 Years	80	16.74	2.95	1-2	0.06
2. 31-40 "	162	16.77	3.65	1-3	1.13
3. 41-50 "	183	17.21	3.54	1-4	3.40 *
4. 50 above "	205	18.05	2.85	2-3	1.15
				2-4	3.68 *
				3-4	2.54
Sex					
1. Male	360	16.04	3.04	1-2	12.33 *
2. Female	270	19.00	2.93		
Qualification					
1. Under Graduate	60	18.22	3.26	1-2	2.71 *
2. Graduate	400	16.99	3.38	1-3	0.98
3. Post Graduate	170	17.74	3.13	2-3	2.56
Designation					
1. Secondary Grade	188	17.45	3.17	1-2	1.62
2. B.Ed., Assistant	342	16.96	3.51	1-3	2.20
3. Head Master	100	18.24	2.78	2-3	3.80 *
Experience					
1. Below 5 yrs	107	16.57	3.17	1-2	0.84
2. 6-10 "	130	16.95	3.71	1-3	2.13
3. 11-15 "	170	17.46	3.68	1-4	3.33 *
4. Above 15 "	223	17.76	2.77	2-3	1.19
				2-4	2.18
				3-4	0.90
Management					
1. Government	97	17.48	3.37	1-2	2.33
2. Local body	312	16.57	3.40	1-3	2.00
3. Private	221	18.28	2.94	2-3	6.18 *

Cont...

1	2	3	4	5	6	7
Location						
1.	Urban	353	16.88	3.31	1-2	3.71 *
2.	Rural	277	17.86	3.28		
Size of Class						
1.	Above 50	285	16.62	3.39	1-2	3.64 *
2.	30-49	252	17.68	3.34	1-3	5.33 *
3.	Below 30	93	18.42	2.62	2-3	2.16

* Significant at 0.01 level

As can be seen from the above table, 10 C.R. Values are significant at 0.01 level out of a total No. of 26 C.R. Values. The following are the findings from this table:

1. In this sample the higher the age group, the higher is its area mean score. Though we find this area mean -score of the higher age-group as higher, when compared to the category Nos. 1 & 2; yet it does not differ from the category No. 3's area-mean score.
2. Female Teachers have a higher mean-score for this area "Teaching Ability" than Male Teachers as in the case of Personality Factors.
3. The Under Graduate Teachers and Graduate Teachers have shown significant differences in their area mean scores. The Under Graduate Teachers' mean-score for this area "Teaching Ability" is higher than the Graduate Trained Teachers' mean-score. In the case of Post-graduate Teachers, their area mean-score is, however, not so significantly different from that of the other two categories. Evidently, this sub-area doesn't influence the morale of Post-graduate Teachers.
4. Designation wise, the B.Ed Teachers and Head Masters have significantly different area mean scores with a higher score in favour of Head Masters. However in the case of Secondary Grade Trained Teachers, their area-mean score does't differ significantly from those of the other two categories.
5. Inexperienced teachers and Experienced Teachers showed significantly different area means. The Teaching Ability area mean score of experienced teachers is higher than that of inexperienced teachers. But, the impact of this sub area,

Teaching ability, seems to increase, significantly, only after one acquires an experience of 15 years, in view of the fact that the mean-score of the category with highest experience is significantly a higher one than that of the category No.1 alone, i.e., those with lowest experience, while the mean-scores of the other middle categories of respondents don't differ so significantly from those of the former, nor from among themselves.

6. While the Teachers working in Private Management Schools and Government Management Schools show no significant difference, of mean-scores in this sub area, the mean-scores of the teachers working in Local Body Schools and Private Management Schools differ significantly. Thus, in the area of Teaching Ability the Private Management School Teachers show a higher area mean than Local Body School Teachers. However, the mean-score of Government School Teachers doesn't differ significantly from those of the other two categories, which might mean that the impact of this sub area on the Government School Teachers in terms of their morale is very meagre.
7. Location wise the Teaching Ability area mean of Rural School Teachers is significantly higher than Urban School Teachers, in this sub area, as in the case of the preceding three sub areas.
8. In the area of Teaching Ability, teachers handling Small size classes and median size classes have shown higher means than teachers handling large size classes. However, the mean-scores of the former two categories don't differ significantly from those of each other. Probably, this sub area doesn't affect the morale level of these two categories which don't seem to differ from each other.

TABLE—23

Table showing the data of area 3 (c) Organising skills.

Variable and its Categories	N	Mean	S.D.	Categories related	C.R.
1 2	3	4	5	6	7
Age					
1. 26-30 Years	80	14.83	2.51	1-2	0.14
2. 31-40 "	162	14.77	3.13	1-3	1.09

Cont...

1	2	3	4	5	6	7
3.	41-50 "	183	15.22	3.07	1-4	3.68 *
4.	50 above "	205	16.04	2.48	2-3	1.34
					2-4	4.21 *
					3-4	2.87 *
Sex						
1.	Male	360	15.16	2.87	1-2	1.66
2.	Female	270	15.54	2.89		
Qualification						
1.	Under Graduate	60	16.35	3.10	1-2	3.15*
2.	Graduate	400	15.01	2.88	1-3	1.48
3.	Post Graduate	170	15.68	2.69	2-3	2.66 *
Designation						
1.	Secondary Grade	188	15.92	2.70	1-2	4.54 *
2.	B.Ed., Assistant	342	14.77	2.93	1-3	0.45
3.	Head Master	100	16.07	2.67	2-3	4.18 *
Experience						
1.	Below 5 yrs	107	14.46	2.68	1-2	1.95
2.	6-10 "	130	15.21	3.24	1-3	2.53
3.	11-15 "	170	15.36	3.19	1-4	4.32 *
4.	Above 15 "	223	15.77	2.38	2-3	0.40
					2-4	1.73
					3-4	1.41
Management						
1.	Government	97	14.89	2.92	1-2	0.46
2.	Local Body	312	15.04	3.00	1-3	2.94 *
3.	Private	221	15.90	2.61	2-3	3.50 *
Location						
1.	Urban	353	15.09	2.85	1-2	2.29
2.	Rural	277	15.62	2.90		
Size of Class						
1.	Above 50	285	14.84	2.84	1-2	2.93 *
2.	30-49	252	15.57	2.96	1-3	4.13 *
3.	Below 30	93	16.13	2.55	2-3	1.72

* Significant at 0.01 level.

As can be seen from the above table, 12 C.R. Values are significant at 0.01 level out of the 26 C.R. Values in this area:

1. The variables Sex, and Location don't seem to be the influencing variables.
2. The variables that are associated significantly with the area "Organising Skills" are Age, Qualification, Designation, Teaching Experience, Management and Size of the class.
3. The maxim the higher the age, the greater is the morale level of Teachers holds good in this sub area also. The senior age group of Teachers above 50 years differs in its mean-score from those of the other three age groups significantly and yet the latter three age groups don't differ from one another in their morale levels significantly. Evidently the sub area "Organising Skills of Teaching" hasn't much impact on these three age groups in terms of their morale.
4. Under Graduate Teachers and Post-graduate Teachers differ from Graduate Teachers. The former have shown significantly higher mean than the latter. The Head Masters and Secondary Grade Teachers show higher means than B.Ed., Teachers. And also, the former two categories don't differ from each other in their morale levels in terms of this subarea, though their Qualifications differ much, together with their Teaching Experience. Probably, the Qualification based designation hasn't much impact on this sub area in terms of Teacher-morale.
5. As far as the variable 'Experience' is concerned inexperienced teachers show a significant difference from Experienced teachers in the levels of their morale in this sub area. Besides, as found, in some of the previous findings under this section and the other section pertaining to variable wise and tool wise data, this sub area seems to have much impact only on the category of respondents with the highest experience (above 15 years); which alone differed from the category with the least experience (five years and below) in their mean-scores in this sub area. Probably, the impact of this sub area is perceptibly high, only after one acquires 15 years' experience.
6. As for the variable, 'Management', though the Government School Teachers and Local Body School Teachers don't differ, both of them show a lower mean than the teachers working in Private Management Schools, in this area Organising Skills.

7. As for the variable, size of the class, the teachers handling small size classes are better in the area 'Organising Skills' than the teachers handling large size classes. Teachers handling the median size classes have a higher mean-score than only those handling large size classes, but not those handling small size classes. Probably, the impact of this sub area on teachers handling median size classes and small classes appears to be equal.

As can be seen from the Table—24, shown on page No. 156 7 C.R. Values are significant at 0.01 level, out of a total No. of 26 C.R. Values.

1. An examination of the C.R. Values shows that the variables of Age, Designation, and Teaching Experience are not influencing the Linguistic Proficiency. Only the other variables of Sex, Qualifications, Management, Location and size of Class influence the Linguistic Proficiency.
2. Female Teachers have shown a higher mean in this area of Linguistic Proficiency than Male Teachers, unlike in the "Organising Skills", under the Professional Skills wherein this variable sex hasn't influenced the Teachers' morale in terms of this sub area.
3. The under Graduate Teachers and Post-graduate Teachers do not differ from each other in their mean-scores, in the area of Linguistic Proficiency. Both of them show a higher mean than Graduate Teachers in this area of Linguistic Proficiency. We may therefore infer that the Under Graduate Teachers are able to get a higher morale than Graduate Teachers in terms of this sub area; Probably by virtue of their Teaching Experience which involves some Linguistic Proficiency too.
4. While teachers working in Government Schools and Local Body Schools do not differ from each other in this area Linguistic Proficiency, the teachers working in Private Management Schools show a significant difference from Local Body School Teachers. We may perhaps infer from this situation that the Teachers of schools under public management do not have much impact of this sub area in terms of their morale.

TABLE—24

Table showing the data of area 3 (d) Linguistic Proficiency.

Variable and its Categories	N	Mean	S.D.	Categories related	C.R.
Age					
1. 26-30 Years	80	15.16	2.26	1-2	0.23
2. 31-40 "	162	15.24	2.95	1-3	0.18
3. 41-50 "	183	15.22	3.14	1-4	2.38
4. 50 above "	205	15.91	2.64	2-3	0.05
				2-4	2.25
				3-4	2.30
Sex					
1. Male	360	14.39	2.73	1-2	12.13 *
2. Female	270	16.85	2.36		
Qualification					
1. Under Graduate	60	16.50	2.64	1-2	3.80 *
2. Graduate	400	15.09	2.95	1-3	1.55
3. Post-graduate	170	15.89	2.53	2-3	3.29 *
Designation					
1. Secondary Grade	188	15.59	2.77	1-2	1.47
2. B.Ed., Assistant	342	15.21	2.89	1-3	1.12
3. Head Master	100	15.97	2.77	2-3	2.39
Experience					
1. Below 5 yrs	107	15.03	2.47	1-2	1.11
2. 6-10 "	130	15.42	3.01	1-3	1.28
3. 11-15 "	170	15.47	3.25	1-4	2.05
4. Above 15 "	223	15.63	2.57	2-3	0.13
				2-4	0.66
				3-4	0.53
Management					
1. Government	97	15.45	2.89	1-2	1.49
2. Local Body	312	14.95	2.89	1-3	1.98
3. Private	221	16.13	2.62	1-3	4.90 *
Location					
1. Urban	353	15.07	2.91	1-2	3.83 *
2. Rural	277	15.92	2.70		
Size of Class					
1. Above 50	285	14.89	2.90	1-2	3.28 *
2. 30-49	252	15.71	2.91	1-3	5.43 *
3. Below 30	93	16.40	2.10	2-3	2.40

* Significant at 0.01 level.

5. Teachers working in Rural Schools show a higher mean than teachers working in Urban Schools in this area of Linguistic Proficiency as in the other areas of this tool other than Organising Skills.
6. The pattern of C.R. Values for the variable Size of the class seems to indicate that the teachers handling small size classes are more confident about their Linguistic proficiency. Their area mean is significantly higher than the teachers handling large size classes, in the case of teachers handling median size classes, they differ significantly from those handling large size classes in their mean-scores, while they do not differ so from those handling small-size classes.

Tool—II : Environmental Factors

This Tool consists of four areas namely:

1. School Facilities,
2. School Administration,
3. Educational Administration,
4. Environmental Impact:
   (a) Family,
   (b) Community,
   (c) Value system.

Let us try to study the data in Table—25 to 30 pertaining to the areas of this tool, in order to ascertain the influence of these areas in terms of Teacher-morale.

TABLE—25

Table showing the data of area (1) School Facilities.

Variable and its Categories	N	Mean	S.D.	Categories related	C.R.
1 2	3	4	5	6	7
Age					
1. 26-30 Years	80	33.38	5.28	1-2	0.99
2. 31-40 "	162	32.59	6.78	1-3	1.01
3. 41-50 "	183	32.59	6.90	1-4	2.80 *

Cont...

1	2	3	4	5	6	7
4.	50 above "	205	35.38	5.83	2-3	0.01
					2-4	4.17 *
					3-4	4.17 *
Sex						
1.	Male	360	31.38	6.19	1-2	11.00 *
2.	Female	270	36.56	5.58		
Qualification						
1.	Under Graduate	60	35.07	6.32	1-2	2.67 *
2.	Graduate	400	32.71	6.63	1-3	0.10
3.	Post Graduate	170	35.16	5.70	2-3	4.46 *
Designation						
1.	Secondary Grade	188	33.99	6.14	1-2	2.32
2.	B.Ed., Assistant	342	32.65	6.75	1-3	3.07 *
3.	Head Master	100	36.10	5.21	2-3	5.42 *
Experience						
1.	Below 5 yrs	107	33.00	5.53	1-2	0.09
2.	6-10 "	130	32.92	7.16	1-3	0.22
3.	11-15 "	170	32.83	7.18	1-4	2.84 *
4.	Above 15 "	223	34.86	5.66	2-3	0.11
					2-4	2.64 *
					3-4	3.04 *
Management						
1.	Government	97	33.01	7.17	1-2	0.64
2.	Local Body	312	32.49	6.54	1-3	2.94 *
3.	Private	221	35.42	5.58	2-3	5.56 *
Location						
1.	Urban	353	32.74	6.55	1-2	3.82 *
2.	Rural	277	34.69	6.19		
Size of Class						
1.	Above 50	285	32.00	6.53	1-2	4.70 *
2.	30-49	252	34.65	6.55	1-3	5.87 *
3.	Below 30	93	35.63	4.67	2-3	1.54

* Significant at 0.01 level.

As can be seen from the above table, 16 C.R. Values are significant at 0.01 level, out of the total no. of 26 C.R. values in the Area of School Facilities which might mean that this area influences Teacher-morale highly.

1. It can be observed that all the 8 variables are associated with this area.
2. The highest age group has shown higher mean than the other age groups. In this area of Environmental Factors morale it significantly differs from the other 3 age groups chosen for this study. This finding is similar to the one in some of the areas of Teacher Factor (Personality Factors, Professional Aspirations, and Organising Skills).
3. Female Teachers differ from Male Teachers in this area. Female Teachers show higher mean than Male Teachers. This finding is similar to the one in some areas of the Teacher Factor (Personality Factors, Professional Aspirations, Teaching Ability, and Linguistic Proficiency).
4. Post-graduate Teachers and under Graduate Teachers show similar means which are higher than the means of Graduate Training Teachers. This finding is similar to the one in some areas of the Teacher Factor (Personality Factors, Academic Proficiency, Organising Skills, and Linguistic Proficiency).
5. As far as the variable 'Designation' is concerned, the Head Masters show a higher mean, than the B.Ed., Teachers who show the lowest mean. Further more, Secondary Grade Teachers and B.Ed., Teachers manifest an equal level of morale in view of their insignificant mean-differences which might mean that the impact of this area, Schools Facilities, on these two categories of respondents in terms of their morale is too little. Thus, the Head Masters have manifested a highest impact of this area on their morale which is at a higher level when compared to their Teaching Assistants.
6. The experienced teachers show a higher mean in this area of Environmental Factor morale namely School Facilities than all the other categories of inexperienced Teachers.
7. Teachers working in Private Management Schools show a higher mean than the teachers working in Local Body Schools and Government Schools.

8. Teachers working in Rural Schools show a higher mean than the teachers working in Urban Schools.
9. There are reasons to believe that size of the class is an influencing variable, as teachers handling small size classes show a mean score higher than that of the teachers handling large size classes. However, in the case of teachers with median size classes, they show a higher mean-score than those with large size classes, but when compared to those with small size classes, their mean-score is at the same level as that of the latter. Thus, the impact of this area on these two categories of respondents is constant and at the same level.

TABLE—26

Table showing the data of area (2) School Administration.

Variable and its Categories	N	Mean	S.D.	Categories related	C.R.
1 2	3	4	5	6	7
Age					
1. 26–30 Years	80	57.29	8.99	1-2	1.20
2. 31.40 "	162	55.69	11.03	1-3	0.91
3. 41-50 "	183	56.07	11.79	1-4	4.17 *
4. 50 above "	205	62.18	8.65	2-3	0.31
				2-4	6.14 *
				3-4	5.76 *
Sex					
1. Male	360	54.70	10.29	1-2	10.06 *
2. Female	270	62.67	9.47		
Qualification					
1. Under Graduate	60	60.05	10.92	1-2	2.28
2. Graduate	400	56.59	11.13	1-3	0.62
3. Post Graduate	170	61.02	8.67	2-3	5.10 *
Designation					
1. Secondary. Grade	188	58.63	10.09	1-2	2.64 *
2. B.Ed., Assistant	342	56.12	11.12	1-3	5.03 *

Cont...

1	2	3	4	5	6	7
3.	Head Master	100	63.98	7.68	2-3	8.06 *
Experience						
1.	Below 5 yrs	107	56.53	9.87	1-2	0.23
2.	6-10 "	130	56.22	11.27	1-3	0.19
3.	11-15 "	170	56.28	11.99	1-4	4.33 *
4.	Above 15 "	223	61.39	8.75	2-3	0.05
					2-4	4.50 *
					3-4	4.69 *
Management						
1.	Government	97	56.65	12.01	1-2	0.39
2.	Local Body	312	56.12	10.96	1-3	3.64 *
3.	Private	221	61.57	8.67	2-3	6.41 *
Location						
1.	Urban	353	56.27	10.99	1-2	5.06 *
2.	Rural	277	60.47	9.82		
Size of Class						
1.	Above 50	285	55.38	10.92	1-2	4.46 *
2.	30-49	252	59.53	10.64	1-3	7.33 *
3.	Below 30	93	62.69	7.32	2-3	3.12 *

* Significant at 0.01 level

As can be seen from the above Table, 17 C.R. Values are significant at 0.01 level out of a total no. of 26 C.R. values. It can be observed from the table that all the 8 variables are associated with this area, manifesting significant mean differences.

1. Teachers above the age group of 50 years have shown a higher mean than the other lower age groups.
2. The mean score of Female Teachers is higher than the Male Teachers.
3. All the sub-samples of Secondary Grade Teachers, B.Ed., Teachers and Head Masters differ from each other. The Head Masters show a higher mean while the B.Ed., Teachers show a lower mean.
4. The Under Graduate Teachers and Post-graduate Teachers show similar means and got higher mean than the Graduate Teachers.
5. Experience is an influencing variable in this area of School Administration. Experienced Teachers showed a higher mean than the other three categories of inexperienced Teachers.

6. The teachers working in Private Management Schools show higher mean than the teachers working in Local Body Schools and Government Schools. However, teachers in the latter two types of school don't differ from each other in their mean scores.
7. Rural School Teachers have shown a higher mean in this area of School Administration than the teachers working in Urban Schools.
8. Size of the Class being an influencing variable, teachers handling small size classes i.e., below 30 have shown a higher mean than the teachers handling average size classes and large size classes. Even in the latter two categories, they differed significantly in 77their mean scores, those with large size classes manifested the lowest mean-score.

TABLE—27

Table showing the data of area (3) Educational Administration.

Variable and its Categories	N	Mean	S.D.	Categories related	C.R.
1 2	3	4	5	6	7
Age					
1. 26-30 years	80	32.85	5.68	1-2	0.72
2. 31-40 "	162	32.27	6.40	1-3	0.22
3. 41-50 "	183	32.67	6.66	1-4	2.57
4. 50 above "	205	34.71	4.98	2-3	0.58
				2-4	3.99 *
				3-4	3.38 *
Sex					
1. Male	360	33.38	5.55	1-2	0.57
2. Female	270	33.09	6.66		
Qualification					
1. Under Graduate	60	35.42	6.60	1-2	3.21 *
2. Graduate	400	32.51	6.06	1-3	1.25
3. Post Graduate	170	34.23	5.48	2-3	3.31 *
Designation					
1. Secondary Grade	188	33.99	5.86	1-2	3.11 *

Cont..

1	2	3	4	5	6	7
2.	B.Ed., Assistant	342	32.29	6.28	1-3	1.80
3.	Head Master	100	35.15	4.84	2-3	4.83 *
Experience						
1.	Below 5 yrs	107	32.58	5.96	1-2	0.09
2.	6-10 "	130	32.65	6.63	1-3	0.49
3.	11-15 "	170	32.96	6.90	1-4	2.37
4.	Above 15 "	223	34.14	4.82	2-3	0.40
					2-4	2.24
					3-4	1.90
Management						
1.	Government	97	32.92	6.61	1-2	0.47
2.	Local Body	312	32.56	6.21	1-3	1.91
3.	Private	221	34.37	5.38	2-3	3.58 *
Location						
1.	Urban	353	32.32	6.03	1-2	4.46 *
2.	Rural	277	34.44	5.87		
Size of Class						
1.	Above 50	285	32.00	6.07	1-2	3.16 *
2.	30-49	252	33.69	6.30	1-3	7.10 *
3.	Below 30	93	35.88	3.97	2-3	3.83 *

* Significant at 0.01 level.

1. As can be observed from the above table, that the variables Sex and Teaching are not the influencing variables. Evidently, the impact of this area, Educational Administration on these two variables is meagre.
2. The influencing variables are, 1. Age, 2. Qualification, 3. Designation, 4. Management, 5. Location, and 6. Size of the Class.
3. There are reasons to believe that the highest age group shows a higher morale in this area of Educational Administration, than only the two middle groups. Peculiarly, the highest age-group manifests their morale in terms of this area, at the same level as the youngest age group.
4. As in the previous areas the Graduate Trained Teachers have shown a lower mean while Under-graduate Teachers and Post-graduate Teachers have shown higher means.

5. Designation wise also, the B.Ed., Teachers have shown a lower mean, where as Head Masters and Secondary Grade Teachers have shown higher mean.
6. In terms of Management, teachers working in private Management Schools show a higher mean than the teachers working in the Local Body Schools and Government Schools, the latter two categories manifesting the same level of morale in view of their insignificant mean-differences.
7. The Teachers working in Rural Schools show a higher mean-score than the teachers working in Urban Schools.
8. There are reasons to believe that the variable 'size of the class' influences the opinions of teachers towards Educational Administration. Teachers handling Small Size Classes showed higher mean than the teachers handling average size and higher size classes. Among the latter two categories, teachers with large size classes manifest the lowest level of morale in view of their significant mean differences with the other two categories.

TABLE—28

Table showing the data of area 4 (a) Family.

Variable and its Categories	N	Mean	S.D.	Categories related	C.R.
1 2	3	4	5	6	7
Age					
1. 26-30 Years	80	10.53	1.65	1-2	0.81
2. 31-40 "	162	10.32	2.17	1-3	0.63
3. 41-50 "	183	10.37	2.35	1-4	3.00 *
4. 50 above "	205	11.20	1.89	2-3	0.19
				2-4	4.10 *
				3-4	3.84 *
Sex					
1. Male	360	10.09	1.99	1-2	7.99 *
2. Female	270	11.39	2.06		
Qualification					
1. Under Graduate	60	11.28	2.11	1-2	3.06 *
2. Graduate	400	10.39	2.19	1-3	0.81

Cont...

1	2	3	4	5	6	7
3.	Post Graduate	170	11.04	1.83	2-3	3.64 *
Designation						
1.	Secondary Grade	188	10.70	1.98	1-2	1.72
2.	B.Ed., Assistant	342	10.38	2.23	1-3	3.35 *
3.	Head Master	100	11.46	1.74	2-3	5.10 *
Experience						
1.	Below 5 Yrs	107	10.43	1.74	1-2	0.11
2.	6-10 "	130	10.40	2.31	1-3	0.40
3.	11-15 "	170	10.53	2.43	1-4	2.67 *
4.	Above 15 "	223	10.99	1.84	2-3	0.47
					2-4	2.47
					3-4	2.04
Management						
1.	Government	97	10.55	2.36	1-2	0.68
2.	Local Body	312	10.37	2.10	1-3	1.99
3.	Private	221	11.09	1.95	2-3	4.10 *
Location						
1.	Urban	353	10.35	2.15	1-2	4.13 *
2.	Rural	277	11.03	2.01		
Size of Class						
1.	Above 50	285	10.19	2.13	1-2	3.82*
2.	30-49	252	10.90	2.17	1-3	5.94 *
3.	Below 30	93	11.39	1.52	2-3	2.35

* Significant at 0.01 level

1. As can be seen from the above table, 13 C.R. Values are significant at 0.01 level out of a total No. of 26 C.R. Values. All the 8 variables are associated with the opinions towards this area, manifesting significant mean-differences.
2. Teachers in the Age Group of 50 and above, show a significantly higher mean than the other 3 categories of low age groups. But, peculiarly, the latter manifest more or less the same level of morale.

3. Female Teachers show significantly higher mean than Male Teachers.
4. While Under-Graduate Teachers and Post-graduate Teachers show similar means without significant differences between them, the Graduate Teachers show a lower mean.
5. The Secondary Grade Teachers and B.Ed., Teachers showed similar means without significant differences between them, but both of them differ from Head Masters who showed a higher mean.
6. There is a difference only between the most inexperienced teachers and the most Experienced Teachers in this area family. Thus, the most experienced Teachers show a higher mean score than the most inexperienced teachers. However the other two middle categories don't differ from any of the categories. Evidently, the variable of experience has low impact on Teachers' morale in terms of this area.
7. Teachers working in Private Management Schools show higher mean than the Teachers working in Local Body Schools. However, they show the same level of morale with the Government School Teachers.
8. The Rural Teachers seem to manifest a higher level of morale in terms of this area, than the Urban Teachers.
9. Size of the class is associated significantly with the opinions of the sample towards family, as teachers handling large classes significantly differ from teachers handling small size classes, the mean of the teachers handling small classes being higher. However, the teachers handling median size classes show a higher level of morale than teachers with large size classes while they manifest more or less the same level of morale as the teachers with small size classes.

TABLE—29

Table showing the data of area 4 (b) Community.

Variable and its Categories		N	Mean	S.D.	Categories related	C.R.
1	2	3	4	5	6	7
Age						
1.	26-30 Years	80	19.63	3.99	1-2	0.47
2.	31-40 "	162	19.96	4.84	1-3	0.10
3.	41-50 "	183	19.74	5.08	1-4	3.08 *
4.	50 above "	205	21.35	4.31	2-3	0.41
					2-4	2.85 *
					3-4	3.33 *
Sex						
1.	Male	360	18.92	4.27	1-2	9.08 *
2.	Female	270	22.18	4.60		
Qualification						
1.	Under Graduate	60	22.18	4.91	1-2	3.51 *
2.	Graduate	400	19.81	4.73	1-3	1.87
3.	Post Graduate	170	20.84	4.33	2.3	2.53
Designation						
1.	Secondary Grade	188	20.80	4.36	1-2	2.87 *
2.	B.Ed., Assistant	342	19.61	4.92	1-3	1.92
3.	Head Master	100	21.79	4.06	2-3	4.49 *
Experience						
1.	Below 5 yrs	107	19.87	4.13	1-2	0.28
2.	6-10 "	130	20.04	5.17	1-3	0.28
3.	11-15 "	170	20.03	5.38	1-4	2.15
4.	Above 15 "	223	20.91	4.01	2-3	0.01
					2-4	1.65
					3-4	1.78
Management						
1.	Government	97	20.27	5.27	1-2	1.32
2.	Local Body	312	19.48	4.52	1-3	2.02
3.	Private	221	21.51	4.42	2-3	5.15 *

Cont...

1 2	3	4	5	6	7
Location					
1. Urban	353	19.79	4.67	1-2	3.17 *
2. Rural	277	20.98	4.65		
Size of Class					
1. Above 50	285	19.35	4.58	1-2	3.83 *
2. 30-49	252	20.92	4.89	1-3	4.62 *
3. Below 30	93	21.60	3.90	2-3	1.33

* Significant at 0.01 level

As can be seen from the above table, 11 C.R. Values are significant at 0.01 level out of a total no. of 26 C.R. Values.

1. The variable Teaching Experience is not associated significantly with the community and hence it is not an influencing variable on this area.
2. Teachers above the age group of 50 years show a higher mean in this area than the other lower age groups. But peculiarly the latter three categories manifest more or less the same level of morale.
3. Female Teachers have show a higher mean than Male Teachers in this area.
4. Under Graduate Teachers and Post-graduate Teachers show more or less the same level of morale in view of their insignificant mean-differences. But Under Graduate Teachers show a higher mean than Graduate Teachers. Probably the impact of community on the Graduate Teachers is the lowest in terms of their morale.
5. The Head Masters show a higher mean than B.Ed., Teachers, i.e., who showed the lowest mean, As for the Secondary Grade Teachers, they manifest a higher level of morale than B.Ed., Teachers in terms of this area, showing more or less the same level of morale as Head Masters.
6. The Teachers working in Private Management Schools have shown a higher mean than the teachers working in Local Body Schools in this area community . However, Government School Teachers have shown more or less the same level of morale as the other two categories of Teachers.

7. The Teachers working in Rural Schools show higher mean than the Teachers working in Urban Schools.
8. Teachers handling small size classes showed a higher mean than the teachers handling large size classes. In the case of Teachers with median size classes, they manifest a higher level of morale than those with large size classes, while they don't differ in their mean scores, from those with small size classes.

TABLE—30

Table showing the data of area 4 (c) Value System.

Variable and its Categories	N	Mean	S.D.	Categories related	C.R.
1 2	3	4	5	6	7
Age					
1. 26-30 Years	80	19.38	3.78	1-2	0.82
2. 31-40 "	162	19.83	4.49	1-3	1.28
3. 41-50 "	183	20.08	4.73	1-4	3.77 *
4. 50 above "	205	21.28	3.99	2-3	0.50
				2-4	3.24 *
				3-4	2.70 *
Sex					
1. Male	360	20.27	4.06	1-2	0.32
2. Female	270	20.38	4.77		
Qualification					
1. Under Graduate	60	22.18	4.51	1-2	3.74 *
2. Graduate	400	19.86	4.37	1-3	2.17
3. Post Graduate	170	20.74	4.13	2-3	2.30
Designation					
1. Secondary Grade	188	20.95	4.22	1-2	3.68 *
2. B. Ed., Assistant	342	19.51	4.48	1-3	1.93
3. Head Master	100	21.87	3.67	2-3	5.41 *
Experience					
1. Below 5 yrs	107	19.44	3.91	1-2	1.33

Cont...

1	2	3	4	5	6	7
2.	6-10 "	130	20.19	4.79	1-3	1.51
3.	11-15 "	170	20.26	5.08	1-4	3.15 *
4.	Above 15 "	223	20.85	3.61	2-3	0.12
					2-4	1.36
					3-4	1.29
Management						
1.	Government	97	20.32	4.93	1-2	0.85
2.	Local Body	312	19.85	4.29	1-3	1.14
3.	Private	221	20.97	4.16	2-3	3.03 *
Location						
1.	Urban	353	19.79	4.31	1-2	3.41 *
2.	Rural	277	20.98	4.36		
Size of Class						
1.	Above 50	285	19.54	4.20	1-2	3.01 *
2.	30-49	252	20.70	4.67	1-3	4.76 *
3.	Below 30	93	21.66	3.55	2-3	2.03

* Significant at 0.01 level.

As can be seen from the above Table, 11 C.R. Values are significant at 0.01 level out of a total no. of 26 C.R. Values.

1. The variable Sex is not associated with the opinions of teachers towards value system, as the mean scores there under have no significant mean-differences, which would mean that the Sex variable has no impact on the scores of the sample in this area.
2. Age is a variable associated significantly with the value system. Teachers above the age of 50 years show a higher mean than all the other three categories in the sample; the latter, however, manifest more or less the same level of morale, in view of the insignificance of their mean-differences from one another.
3. While Under Graduate Teachers and Post-graduate Teachers don't differ much, the Under Graduate Teachers have a higher mean than the Graduate Teachers towards value system. Besides, Graduate Teachers manifest more or less the same level of morale as Post-graduate Teachers.
4. Designation wise, the mean-score of Head Masters is higher than that of B.Ed., Assistants. The latter differ in their means from the mean-scores of Secondary Grade Teachers, which may mean

TABLE —31

Abstract of Tables—16, 17 & 18 show certain particulars of variations on account of Mean–Differences—Variable-wise and Area- wise.

Sl. No.	Area	Table No.	Age		Sex		Qualification		Designation		Experience		Management		Location		Size of class	
			A	B	A	B	A	B	A	B	A	B	A	B	A	B	A	B
1.	Whole opinionnaire	16	1-4 2-4 3-4	6/3	1-2	1/1	1-2 2-3	3/2	1-2 2-3	3/2	1-4 2-4 3-4	6/3	1-3 2-3	3/2	1-2	1/1	All	3/3
2.	Teacher Factor Too I	17	1-4 2-4 3-4	6/3	1-2	1/1	1-2 2-3	3/2	1-2 2-3	3/2	1-4	6/1	1-3 2-3	3/2	1-2	1/1	All	3/3
3.	Environmental Factors Tool II	118	1-4 2-4 3-4	6/3	1-2	1/1	1-2 2-3	3/2	All	3/3	-do-		-do-		-do-		-do-	

Index: A: Pairs of categories with significant C.R. Values.
B: No. of Pairs with the above C.R. Values.

TABLE—32

Abstract of Table—19,20 to show certain particulars of variations on account of Mean- Differences—Variable-wise and Area-wise.

Sl. No.	Area	Table No.	Age		Sex		Qualification		Designation		Experience		Management		Location		Size of Class	
			A	B	A	B	A	B	A	B	A	B	A	B	A	B	A	B
1.	Personality Factors	19	1-4 2-4 3-4	6/3	1-2	1/1	1-2 2-3	3/2	1-2 2-3	3/2	1-4 3-4	6/2	1-3 2-3	3/2	1-2	1/1	1-2 1-3	3/2
2.	Professional Aspirations	20	1-4 2-4 3-4	6/3	1-2	1/1	2-3	3/1	1-2 2-3	3/2	1-4	6/1	1-3 2-3	3/2	1-2	1/1	1-2 1-3 2-3	3/3

Index: A : Pairs of categories with significant C.R. Values.
B : No, of pairs with the above C.R. Values.

TABLE —33

Abstract of Tables—21, 22, 23, 24 to show certain particulars of variations on account of Mean-Differences—Variable-wise and Area-wise.

Sl. No.	Area	Table No.	Age		Sex		Qualification		Designation		Experience		Management		Location		Size of class	
			A	B	A	B	A	B	A	B	A	B	A	B	A	B	A	B
1. 3 (a)	Academic Proficiency	21	Nil	6/0	Nil	1/0	1-2 2-3	3/2	1-2	3/1	Nil	6/0	2-3	3/1	1-2	1/1	1-3	3/1
2. 3 (b)	Teaching Ability	22	1-4 2-4	6/2	1-2	1/1	1-2	3/1	2-3	3/1	1-4	6/1	2-3	3/1	1-2	1/1	1-2 1-3	3/2
3. 3 (c)	Organizing Skills	23	1-4 2-4 3-4	6/3	Nil	1/0	1-2 2-3	3/2	1-2 2-3	3/2	1-4	6/1	1-3 2-3	3/2	Nil	1/0	1-2 1-3	3/2
4. 3 (d)	Linguistic Proficiency	24	Nil	6/0	1-2	1/1	1-2 2-3	3/2	Nil	3/0	Nil	6/0	2-3	3/1	1-2	1/1	1-2 1-3	3/2

Index: A : Pairs of categories with significant C.R. Values.

B : No. of pairs with the above C.R. Values.

TABLE—34

Abstract of Tables —25, 26 and 27 to show certain particulars of variations on account of Mean—Differences Variable-wise and Area-wise.

Sl. No.	Area	Table No.	Age		Sex		Qualification		Designation		Experience		Management		Location		Size of classes	
			A	B	A	B	A	B	A	B	A	B	A	B	A	B	A	B
1.	School Facilities	25	1-4 2-4 3-4	6/3	1-2	1/1	1-2 2-3	3/2	1-3 2-3	3/2	1-4 2-4 3-4	6/3	1-3 2-3	3/2	1-2	1/1	1-2 1-3	3/2
2.	School Administration	26	1-4 2-4 3-4	6/3	1-2	1/1	2-3	3/1	1-3 1-2 2-3	3/3	1-4 2-4 3-4	6/3	1-3 2-3	3/2	1-2	1/1	1-2 1-3 2-3	3/3
3.	Educational Administration	27	2-4 3-4	6/2	Nil	1/0	1-2 2-3	3/2	1-2 2-3	3/2	Nil	6/0	2-3	3/1	1-2	1/1	1-2 1-3 2-3	3/3

Index : A : Pairs of categories with significant C.R. Values.
B : No. of pairs with the above C.R. Values.

TABLE—35

Abstract of Tables—28, 29 and 30 to show certain particulars of variations on account of Mean-Differences—Variable-wise and Area-wise.

Sl. No.	Area	Table No.	Age		Sex		Qualification		Designation		Experience		Management		Location		Size of classes	
			A	B	A	B	A	B	A	B	A	B	A	B	A	B	A	B
1.	4. Environmental Impact (a) Family	28	1-4 2-4 3-4	6/3	1-2	1/1	1-2 2-3	3/2	1-3 2-3	3/2	1-4	6/1	2-3	3/1	1-2	1/1	1-2 1-3	3/2
2.	4. Environmental Impact (b) Community	29	1-4 2-4 3-4	6/3	1-2	1/1	1-2	3/1	1-2 2-3	3/2	Nil	6/0	2-3	3/1	1-2	1/1	1-2 1-3	3/2
3.	4. Environmental Impact (c) Value System	30	1-4 2-4 3-4	6/3	Nil	1/0	1-2	3/1	1-2 2-3	3/2	1-4	6/1	2-3	3/1	1-2	1/1	1-2 1-3	3/2

Index A : Pairs of categories with significant C.R. Values.
B : No. of pairs with the above C.R. Values.

that Teacher-morale doesn't seem to be dependent on Educational Qualification or the grade of a Teaching Assistant in the School.

5. There are reasons to believe that experience is an influencing variable in this area. The experienced teachers showed higher mean than the in-experienced teachers. But this difference is manifest significantly, only between the most experienced teachers and the least experienced teachers.
6. Teachers working in Private Management Schools show a higher mean than the teachers working in Local Body Schools. But the Government School Teachers seem to manifest more or less the same level of morale as that of the other two categories of Teachers.
7. The Teachers working in Rural Schools have shown a high mean score than the teachers working in Urban Schools.
8. Size of the class appears to be associated significantly with opinions towards value system. Teachers handling small size classes have shown a higher mean score than the teachers handling large size classes. However, the teachers with median size classes manifest a higher morale than only those with large size classes.

Tables—31 to 35 shown in page 171-175, consolidate the Variable-wise and the Area-wise C.Rs in Tables— 16 to 30, in order to give a glance at them simultaneously and thereby consider, Area-wise, the impact of each Variable.

In Tables—31 to 35 the investigator consolidated the C.Rs of Tools-I and II as revealed in Tables—16 to 30 in order to provide a glance at them both variable wise and area–wise. Some of these C.Rs. are at significant levels of mean differences. In these cases the related sub samples vary in their Teacher Morale mean scores. Unfortunately the investigator couldn't make regression analysis due to time constraint; yet, the pairs of sub-samples that showed varying levels of significance in their mean differences under a variable like Age or Sex compare area-wise under it, by common sense. For example, Null Hypothesis on Sex variable could be manifest, in the Areas Nos. 3 (a) and (c) Academic Proficiency and Organising Skills, while in all the other four Area Nos. 1,2,3 (b) and 3 (d), the Sex variable manifests its impact significantly. The investigator could observe it direct by way of ready reference in Tables—32 to 33. In Tables Nos. 34 and 35 also, a similar phenomenon could be observed directly, under Area Nos. 3, and 4 (c)—Educational Administration and Value system of the Environmental Factors Morale, in which the investigator could not find significant Mean-differences under the Sex Variable. Hence Tables—31 to 35 serve to indicate such variations in Teacher-Morale Mean-Scores area-wise under a variable. However, they couldn't be used for the purpose of variable-wise comparison, due to want of Regression—Analysis.

Observations from Tables 31 to 35

1. Area No. 3 (a) Academic Proficiency of Tool—I does not manifest any significant Mean—Differences under the variables of Age, Sex and Experience while it has manifested the same under the other five variables, vide Table—33.
2. Similarly, Area no. 3(c) of Organizing Skills in Tool—I does not manifest it under the variables of Sex and Location under Table No. 33 while it has manifested the same under all the other six variables.
3. Again, Area no. 3 (d) Linguistic Proficiency in Tool—I does not manifest it under the variables of Age, Designation and Experience, while it has manifested the same under all the other five variables, vide Table—33.
4. The other three Areas of Tool—I and also the whole Opinionnaire including its two tools manifested significant Mean-Differences under all the eight variables, vide Tables—31, 32 to 33.
5. Area No. 3 of Tool—II (Educational Administration) has not manifested any significant Mean-Differences under the variables of Sex and Experience, vide Table—34.
6. Again, Area No. 4(b) of Tool—II (Environmental Impact–Community) has not manifested the same under the variable of Experience, vide Table—35.
7. Similarly, Area No. 4 (c) of Tool—II (Environmental Impact--Value System) has not manifested the same under the variable of Sex, vide Table—35.
8. All the other three Areas of Tool—II have manifested the same under each one of the eight variables, vide Tables—34 & 35.

Comparison of the Area—Means of Teacher Factor Tool and Environmental Factor Tool

The number of statements in each area is unevenly distributed. So, in order to make an area-wise comparison, area means were calculated.

TABLE—36

Table showing a comparison of the Area—Means of Teacher Factor Tool.

Sl. No.	Area	Area MeanScore	Rank Order
1.	1 Personality Factors	2.407	1
2.	2 Professional Aspirations	2.378	2
	3 Professional Skills:		
3.	(d) Linguistic Proficiency	2.206	3
4.	(c) Organising Skills	2.188	4
5.	(b) Teaching Ability	2.163	5
6.	(a) Academic Proficiency	2.143	6

As can be seen from the above table none of the area means is higher than 2.5. It means that the sample maintains a Neutral Opinion towards all these areas in the Teacher Factor.

Under the area-wise mean-scores of Tool—I, it is observed that the Area—1; Personality Factors and Area—2; Professional Aspirations in Teacher Factor Tool got the highest mean-scores. This leads to an inference that the subjects expressed more favourable opinions on the items given in these two areas. In the case of Professional Skills, the sample has ranked this area last.

Within this area of Professional Skills, which comprises four constituent skills, low weightage is found in the case of Area—3 (a) Academic Proficiency in Teacher Factor Tool. This shows the low acceptance of sample to the items given in Academic Proficiency.

TABLE—37

Table showing a comparison of the Area—means of Environmental Factors Tool.

Sl. No.	Area	Area MeanScore	Rank Order
1.	2 School Administration	2.324	1
2.	1 School Facilities	2.240	2
3.	3 Educational Administration	2.216	3
	4 Environmental Impact :		
4.	(a) Family	2.130	4
5.	(b) Community	2.031	5
6.	(c) Value System	2.031	5

Table—37 shows teacher morale levels with regard to Environmental Factors. Here also none of the area means is above 2.5 as in the case of Teacher Factor. Hence we may infer that the sample maintains a neutral level rather than a level of negative response.

1. The highest preference is given to School Administration, the next importance was given to School Facilities.
2. Morale level with regard to Community and Value system is of lowest level.

As can be seen from the above tables—38 to 39, Teacher Factor Tool shows 15 coefficients of correlations. Below are given the areas that got the first three ranks and the last three ranks in the Tool—I :

The highest correlation (Rank No.1) is between the areas of Academic Proficiency and Organising Skills (0.797),

The second highest correlation (Rank No.2) is between the areas of Professional Aspirations and Organising Skills (0.788).

The third highest correlation (Rank No. 3) is between the areas of Personality Factors and Teaching Ability (0.775) and also Linguistic Proficiency and Teaching Ability (0.775).

TABLE —38

Table showing the coefficients of correlation between the Areas of Teacher Factor Tool and Environmental Factor Tool.

Sl.No.	Area	Tool - I						Tool - II					
		P.F. 1	Pr.A. 2	A.P. 3	T.A. 4	O.S. 5	L.P. 6	S.F. 7	S.A. 8	E.A. 9	F. 10	C. 11	V.S. 12
	Tool —I												
1.	1. P.F.												
2.	2. Pr.A.	0.749											
3.	3. (a) A.P.	0.600	0.756										
4.	(b) T.A.	0.775	0.645	0.476									
5.	(c) O.S.	0.642	0.788	0.797	0.610								
6.	(d) L.P.	0.754	0.630	0.534	0.775	0.590							
	Tool —II												
7.	1. S.F.	0.722	0.601	0.519	0.699	0.581	0.688						
8.	2. S.A.	0.742	0.664	0.558	0.704	0.609	0.695	0.921					
9.	3. E.A.	0.542	0.613	0.608	0.560	0.641	0.562	0.762	0.781				
10.	4. (a) F.	0.645	0.561	0.527	0.649	0.553	0.650	0.859	0.852	0.753			
11.	(b) C.	0.680	0.608	0.581	0.688	0.605	0.698	0.867	0.849	0.748	0.821		
12.	(c) V.S.	0.523	0.597	0.654	0.547	0.664	0.566	0.725	0.743	0.848	0.734	0.792	
	Total :	11	10	9	8	7	6	5	4	3	2	1	= 66
	Grand Total :	66											

Index: 1. P.F.—Personality Factors; 2. Pr. A.— Professional Aspirations; 3. A.P. —Academic Proficiency; 4 T.A.—Teaching Ability ; 5. O.S.—Organising Skills; 6. L.P.—Linguistic Proficiency; 7. S.F.— School Facilities; 8. S.A.—School Administration; 9. E.A.—Educational Administration; 10 F.—Family; 11. C—Community; 12. V.S.—Value System.

TABLE—39

Table showing the co-efficients of correlation arranged in Rank Order, in the various areas within Tools—I & II and also their External Correlation.

Sl. No.	Areas of the Correlates	Coefficient of Correlation	Rank order of areas in Tools		
			I	II	I & II
1	2	3	4	5	6
1.	School Administration & School Facilities	0.921		1	
2.	Community & School Facilities	0.867		2	
3.	Family & School Facilities	0.859		3	
4.	Family & School Administration	0.852		4	
5.	Community & School Administration	0.849		5	
6.	Value System & Educational Administration	0.848		6	
7.	Community & Family	0.821		7	
8.	Organising skills & Academic Proficiency	0.797	1		
9.	Value System & Community	0.792		8	
10.	Organising Skills & Professional Aspirations	0.788	2		
11.	Educational Administration & School Administration	0.781		9	
12.	Teaching Ability & Personality Factors	0.775	3.5		
13.	Linguistic Proficiency & Teaching Ability	0.775	3.5		
14.	Educational Administration & School Facilities	0.762		10	
15.	Academic Proficiency & Professional Aspirations	0.756	5		
16.	Linguistic Proficiency & Personality Factors	0.754	6		
17.	Family & Educational Administration	0.753		11	

1	2	3	4	5	6
18.	Professional Aspirations & Personality Factors	0.749	7		
19.	Community & Educational Administration	0.748		12	
20.	Value System & school Administration	0.743		13	
21.	School Administration & Personality Factors	0.742			1
22.	Value System & Family	0.734		14	
23.	Value System & School Facilities	0.725		15	
24.	School Facilities & Personality Factors	0.722			2
25.	School Administration & Teaching Ability	0.704			3
26.	School Facilities & Teaching Ability	0.699			4
27.	Community & Linguistic Proficiency	0.698			5
28.	School Administration & Linguistic Proficiency	0.695			6
29.	School Facilities & Linguistic Proficiency	0.688			7.5
30.	Community & Teaching Ability	0.688			7.5
31.	Community & Personality Factors	0.680			9
32.	School Administration & Professional Aspirations	0.664			10.5
33.	Value System & Organising Skills	0.664			10.5
34.	Value System Academic Proficiency	0.654			12
35.	Family & linguistic proficiency	0.650			13
36.	Family & Teaching Ability	0.649			14
37.	Family & Personality Factors	0.645			15
38.	Teaching Ability & Professional Aspirations	0.645	8		
39.	Organising Skills & Personality Factors	0.642	9		
40.	Educational Administration & Organising Skills	0.641			16
41.	Linguistic Proficiency & Professional Aspirations	0.630	10		
42.	Educational Administration & organising Skills	0.613			17
1	2	3	4	5	6

43.	Organising Skills & Teaching Ability	0.610	11	
44.	School Administration & Organising Skills	0.609		18
45.	Educational Administration & Academic Proficiency	0.608		19.5
46.	Community & Professional Aspirations	0.608		19.5
47.	Community & Organising Skills	0.605		21
48.	School Facilities & Professional Aspirations	0.601		22
49.	Academic proficiency & personality Factors	0.600	12	
50.	Value System & Professional Aspirations	0.597		23
51.	Linguistic Proficiency & Organising Skills	0.590	13	
52.	School Facilities & Organising Skills	0.581		24.5
53.	Community & Academic Proficiency	0.581		24.25
54.	Value System & Linguistic Proficiency	0.566		26
55.	Educational Administration & Linguistic Proficiency	0.562		27
56.	Family & Professional Aspirations	0.561		28
57.	Educational Administration & Teaching Ability	0.560		29
58.	School Administration & Academic Proficiency	0.558		30
59.	Family & Organising Skills	0.553		31
60.	Value system & Teaching ability	0.547		32
61.	Educational Administration & Personality Factors	0.542		33
62.	Linguistic Proficiency & Academic Proficiency	0.534	14	
63.	Family & Academic Proficiency	0.527		34
64.	Value system & Personality Factors	0.523		35
65.	School Facilities & Academic Proficiency	0.519		36
66.	Teaching Ability & Academic Proficiency	0.476	15	

The lowest correlation (Last rank—Rank No. 15) is between the areas of Academic Proficiency and Teaching Ability (0.476).

The second lowest correlation (Rank No. 14) is between the areas of Linguistic Proficiency and Academic Proficiency (0.534).

The third lowest correlation (Rank No. 13) is between the areas of Linguistic Proficiency and Organising Skills (0.590).

Tooi—II

As can be seen from the above Table Nos. 38 & 39, Environmental Factors Tool shows fifteen co-efficients of correlations.

Below are given the areas that got the first three ranks and the last three ranks, in the Tool—II.

The highest correlation (Rank No.1) is between the areas of School Administration and School facilities (0.921).

The second highest correlation (Rank No.2) is found between the areas of Community and School facilities (0.867).

The third highest correlation (Rank No. 3) is found between the areas of Family and School facilities (0.859).

The lowest correlation (Last rank–Rank No. 15) is between the areas of School Facilities and Value system (0.725)

The second lowest correlation (Rank No. 14) is found between the areas of Family and Value system (0.734).

The third lowest correlation (Rank No. 13) is found between the area of School Administration and Value system (0.743).

Tools—I and II

As can be seen from the above Table Nos. 38 and 39 there are 36 coefficients of external correlations (between the areas of Tool-I and II). Below are given the areas that got the first three ranks and the last three ranks in these external correlations.

The highest correlation (Rank No.1) is in the area of Personality Factors in Tool—I and School Administration in Tool—II (0.742).

The second highest correlation (Rank No.2) is found in the areas of Personality Factors and School Facilities (0.722).

The third highest correlation (Rank No.3) is found in the areas of Teaching Ability and School Administration (0.704).

The lowest correlation (Rank No. 36) is found between the areas of Academic Proficiency and School Facilities (0.519).

The second lowest correlation (Rank No. 35) is found between the areas of Personality Factors and Value system (0.523).

The third lowest (Last Rank—Rank No. 34) is found between the areas of Academic Proficiency and Family (0.527).

The coefficients of correlation under the six areas of Teacher Factor (Tool—I) range from 0.476 (between Academic Proficiency and Teaching Ability) to 0.797 (between Academic Proficiency and Organising Skills).

The range under the six areas of Environmental Factors (Tool–II) from 0.725 (between School Facilities and Value System) to 0.921 (between School Facilities and School Administration).

The coefficients of correlation found externally between the areas of the two different Tools, range from 0.519 (between Academic Proficiency and School Facilities) to 0.742 (between Personality Factors and School Administration.

Thus a higher correlation is found in the areas of Environmental Factors, than in those of Teacher Factor. However the co-efficients of correlation range more widely in the areas of Teacher Factor. The matrix of correlations is much wider externally than internally, as the external correlations occured more extensively than the internal correlations. On the whole the areas of the two constituent factors, particularly those of the Environmental Factors, have more positive interrelations.

SECTION –D

Analysis of the Item -wise Data

Item-Mean Scores were calculated for the whole sample and sub samples. So, the opinions of the teachers towards each item are identified. Item-Mean Scores were corrected to their first decimals and reported.

The following system of interpretation is adopted for Positive and Negative Items.

For Positive Items

An Item-Mean Score of 1.0 to 1.4 denotes Disagreement of the sample to the item. An item-Mean Score of 1.5 to 2.4 denotes Neutral opinion of the sample to the item. An Item-Mean Score of 2.5 to 3.00 denotes Agreement of the sample to the item.

For Negative Items

There are 15 Negative Items in the Whole Opinionnaire. A reverse scoring is adopted to assess the responses in them. Below are given the related particulars of one of the Negative Items in Table—40.

TABLE—40

Table showing the data regarding reverse scoring and Item-Mean Score of one of the Negative Items.

Sl. No.	Item No.	Item	Frequencies of the responses under A	N	D	Item Mean Score
1.	2	I discourage them to think independently	43	20	567	2.8

Under the three grades i.e., Agree / Neutral Opinion and disagree, scores of 1, 2, and 3 are given respectively. For example in the above table, item no. 2 got the Mean-Score of 2.8. In this item, forty three respondents agreed with the item (negatively). As their score comes to 1 per head, the total score of 43 respondents comes to 43 (43x1); In case of Neutral Opinion, 20 respondents maintained neutrality. As their score is two per head, their total score comes to 40 (20x2). 567 respondents disagreed with this statement. As their score comes to 3 individually, their total score comes to 1701 (567x3). Thus the aggregate score for this item in the case of 630 respondents comes to (43+40+1701) 1784. Hence, the Item-Mean Score is 1784 ÷ 630 = 2.83. In this way, Mean-Scores of all Negative items are calculated in this study.

Hence, in case of this item the whole sample disagreed to discourage the pupils to think independently. In other words, the sample agreed positively to encourage the pupils to think independently. So, in table nos 41 to 52 the response points of Negative Items are shown as 'A' (Positive) or otherwise, on par with positive Items.

Thus, Mean-Scores of these Negative Items are placed on par with the Mean-Scores of Positive Items. In this way a parity is established between the scores of Positive and Negative Items to facilitate their comparison.

Thus, Item-wise data have been taken up with reference to the Item-wise Teacher-Responses, which have been analysed area-wise for the sake of convenience, to indicate the point allotted to an item, based on these responses and the Item-wise Mean-Score. These Mean-Scores would reveal the morale level of the respondents to each item.

These response points are indicated Item-wise by the following abbreviated symbols:

Sl. No.	Response-point level	Abbreviated Symbol adopted
1.	Agree	A
2.	Neutral Opinion	N
3.	Disagree	D

Tool—I : Teacher Factor

Table showing the Item-wise data in the Area-I: Personality Factors.

TABLE—41

Sl. No.	Item	Item Mean Score	Interpretation
1.	I motivate my pupils to learn well.	2.8	A
2.	I discourage them to think independently. (N)	2.8	A
3.	I encourage their original ideas.	2.2	N
4.	I exchange my ideas with them.	2.0	N
5.	I encourage them to make their own decisions in class room management.	2.0	N
6.	I guide them to cultivate good habits.	2.4	N
7.	I tolerate the errors in their behavioural changes (Intellectual and moral) in order to develop them constructively.	2.1	N
8.	I maintain cordial relations with them	2.3	N
9.	I act as a loco-parent for them.	2.3	N
10.	I act as a friend, guide and philosopher to them.	2.5	A
11.	I am impartial in assessing their academic work	2.8	A
12.	I maintain emotional balance with them.	2.1	N
13.	My colleagues give respect to my ideas.	2.1	N
14.	I maintain cordial relations with my colleagues.	2.1	N
15.	I am undemocratic in class-room management (N)	2.8	A
16.	The size of the class has no impact on my teaching.	2.1	N
17.	I find no monotony in my routine class work	2.1	N
18.	I take my classes punctually	2.9	A
19.	I am conscientious in performing my duties.	2.8	A
20.	I attend the Daily Assembly in my school.	2.8	A
21.	I take part in additional duties such as polling, census work etc, willingly.	2.4	N
22.	I welcome suggestions on my academic activities.	2.1	N
23.	I enjoy the freedom of expression in my profession.	2.0	N
24.	I discourage malpractices in examinations.	2.7	A
25.	I do so paying scant attention to the results.	2.6	A

As can be seen from the above table the whole sample has agreed with eight (8) positive items and disagreed with two (2) negative items. It denotes that a total of 10 items are accepted by the whole sample. It indicates the whole sample opined that these ten (10) items are main factors which contribute in promoting Teacher-morale. The content of these items is as follows.

Sl. No.	Item No.	Item
1.	1	Motivating the pupils to learn well.
2.	2	Encouraging the students to think independently.
3.	10	Acting as a friend, guide and philosopher to the students.
4.	11	Maintaining impartiality in assessing the work of the pupils;
5.	15	Maintaining a democratic approach in the class room management.
6.	18	Observing punctuality in taking classes.
7.	19	Performing the duties conscientiously.
8.	20	Attending the daily school Assembly.
9.	24	Discouraging the mal-practices in exainations and
10.	25.	Refusing to pay more attention to more examination results.

On the remaining 15 positive items, the whole sample expressed neutral opinion. The content of these items is as follows:

Sl. No.	Item No.	Item
1.	3	Encouraging the pupils' original ideas,
2.	4	Exchanging Teachers ideas with pupils.
3.	5	Encouraging the pupils to make their own decisions in class-room management.
4.	6	Guiding them to cultivate good habits.
5.	7	Tolerating errors of pupils' behaviour to help them learn to improve upon them.
6.	8	Maintaining cordial relations with them.
7.	9	Acting as their loco-parent.
8.	12	Maintaining emotional balance with them.
9.	13	Commanding respect from colleagues.
10.	14	Maintaining cordial relations with them
11.	16	Teaching in large size classes without any adverse effect.
12.	17	Feeling monotony in the class-work.
13.	21	Taking part in additional duties of national importance, willingly.
14.	22	Welcoming suggestions on academic activities.
15.	23	Enjoying the freedom of expression in teaching profession.

There are no items with negative response in this area nor in the other areas of the whole opinionnaire.

TABLE—42

Table showing the Item-wise data in the Area—2; Professional Aspirations.

Sl. No.	Item	Item Mean Score	Inter-pretation
1	2	3	4
26.	I make myself available to my pupils out of the school hours also, for their guidance.	2.8	A
27.	I give them educational as well as vocational guidance.	2.2	N
28.	I discourage creativeness among them. (N)	2.8	A
29.	I develop logical reasoning in them through my class work.	2.2	N
30.	I adapt my teaching to the needs of individual differences among them.	2.2	N
31.	I co-operate with my colleagues for our mutual constructive guidance.	2.2	N
32.	I discuss with my colleagues on academic matters.	2.2	N
33.	I conduct private tuitions to supplement my income. (N)	2.7	A
34.	I take decisions for the proper management of the classes.	2.0	N
35.	I conduct the school programmes in such a way as to serve the needs of the local community.	2.1	N
36.	I use my professional security for the benefit of my pupils.	2.1	N
37.	In view of the security of my job, I work without fear or favour.	2.1	N
38.	I use the opportunities available to improve my academic qualifications.	2.8	A
39.	I keep in touch with the latest developments in the methods of teaching my subjects.	2.9	A
40.	I read books and journals for my professional growth.	2.8	A
41.	I strive for my professional growth by participating in the in-service programmes, willingly.	2.8	A
42.	I secure professional growth by undertaking action research.	2.3	N
43.	I see the T.V. News - Bulletins regularly.	2.1	N
44.	I use general knowledge in teaching, wherever it is applicable.	2.6	A
45.	I am very much benefited with the subject of psychological foundations of education in my class-room teaching.	2.1	N

Cont...

1	2	3	4
46.	I grade the questions in school examinations in terms of their difficulty level.	2.1	N
47.	I use the PUPILS' responses in examinations, to give them remedial instruction.	2.2	N
48.	I love to work in professional organisations	1.8	N
49.	I enjoy my professional status.	2.2	N
50.	I am personally interested in the teaching profession.	2.9	A

As can be seen from the above table the whole sample has agreed with seven (7) positive items and disagreed with two (2) negative items. It denotes that a total of the (9) items are accepted positively by the whole sample, as can be seen from their item mean-scores. It indicates the whole sample opined that these nine (9) items are main factors which contribute in promoting teacher-morale. The content of these items is as follows:

Sl. No.	Item No.	Item
1.	26	Teacher's availability to pupils out of the school hours for their guidance.
2.	28	Encouraging the creativeness among pupils.
3.	33	Not resorting to private tuitions for extra income.
4.	38	Using the opportunities to improve the academic qualifications.
5.	39	Keeping in touch with the latest developments in the methods of teaching.
6.	40	Reading books and journals for professional growth.
7.	41	Striving for Professional growth by participating in the in-service programmes for Professional growth.
8	44	Using general knowledge in teaching.
9.	50	Developing personal interest in the profession.

On the remaining sixteen (16) positive items, the whole sample expressed neutral opinion. The content of these items is as follows:

Sl. No.	Item No.	Item
1.	27	Giving educational and Vocational guidance to pupils.
2.	29	Developing logical reasoning among the pupils.
3.	30	Adapting suitable teaching in accordance with individual differences.
4.	31	Co-operating with colleagues for mutual constructive guidance.
5.	32	Discussing with colleagues on academic matters.
6.	34	Taking decisions for the proper management of the classes.
7.	35	Serving the needs of Local Community through school programmes.
8.	36	Using professional security of the Teacher for the benefit of the pupils.
9.	37	Working without fear or favour in view of the security of service of the Teacher.
10.	42	Securing professional growth by undertaking action research.
11.	43	Using the T.V. News - Bulletins regularly.
12.	45	Benefit from psychological foundations of Education in the teacher's class work.
13.	46	Grading the Questions of examinations in terms of their difficulty level.
14.	47	Giving remedial instruction to the pupils by using their responses in examinations.
15.	48	Working in professional organisations.
16.	49	Enjoying one's professional status.

TABLE —43

Table showing the Item-wise data in the Area—3: (a) Academic Proficiency.

Sl. No.	Item	Item Mean Score	Inter-preta-tion
51.	I clarify the doubts of my pupils in my subjects.	2.5	A
52.	I work hard to acquire an upto-date knowledge in my school subjects.	1.9	N
53.	I strive to enrich my knowledge of the content in the subjects I teach.	2.8	A
54.	I evince keen interest in attending the library.	2.6	A
55.	I am satisfied with the library accommodation in my school.	1.5	N
56.	I utilise my leisure time for writing articles on education.	1.5	N
57.	I use my leisure time to prepare instructional materials regularly.	2.6	A
58.	I Participate in the academic meetings held by Education Department and others.	1.5	N

As can be seen from the above table the whole sample has agreed with four (4) positive items. It indicates the whole sample opined that these four (4) items are the main factors which contribute in promoting Teacher-morale. The content of these items is as follows:

Sl. No.	Item No.	Item
1.	51	Clarifying the doubts of the pupils.
2.	53	Enriching the Teacher's knowledge of the content in the subjects.
3.	54	Evincing keen interest in attending the library.
4.	57	Using the teacher's leisure time to prepare instructional materials.

On the remaining four (4) positive items the whole sample expressed neutral opinion. The content of these items is as follows:

Sl. No.	Item No.	Item
1.	52	Acquiring an upto-date knowledge in the subjects concerned.
2.	55	Being satisfied with the library accommodation in the school.
3.	56	Utilising leisure time for writing articles on Education.
4.	58	Participating in the academic meetings held by Education Department and other agencies.

TABLE—44

Table showing the Item-wise data in the Area—3 : (b) Teaching Ability.

Sl. No.	Item	Item Mean Score	Interpretation
59.	I encourage pupils to acquire practical knowledge.	1.8	N
60.	I prepare my daily lesson-plans before going to classes.	2.7	A
61.	I use suitable teaching aids in my classes.	2.3	N
62.	I prepare new models of teaching aids every year.	1.5	N
63.	I don't teach my subjects systematically. (N)	2.9	A
64.	I adopt new teaching methods like team teaching, group discussion etc.	2.6	A
65.	I use electrical gadgets and T.V. in the class-room teaching.	1.8	N
66.	I use Community Resources for enriching my class-room instruction.	1.5	N

As can be seen from the above table the whole sample has agreed with two (2) positive items and disagreed with one (1) negative item. It denotes that a total of three (3) items are agreed positively by the whole sample as can be seen from their item mean-scores. It indicates the whole sample opined that these three (3) items are the main factors which contribute in promoting Teacher-morale. The content of these items is as follows:

Sl. No.	Item No.	Item
1.	60	Preparing the daily lesson plans in advance.
2.	63	Teaching systematically.
3.	64	Adopting new teaching methods like, team-teaching, group discussion etc.

On the remaining five (5) positive items the whole sample expressed neutral opinion. The content of these items is as follows:

Sl. No.	Item No.	Item
1.	59	Encouraging the pupils in acquisition of practical knowledge.
2.	61	Use of teaching aids in the classes.
3.	62	Preparation of new models of teaching aids every year.
4.	65	Use of electrical gadgets and T.V. in the class room teaching.
5.	66	Use of community resources for enriching the class-room instructions.

TABLE—45

Table showing the Item-wise data in the Area—3 :
(c) Organising Skills.

Sl. No.	Item	Item Mean Score	Interpretation
67.	I take up experimental projects to improve my teaching teachniques, procedures and methods.	2.7	A
68.	I participate in the subject club activities.	2.7	A
69.	I participate in the Science fairs/ Science Exhibitions	2.7	A
70.	I discourage my pupils to participate in Dramatic clubs.(N)	2.1	N
71.	I take active part in Intramural competitions.	1.8	N
72.	I involve myself actively in the Annual Day celebrations of my School.	1.7	N
73.	I participate in the Social Service Camps.	1.6	N

As can be seen from the above table the whole sample has agreed with three (3) positive items. It indicates the whole sample opined that these three (3) items are main factors which contribute in promoting Teacher-morale. The content of these items is as follows:

Sl. No.	Item No.	Item
1.	67	Taking up experimental projects in improving the teaching techniques, procedures and methods.
2.	68	Participating in the subject club activities.
3.	69	Participating in the science fairs/ science exhibitions.

On the remaining four (4) items the whole sample express neutral opinion on three (3) positive items and one (1) negative item. The content of these items is as follows:

Sl. No.	Item No.	Item
1.	70	Encourage the pupils participation in Dramatic clubs.
2.	71	Participating in Intramural Competitions.
3.	72	Participating in the Annual Day Celebrations of the school.
4.	73	Participating in the Social Service Camps.

TABLE—46

Table showing the Item-wise data in the Area-3 :
(d) Linguistic Proficiency.

Sl. No.	Item	Item Mean Score	Inter-preta-tion
74.	I make my pronunciation intelligible to all the students in the class.	2.3	N
75.	I use simple language, appropriate to the class level.	2.7	A
76.	I don't like to use simple sentences in my language. (N)	2.8	A
77.	I use colloquial style in my classes.	1.6	N
78.	I speak in the classes with reasonable pauses, intonation and accent.	1.6	N
79.	I observe the necessary modulations while explaining the lesson.	1.6	N
80.	I always learn to use correct language, while communicating to the students.	2.8	A

As can be seen from the above table the whole sample has agreed with two (2) positive items and disagreed with one (1) negative item. It denotes that a total of three (3) items are agreed positively by the whole sample as can be seen from their item mean-score. It indicates the whole sample opined that these three (3) items are the main factors which contribute in promoting Teacher-morale.

Sl. No.	Item No.	Item
1.	75	Using simple language, appropriate to the class level.
2.	76	Using simple sentences in the language.
3.	80	Using correct language, while communicating to the students.

On the remaining four (4) positive items the whole sample expressed neutral opinion. The content of these items is as follows:

Sl. No.	Item No.	Item
1.	74	Using intelligible pronunciation.
2.	77	Using colloquial style in the classes.
3.	78	Speaking in the classes with reasonable pauses, intonation and accent.
4.	79	Observing necessary modulations in speaking.

TABLE—47

Tool—II : Environmental Factors

Table showing the Item-wise data in the Area–I : School Facilities.

Sl. No.	Item	Item Mean Score	Interpretation
1	2	3	4
81.	My School is located in healthy surroundings.	2.3	N
82.	My School has adequate and suitable physical facilities.	2.7	A
83.	My school is having drinking water facilities.	1.9	N
84.	My school has adequate sanitary facilities.	2.3	N
85.	My school authorities maintain the sanitary facilities with proper cleanliness.	1.9	N
86.	A Committee of pupils and Staff assists the School Administration to maintain the sanitary facilities in my school.	1.7	N
87.	My class room is decorated with photos of national and international leaders.	2.8	A

(Cont.)...

1	2	3	4
88.	My school library has out-dated and unsuitable books. (N)	2.8	A
89.	Books are stocked in good and attractive book-shelves at my school library.	1.8	N
90.	There is no qualified librarian in my school. (N)	2.4	N
91.	My school has separate reading room with all the required facilities for reading comfortably.	2.6	A
92.	My school Laboratory has adequate accommodation	2.7	A
93.	It is convenient to conduct all the Science Classes: Demonstration Classes and Experiments in my school laboratory.	1.8	N
94.	My school playground is adequate to conduct a variety of sports and games.	1.8	N
95.	My school has adequate games and sports material	1.9	N

As can be seen from the above table the whole sample has agreed with four (4) positive items and disagreed with one (1) negative item. It denotes that a total of five (5) items are agreed positively by the whole sample as can be seen from their item mean-score. It indicates the whole sample opined that these five (5) items are main factors which contribute in promoting Teacher-morale. The content of these items is as follows:

Sl. No.	Item No.	Item
1.	82	Adequacy of suitable physical facilities.
2.	87	Decoration of the class-rooms with photos of National and International leaders.
3.	88	Well equipping library with up-to-date and suitable books.
4.	91	Providing proper reading room with the required facilities.
5.	92	Adequate laboratory accommodation.

On the remaining ten (10) items, the whole sample expressed neutral opinion on nine (9) positive items and one (1) negative item. The content of these items is as follows:

Sl. No.	Item No.	Item
1.	81	Location of the school.
2.	83	Availability of drinking water facilities.
3.	84	Availability of sanitary facilities.
4.	85	Maintaining the sanitary facilities with proper cleanliness.
5.	86	Democratic approach in managing the sanitary facilities.
6.	89	Organisation of the school library with proper equipment.
7.	90	Need for a qualified librarian to the school.
8.	93	Laboratory facilities in the school.
9.	94	Adequate play-ground to conduct games and sports.
10.	95	Availability of sports and games material.

TABLE—48

Table showing the Item-wise data in the Area—2:
School Administration.

Sl. No.	Item	Item Mean Score	Inter-preta-tion
1	2	3	4
96.	I follow the suggestions given by the Head Master and other authorities.	2.3	N
97.	I involve myself actively in the preparation of institutional plan.	2.0	N
98.	My work-load is optimal i.e., neither too heavy nor tool light.	2.8	A
99.	I treat some of the assignments given by my school Head Master and the other superiors as useless for improving my academic work. (N)	2.9	A
100.	I often accept these assignments to win the favour of my superiors. (N)	3.0	A
101.	My academic talent is properly recognised in my school.	2.8	A
102.	There is team-spirit among my school staff.	2.0	N
103.	My school Head-Master receives good co-operation from his office staff.	2.0	N
104.	The Office Staff co-operates with all the teaching staff in their academic, para-academic and non-academic activities.	1.9	N
105.	I co-operate with my school non-teaching staff in their work.	2.0	N
106.	My school Head-Master maintains friendly relations with all the staff-members.	2.8	A
107.	He does not confer any undue favour on any one of the staff-members.	2.8	A

Cont...

1	2	3	4
108.	He gives proper recognition to the good work done by them.	2.8	A
109.	He is democratic in his school administration.	2.8	A
110.	He adopts a humanitarian approach to his staff.	2.2	N
111.	His supervision provides constructive guidance to the school staff and pupils.	2.1	N
112.	His guidance is available to all the staff, without any exception.	2.1	N
113.	He guides them to prevent their errors.	2.9	A
114.	He pardons them for their errors and also helps them to rectify them.	2.8	A
115.	He takes action against them whenever their errors result in moral turpitude among the pupils.	2.8	A
116.	He guides us to understand the importance of avoiding such errors.	2.4	N
117.	We respect him for his moral stature.	2.1	N
118.	My School Managing Body keeps in touch with all the school activities.	2.0	N
119.	They strive to satisfy the felt needs of my school periodically.	2.7	A
120.	My school assists all the Teacher- Welfare Activities.	2.6	A

As can be seen from the above table the whole sample has agreed with eleven (11) positive items and disagreed with two (2) negative items. It denots that a total of thirteen (13) items are agreed positively by the whole sample as can be seen from their item mean-score. It indicates the whole sample opined that these thirteen (13) items are main factors which contribute in promoting Teacher-morale. The content of these items is as follows:

Sl. No.	Item No.	Item
1	2	3
1.	98	Optimal work load.
2.	99	Treating the assignments given by the Head-master and other superiors as useful for improving the academic work.
3.	100	Accepting the assignments not to win the favour of the superiors.
4.	101	Recognising the academic talent of the teacher.
5.	106	Cordial and friendly relations of Head-master with the staff members.

Cont...

1	2	3
6.	107	Impartiality of Head master towards teachers.
7.	108	Proper recognition given to the teachers' good work in the school by Head master.
8.	109	Democratic approach of Head master in Administration.
9.	113	Availability of the Head master's guidance to all the staff members to prevent their errors.
10.	114	Pardoning them for their errors and helping them to rectify them.
11.	115	Taking action by the Head-master against the teachers, whenever their errors result in moral turpitude among the pupils.
12.	119	Satisfying the needs of the school by managing body.
13.	120	Assisting the Teacher-Welfare activities by the school.

On the remaining twelve (12) positive items, the whole sample expressed neutral opinion. The content of these items is as follows:

Sl. No.	Item No.	Item
1.	96	Compliance with the suggestions given by school authorities.
2.	97	Teachers role in preparation of Institutional plan.
3.	102	Team spirit in the staff.
4.	103	Co-operation of the office staff to the Head mater.
5.	104	Co-operation of the office staff to the teachers in school activities.
6.	105	Teacher's co-operation with the non-teaching staff in their work.
7.	110	Head-master's humanitarian approach towards his staff.
8.	111	Head-master's constructive supervision and guidance to the staff and pupils.
9.	112	Availability of the Headmaster's guidance to all the staff.
10.	116	The Headmaster's guidance to the teachers to understand the importance of avoiding certain errors.
11.	117	Giving respect to the Head master's moral stature.
12.	118	Managing body being in touch with all the school activities.

TABLE—49

Table showing the Item-wise data in the Area—3 :
Educational Administration.

Sl. No.	Item	Item Mean Score	Interpretation
121.	My school provides good working conditions to all its staff by		
	a) protecting their seniority.	2.4	N
	b) Sanctioning their normal increments every year.	2.0	N
	c) Granting leave as per rules.	1.8	N
	d) Providing the academic requirements and the necessary infra-structure for the proper functioning of the school.	1.8	N
122.	I explain to the pupils the need for the rules and regulations issued by the State.	1.7	N
123.	I help neither the gifted pupils nor the slow learners in my classes. (N)	2.9	A
124.	I co-operate with school administration to involve the students in matters such as fixing holdings, dates of examinations, etc.,	1.8	N
125.	I help my school to satisfy all the conditions, prescribed for its recognition.	1.9	N
126.	I co-operate with the school authorities for the smooth conduct of all the school and public examinations.	2.8	A
127.	I co-operate with my school authorities in Adminission work.	1.9	N
128.	I follow the syllabus prescribed by the Government.	2.8	A
129.	I implement the suggestions given in the syllabus for pupil's practical activities also.	1.8	N
130.	I don't follow the suggestions given at the annual inspection of my school. (N)	2.8	A
131.	I endeavour to achieve the objects of non-detention policy to evaluate and improve my pupils' learning.	2.2	N
132.	I work hard to win distinctions such as National awards in my profession.	2.8	A

As can be seen from the above table the whole sample has agreed with three (3) positive items and disagreed with two (2) negative items. It denotes that a total of five (5) items are agreed positively by the whole sample as can be seen from their item mean-scores. It indicates the whole sample opined that these five (5) items are main factors which contribute in promoting Teacher-morale. The content of these items is as follows:

Sl. No.	Item No.	Item
1.	123	Helping the gifted pupils and the slow learners in the class.
2.	126	Co-operating with the school authorities for the smooth conduct of examinations.
3.	128	Following the syllabus prescribed by the Government.
4.	130	Following the suggestions given in the annual inspection.
5.	132	Hard working for winning national awards.

On the remaining ten (10) positive items, the whole sample expressed neutral opinion. The content of these items is as follows:

Sl. No.	Item No.	Item
1.	121 (a)	The school provides working conditions for protecting the seniority.
2.	" (b)	The school provides working conditions for providing the increments to all the staff.
3.	" (c)	The school provides working conditions for granting leave to all the staff.
4.	" (d)	The school provides working conditions as per the academic requirements and the necessary infra-structure to the school.
5.	122	Explaining to the pupils the need for rules and regulations issued by the state.
6.	124	Democratic approach in fixing holidays and dates of examinations.
7.	125	Helping the school to meet the conditions for recognition.
8.	127	Co-operate in admission work.
9.	129	Adherence to the suggestions given in the syllabus for practical work.
10.	131	Striving to achieve the objectives of non-detention policy.

TABLE—50

Table showing the Item-wise data in the Area—4:

(a) Family.

Sl. No.	Item	Item Mean Score	Interpretation
1	2	3	4
133.	My parents have helped me to develop certain favourable attitudes towards others.	1.6	N
134.	My family members refuse to support my professional aspirations. (N)	2.5	A

Cont..

1	2	3	4
135.	I avoid projecting my family worries into my school work.	2.7	A
136.	I think aloud with my family members about my school problems.	1.6	N
137.	I try out my plans of innovative teaching on children.	1.9	N

As can be seen from the above table the whole sample has agreed with one (1) positive item and disagreed with one (1) negative item. It denotes that a total of two (2) items are agreed positively by the whole sample as can be seen from their item mean-scores. It indicates the whole sample opined that these two (2) items are the main factors which contribute in promoting Teacher-morale. The content of these items is as follows:

Sl. No.	Item No.	Item
1.	134	Support from the family members in realising the professional aspirations.
2.	135	Avoiding the projection of family worries in the school.

On the remaining three (3) positive items, the whole sample expressed neutral opinion. The content of these items is as follows:

Sl. No.	Item No.	Item
1.	133	Co-operation of family members in developing favourable attitudes towards school personnel and others.
2.	136	Consultation with family members about school problems.
3.	137	Tryout of innovative teaching plans on children/ out side the school.

TABLE—51

Table showing the Item-wise data in the Area—4 :
(b) community.

Sl. No.	Item	Item Mean Score	Interpretation
138.	My school parent-teacher association gives its support to my school activities.	2.8	A
139.	I inform the parents of the progress of their wards as well as their difficulties if any, from time to time.	2.9	A
140.	My school resources are made available for the programmes of the local community, without detriment to school activities.	1.8	N
141.	My school participates in the social and cultural functions of the local community.	1.6	N
142.	My school organizes its social service programmes to serve the local community.	1.6	N
143.	My school receives community-support for its activities.	1.8	N
144.	My sincerity and commitment help me to command respect from all sections of the society.	2.3	N
145.	My school authorities deal effectively with the pressure groups who approach them in matters of admissions, conduct of examinations etc.	2.2	N
146.	They study the demand in realistic situation.	1.5	N
147.	They open a dialogue with them in a friendly atmosphere.	1.6	N

As can be seen from the above table the whole sample has agreed with two (2) positive items. It indicates the whole sample opined that these two (2) items are main factors which contribute in promoting Teacher-morale. The content of these items is as follows:

Sl. No.	Item No.	Item
1.	138	Co-operation of the Parent-Teacher association in the school activities.
2.	139	Informing the students' progesss and their difficulties to the parents.

On the remaining eight (8) positive items, the whole sample expressed neutral opinion. The content of these items is as follows:

Sl. No.	Item No.	Item
1.	140	Providing the school resources for the programmes of the local community.
2.	141	Participation of the school in the social and cultural functions of the local community.
3.	142	Organising the social service programmes for the development of local community.
4.	143	Receiving community support for school activities.
5.	144	Commanding respect from society.
6.	145	Dealing effectively with the pressure groups.
7.	146	Dealing with pressure groups in a realistic situation.
8.	147	Opening a dialogue with them, in a friendly atmosphere.

TABLE—52

Table showing the Item-wise data in the Area—4 :

(c) Value system.

Sl. No.	Item	Item Mean Score	Interpretation
148.	All my school personnel keep aloof from local politics.	2.8	A
149.	My school authorities politicize the school issues. (N)	2.9	A
150.	They are guided mostly by social values in disposing of these issues.	2.1	N
151.	They are guided by similar values *i.e.,* higher values in dealing with the caste and religious groups of the community.	2.8	A
152.	They don't allow any pressure-group of the community to pressurize the legitimate interests of their school work.	1.5	N
153.	They deal with all these pressure groups democratically, on a higher ethical basis.	1.9	N
154.	They strive to keep up their school morale in spite of the problems created by these groups.	1.5	N
155.	They manifest their belief in their behaviour that a person with low morale may get temporary pleasures with these groups, but will fall ultimately.	1.5	N
156.	They maintain high morale even if they are tempted with money and other material benefits by these groups.	1.6	N
157.	They caution the teachers having low morale to be careful with these groups.	1.5	N

As can be seen from the above table the whole sample has agreed with two (2) positive items and disagreed with one (1) negative item. It denotes that a total of three (3) items are agreed positively by the whole sample as can be seen from their item mean-scores. It indicates the whole sample opined that these three (3) items are main factors which contribute in promoting Teacher-morale. The content of these items is as follows:

Sl. No.	Item No.	Item
1.	148	Non-interference of the school personnel in local politics.
2.	149	Refusing to politicize the school issues by school authorities.
3.	151	Following the higher values in dealing with the caste and religious groups of the community.

On the remaining seven (7) positive items, the whole sample expressed neutral opinion. The content of these items is as follows:

Sl. No.	Item No.	Item
1.	150	Adherence to social values in disposing the school issues.
2.	152	Avoiding the pressurization from local community on school work.
3.	153	Dealing with pressure groups on an ethical basis.
4.	154	Importance of keeping up the school morale.
5.	155	Certain inconveniences of teachers with low morale.
6.	156	Importance of maintaining high morale against odds.
7.	157	Some caution to the teachers with low morale.

Tables 53 and 54

Based upon the data in Tables—41 to 52, almost a consolidation of these data is given in Tables—53 and 54 to show the area-wise distribution of the positive as well as neutral responses in Tools—I and II.

TABLE —53

Table showing the Area-wise distribution of Positive and Neutral Respponses in Tool —1

Sl.	Area	Table No.	Total No. of Items	No. of P.R.	%	No. of N.R.	%
1.	1. P.F.	41	25	10	40%	15	60%
2.	2. Pr.A.	42	25	9	36%	16	64%
3.	3. (a) A.P.	43	8	4	50%	4	50%
4.	(b) T.A.	44	8	3	37.5%	5	62.5%
5.	(c) O.S.	45	7	3	43%	4	57%
6.	(d) L.P.	46	7	3	43%	4	57%
			80	32	40%	48	60%

Index: No. of P.R. : No. of Positive Responses.
No. of N.R. : No. of Neutral Responses.
% : Percentage.
1. P.F. : Personality Factors
2. Pr.A. : Professional Aspirations
3. (a) A.P. : Academic Proficiency
(b) T.A : Teaching Ability
(c) O.S : Organising Skills
(d) L.P. : Linguistic Proficiency.

TABLE—54

Table showing the Area-wise distribution of Positive and Neutral Responses in Tool —II.

Sl.	Area	Table No.	Total No. of Items	No. of P.R.	%	No. of N.R.	%
1.	1. S.F.	47	15	5	33.3%	10	66.6%
2.	2. S.A.	48	25	13	52%	12	48%
3.	3 E.A.	49	15	5	33.3%	10	66.6%
4.	4. (a) F.	50	5	2	40%	8	60%
5.	(b) C.	51	10	2	20%	8	80%
6.	(c) V.S.	52	10	3	30%	7	70%
			80	30	37.5%	50	62.5%

Index: No, of P.R. : No. of Positive Responses.
No. of N.R. : No. of Neutral Responses.
% : Percentage.

The data given in the two Table Nos. 53 and 54 show that a considerable No. of items received Positive Response, while the sample was Undecided on a larger No. of items in the Tools—I and II.

We may observe the following too, in the above Tables:

(a) We have found in the responses given to the 160 items in the Tools—I and II, two types of the same; P.r. (2.5 to 3.0) and N.R. (1.5 to 2.4) based upon the Item-mean-scores.

None of the 160 items received negative responses, as their mean-scores didn't fall below 1.5.

(b) In Tool—I Positive Responses are 40%, while neutral responses are 60%; they (the former) are respectively 37.5% and 62.5%, in Tool—II.
(c) In Tool—I, Positive Responses are in largest number (50%) under Area No. 3 (a) 'Academic Proficiency'. Consequently, Neutral Responses too are equal in it. However, they are in largest number in Area No.3 (b) 'Teaching Ability'.
(d) Again, in Tool—I, Positive Responses are in smallest number in Area No. 3 (b) 'Teaching Ability', (37.5%).
(e) Neutral Responses are in smallest number, (50%) in Area No.3 (a) 'Academic Proficiency' in Tool—I.
(f) As for Tool—II, Positive Responses are in largest number under School Administration (Area No. 2) (52%) in which Neutral Responses are in smallest number (48%). Positive Responses are in smallest number in Area No. 4 (b) Community, in which Neutral Responses are in largest number (80%).

Index: 1.S.F. : School Facilities
2. S.A. : School Administration
3. E.A. : Educational Administration
4. (a) F. : Family
(b) C. : Community
(c) V.S.: Value system.

A further study of the Table Nos. 41 to 52

The above said two levels of Positive and Neutral Responses given to the 160 items under this study, are respectively with item mean-scores of 2.5 to 3.0 (Positive Response Level), and 1.5 to 2.4 (Neutral Response Level). The larger incidence of Neutral Responses as per the Item-wise mean scores, and the absence of Negative Responses are apparently very peculiar phenomena. Kind attention is invited to the following in this connection, in the observations made earlier with reference to the Tool-wise and the Area-wise Mean-scores.

(a) Tool-wise also, the average Item Mean-Score falls within the Neutral Response points only, rather than the Positive Response points. It is actually: 2.31 in Teacher Factor Morale and 2.20, in Environmental Factors Morale vide Table No. 11. Besides, these two tools differ in their mean scores significantly at 0.01 level, vide Table No. 11. Hence the higher morale in the Teacher Factor, as already found.
(b) Even area-wise, it is within the Neutral Response points, ranging in the Teacher Factor Morale from 2.1 to 2.4; and in the Environmental Factors Morale from 2.0 to 2.3, vide Table Nos. 36 and 37.
(c) However, under the impact of certain variables, only in three areas, (Personality Factors; Professional Aspirations, and School Administration) it goes up, so as to fall within the Positive Response points, as per Table No. 55. Evidently, the morale is higher in these three areas, only under the impact of the related variables.

An endeavour to differentiate between the Positive and the Neutral Responses obtained in this study will show that the latter have, probably, a greater disagreement, as against the former. Besides, the two phenomena caused by the two types of responses cannot but have some variations in the various items of the opinionnaire; they may not, probably, be uniform in them. Thus, even the positive responses, (2.5 to 3.0), seem to be manifest at two different levels; one may be highly positive response (2.8 to 3.0) while the other may be moderately positive response, (2.5 to 2.7) ; under Neutral Responses, too, three such levels may be, perhaps, expected, and, the investigator may perhaps, find even a reverberation in some of the responses into a Negative type. These three levels may be, therefore,

(a) Moderately Neutral Response (i) inclined towards the positive side

(b) Highly Neutral Response inclined towards neither the positive side nor the negative side, i.e., at the median level, and
(c) Moderately Neutral Response (ii) inclined towards the negative side.

With these assumptions, and also in view of (a) this compressed assessment at two points only, under the study on hand, and also (b) a wider range for the Neutral Response scores from 1.5 to 2.4, when compared to that of the Positive and the Negative Response scores, the Investigator may, perhaps, reclassify all the 160 items into the following five categories, as though in a five point scale for the sake of a broader analysis:

(a) Items that received a Highly Positive Acceptance with mean-scores of 2.8 to 3.0 (a total no. of 41 items).
(b) Items that received a Moderately Positive Acceptance with mean-scores of 2.5 to 2.7 (a total no. of 21 items).
(c) Items that received A Moderately Neutral Response on the positive side with mean-score of 2.1 to 2.4 (a total no. of 43 items).
(d) Items that received A highly Neutral Response at the median level with mean-scores of 1.8 to 2.0 (a total no. of 32 items), and
(e) Items that received a moderately neutral response on the negative side with mean-scores of 1.5 to 1.7 (a total no. of 23 items).

Below are given the 160 items, category-wise as per the above reclassification:

A. Item that received *A Highly Positive Acceptance* with item-wise mean-scores of 2.8 to 3.0 as per Table Nos 41 to 52 are as follows:

TABLE—55

Table showing the impact of certain Variables on the Areas of Teacher Factor and Environmental Factors.

Sl. No.	Area	Table No.	Variable	Category of the Variable	No. of the category	Area Mean Score	No. of Items in Area	Average Item Mean Score
1.	Personality Factors	19	Age	Teachers of 50 Yrs & above	205	62.84	25	2.5
2.	" "	19	Sex	Women Teachers	270	65.89	25	2.6
3.	" "	19	Designation	Head Masters	100	62.5	25	2.5
4.	" "	19	Management	T.P.I.	221	63.71	25	2.6
5.	" "	19	Class-Size	T.H.S.S.C.	93	63.60	25	2.5
6.	Professional Aspirations	20	"	"	93	63.29	25	2.5
7.	School Administration	26	Sex	Women Teachers	270	62.67	25	2.5
8.	" "	26	Designation	Head Masters	100	63.98	25	2.6
9.	" "	26	Class-Size	T.P.I	93	62.69	25	2.5

Index: T.P.I. : Teachers working under Private Institutions.
T.H.S.S.C. : Teachers Handling Small-size Classes below 30.

Sl. No.	Item No.	Content of the Item
1	2	3
TOOL–I : TEACHER FACTOR		
		Area–(1) Personality Factors:
1.	1	Motivating the pupils to learn well;
2.	2	Encouraging the students to think independently ;
3.	11	Maintaining impartiality in assessing the work of the pupils;
4.	15	Maintaining a democratic approach in the class room management.
5.	18	Observing punctuality in taking classes.
6.	19	Performing the duties conscientiously.
7.	20	Attending the daily school Assembly.
		Area—(2): Professional Aspirations:
8.	26	Teacher's availability to pupils out of the school hours for their guidance.
9.	28	Encouraging the creativeness among pupils.
10.	38	Using the opportunities to improve the academic qualifications.
11.	39	Keeping in touch with the latest developments in the methods of teaching.
12.	40	Reading books and journals for professional growth.
13.	41	Striving for Professional growth by participating in the in-service programmes for Professional growth.
14.	50	Developing personal interest in the profession.
		Area–(3) : Professional Skills
		(a) : Academic Proficiency:
15.	53	Enriching the Teacher's knowledge of the content in the subjects.
		(b) *Teaching Ability:*
16.	63	Teaching systematically.
		(c) Organising Skills:
		Nil
		(d) Linguistic Proficiency:
17.	76	Using simple sentences in the language.
18.	80	Using correct language, while communicating to the students.
		Tool–II : Environmental Factors
		Area–(1) : School Facilities
19.	87	Decoration of the class-rooms with photos of National and International leaders.
20.	88	Well equipping library with up-to-date and suitable books.

Cont..

1	2	3
		Area–(2): School Administration
21.	98	Optimal work load.
22.	99	Treating the assignments given by the Head-master and other superiors as useful for improving the academic work.
23.	100	Accepting the assignments not to win the favour of the superiors.
24.	101	Recognising the academic talent of the teacher.
25.	106	Cordial and friendly relations of Head Master with the staff members.
26.	107	Impartiality of Head Master towards teachers.
27.	108	Proper recognition given to the teachers' good work in the school by Head Master.
28.	109	Democratic approach of Head Master in Administration.
29.	113	Availability of the Head Master's guidance to all the staff members to prevent their errors.
30.	114	Pardoning them for their errors and helping them to rectify them.
31.	115	Taking action by the Head Master against the Teachers, whenever their errors result in moral turpitude among the pupils.
		Area–(3) : Educational Administration:
32.	123	Helping the gifted pupils and the slow learners in the class.
33.	126	Co-operating with the school authorities for the smooth conduct of examinations.
34.	128	Following the syllabus prescribed by the Government.
35.	132	Hard working for winning national awards.
36.	130	Following the suggestions given in the annual inspection.
		Area—(4) : Environmental impact:
		(a) : Family :
		Nil
		(b): Community:
37.	138	Co-operation of the parent-teacher association in the school activities.
38.	139	Informing the students' progress and their difficulties to the parents.
		(c): Value System:
39.	148	Non-interference of the school personnel in local politics.
40.	149	Refusing to politicize the school issues by school authorities.
41.	150	Adherence to social values in disposing the school issues.

B. Items that receive *A Moderately Positive Acceptance* with item-wise mean-scores of 2.5 to 2.7 as per the (Tables—41 to 52), are as follows:

Sl. No.	Item No.	Content of the Item
		TOOL—1: TEACHER FACTOR
		Area—(1) Personality Factors:
1.	10	Acting as a friend, guide and philosopher to the students;
2.	24	Discouraging the malpractices in examinations and
3.	25	Refusing to pay more attention to more examination results.
		Area—(2) : Professional Aspirations:
4.	33	Not resorting to private tuitions for extra income.
5.	44	Using General Knowledge in teaching.
		Area—(3) : Professional Skills:
		(a) : Academic Proficiency:
6.	51	Clarifying the doubts of the pupils.
7.	54	Evincing keep interest in attending the library.
8.	57	Using the teacher's leisure time to prepare instructional materials.
		(b) Teaching Ability
9.	60	Preparing the daily lesson plans in advance.
10.	64	Adopting new teaching methods like, team-teaching, group discussion etc.
		(c) Organising Skills:
11.	67	Taking up experimental projects in improving the teaching techniques, procedures and methods.
12.	68	Participating in the subject club activities.
13.	69	Participating in the science fairs /science exhibitions.
		(d) Linguistic Proficiency:
14.	75	Using simple language, appropriate to the class level.
		TOOL-II: ENVIRONMENTAL FACTORS:
		Area–(1) School Facilities:
15.	82	Adequacy of suitable physical facilities.
16.	91	Providing proper reading room with the required facilities.
17.	92	Adequate laboratory accommodation.
		Area–(2) : School Administration:
18.	119	Satisfying the needs of the school by managing body.
19.	120	Assisting the Teacher-Welfare activities by the school.
		Area–(3) : Educational Administration:
		Nil
		Area–(4) : Environmental Impact:
		(a) : Family:
20.	134	Support from the family members in realising the professional aspirations.
21.	135	Avoiding the projection of family worries in the school.
		(b) Community:
		Nil
		(c) Value System:
		Nil

C. Items that received *A Moderately Neutral Response on the Positive Side* with item-wise mean-scores of 2.1 to 2.4 as per Table Nos. 41 to 52, are as follows:

Sl. No.	Item No.	Content of the Item
1	2	3
		TOOL—I : TEACHER FACTOR:
		Area—(1) : Personality Factors:
1.	3	Encouraging the pupils' original ideas.
2.	6	Guiding them to cultivate good habits.
3.	7	Tolerating errors of pupils' behaviour to help them learn to improve upon them.
4.	8	Maintaining cordial relations with them.
5.	9	Acting as their loco-parent.
6.	12	Maintaining emotional balance with them.
7.	13	Commanding respect from colleagues.
8.	14	Maintaining cordial relations with them.
9.	16	Teaching even large size classes without any adverse effect.
10.	17	Feeling monotony in the class-work.
11.	21	Taking part in additional duties of national importance willingly.
12.	22	Welcoming suggestions on academic activities.
		Area—(2) : Professional Aspirations:
13.	27	Giving educational and Vocational guidance to pupils.
14.	29	Developing logical reasoning among the pupils.
15.	30	Adapting suitable teaching in accordance with individual differences.
16.	31	Co-operating with colleagues for mutual constructive guidance.
17.	32	Discussing with colleagues on academic matters.
18.	35	Serving the needs of Local Community through school programmes.
19.	36	Using professional security of the Teacher for the benefit of the pupils.
20.	37	Working without fear or favour in view of the security of service of the Teacher.
21.	42	Securing professional growth by undertaking action research.
22.	43	Using the T.V. News – Bulletins regularly.
23.	45	Benefit from psychological foundations of Education in the teacher's class work.
24.	46	Grading the Questions of examinations in terms of their difficulty level.
25.	47	Giving remedial instruction to the pupils by using their responses in examinations.
26.	49	Enjoy one's professional status.
		Area—(3) : Professional Skills:
		(a) : Academic Proficiency:
		Nil

1	2	3
		(b) Teaching Ability:
27.	61	Use of teaching aids in the classes.
		(c) Organising Skills:
28.	70	Encourage the pupils participation in Dramatic clubs.
		(d) Linguistic Proficiency:
29.	74	Using intelligible pronunciation.
		TOOL -II; ENVIRONMENTAL FACTORS:
		Area–(1) : School Facilities:
30.	81	Location of the school.
31.	84	Availability of sanitary facilities.
32.	90	Need for a qualified librarian to the school
		Area–(2) : School Administration:
33.	96	Compliance with the suggestions given by school authorities.
34.	110	Head Master's humanitarian approach towards his staff.
35.	111	Head Master's constructive supervision and guidance to the staff and pupils.
36.	112	Availability of the Head Master's guidance to all the staff.
37.	116	The Head Master's guidance to the teachers to understand the importance of avoiding certain errors.
38.	117	Giving respect to the Head Master's moral stature.
		Area–(3) : Educational Administration:
39.	131.	Striving to achieve the objectives of non-detention policy.
40.	121	(a) The school provides working conditions for protecting the seniority.
		Area—(4) : Environmental impact:
		(a) : Family :
		Nil
		(b) : Community:
41.	144	Commanding respect from society.
42.	145	Dealing effectively with the pressure groups.
		(c) : Value System:
43.	151	Following the higher values in dealing with the caste and religious groups of the community.

D. Items that received *A Highly Neutral Response at the Median Level* with item-wise mean-scores of 1.8 to 2.0., as per Table Nos 41 to 52 are as follows:

Sl. No.	Item No.	Content of the Item
1	2	3
		TOOL— I : TEACHER FACTOR:
		Area—(1) : Personality Factors:
1.	4	Exchanging the Teacher's ideas with pupils.
2.	5	Encouraging the pupils to make their own decisions in class-room management.
3.	23	Enjoying the freedom of expression in teaching profession.
		Area—(2) : Professional Aspirations:
4.	34	Taking decisions for the proper management of the classes.
5.	48	Working in Professional organisations.
		Area–(3) : Professional Skills:
		(a) : Academic Proficiency:
6.	52	Acquiring an up-to-date knowledge in the subjects concerned.
		(b) Teaching Ability:
7.	59	Encouraging the pupils in acquisition of practical knowledge.
8.	65	Use of electrical gadgets and T.V. in the class room teaching.
		(c) Organising Skills:
9.	71	Participating in Intramural competitions.
		Area–(3) : Linguistic Proficiency :
		Nil
		TOOL-II : ENVIRONMENTAL FACTORS:
		Area–(1) : School Facilities:
10.	83	Availability of drinking water facilities.
11.	85	Maintaining the sanitary facilities with proper cleanliness.
12.	89	Organisation of the school library with proper equipment
13.	93	Laboratory facilities in the school.
14.	94	Adequate play-ground to conduct games and sports.
15.	95	Availability of sports and games material.
		Area–(2) : School Administration
16.	97	Teachers role in preparation of institutional plan.
17.	102	Team spirit in the staff.
18.	103	Co-operation of the office staff to the Head Master.
19.	104	Co-operation of the office staff to the teachers in school activities.
20.	105	Teacher's co-operation with the non-teaching staff in their work.
21.	118	Managing body being in touch with all the school activities.

1	2	3
		Area–(3) : Educational Administration:
22.	121	The school provides working conditions for (b.) Providing the increments to all the staff.
23.		The school provides working conditions for granting leave to all the staff.
24.		(d.) The school provides working conditions as per the academic requirements and the necessary infrastructure to the school.
25.	124	Democratic approach in fixing holidays and dates of examinations.
26.	125	Helping the school to meet the conditions for recognition.
27.	127	Co-operate in admission work.
28.	129	Adherence to the suggestions given in the syllabus for practical work.
		Area–(4) : Environmental impact:
		(a)Family:
29.	137	Tryout of innovative teaching plans on children/ out side the school.
		(b) : Community:
30.	140	Providing the school resources for the programmes of the local community.
31.	143	Receiving community support for school activities.
		(c): Value system
32.	153	Dealing with pressure groups on an ethical basis.

E. Items that received *A Moderately Neutral Response on The Negative Side* with item-wise mean-scores of 1.5 to 1.7 as per Table Nos. 41 to 52, are as follows:

Sl. No.	Item No.	Content of the Item
1	2	3
		TOOL—I : TEACHER FACTOR:
		Area—(1) : Personality Factors:
		Nil
		Area—(2) : Professional Aspirations:
		Nil
		Area—(3) : Professional Skills:
		(a) : Academic Proficiency
1.	55	Being satisfied with the library accommodation in the school.
2.	56	Utilising leisure time for writing articles on Education.
3.	58	Participating in the academic meetings held by Education Department and other agencies.

1	2	3
		(b) : Teaching Ability
4.	62	Preparation of new models of teaching aids every year.
5.	66	Use of community resources for enriching the class-room instruction.
		(c) : Organising Skills:
6.	72	Participating in the Annual Day Celebrations of the school.
7.	73	Participating in the Social Service Camps.
		(d) : Linguistic Proficiency
8.	77	Using colloquial style in the classes.
9.	78	Speaking in classes with reasonable pauses, intonation and accent.
10.	79	Observing necessary modulations in speaking.
		TOOL–II: ENVIRONMENTAL FACTORS:
		Area–(1): School Facilities:
11.	86	Democratic approach in managing the sanitary facilities.
		Area- (2) : School Administration:
		Nil
		Area–(3): Educational Administration:
12.	122	Explaining to the pupils the need for rules and regulations issued by the state.
		Area–(4) : Environmental Impact:
		(a) : Family
13.	133	Co-operation of family members in developing favourable attitudes towards school personnel and others.
14.	136	Consultation with family members about school problems.
		(b) : Community
15.	141	Participation of the school in the social and cultural functions of the Local Community.
16.	142	Organising the social service programmes for the development of Local Community.
17.	146	Dealing with pressure groups in a realistic situation.
18.	147	Opening a dialogue with them, in a friendly atomosphere.
		(c) Value System
19.	152	Avoiding the pressurisation from local community on school work.
20.	154	Importance of keeping up the school morale.
21.	155	Certain inconveniences of teachers with low morale.
22.	156	Importance of maintaining high morale against odds.
23.	157	Some caution to the teachers with low morale.

TABLE—56

Table showing the Area-wise item—frequencies with reference to the response levels under Teacher- Factor.

Sl. No.	Area	No. of items that received responses within the level of										Total
		H.P.A.	%	M.P.A.	%	M.N.R. (i)	%	H.N.R.	%	M.N.R. (ii)	%	
1.	1. P.F.	7	(28%)	3	(12%)	12	(48%)	3	(12%)	Nil		25
2.	2. Pr.A.	7	(28%)	2	(8%)	14	(56%)	2	(8%)	Nil	—	25
3.	3. (a) A.P.	1	(13%)	3	(37%)	Nil	—	1	(13%)	3	(37%)	8
4.	(b) T.A.	1	(13%)	2	(25%)	1	(12%)	2	(25%)	2	(25%)	8
5.	(c) O.S.	Nil	—	3	(43%)	1	(14%)	1	(14%)	2	(29%)	7
6.	(d) L.P.	2	(29%)	1	(14%)	1	(14%)	Nil	—	3	(43%)	7

Index: H.P.A. : Highly Positive Acceptance.
M.P.a. : Moderately Positive Acceptance.
M.N.R. (i) : Moderately Neutral Response items on the Positive side.
H.N.R. : Highly Neutral Response items at the median level.
M.N.R. (ii) : Moderately Neutral Response items on the negative side.

The figures within brackets reveal percentages of items in each area at the five levels.

TABLE—57

Table showing the Area-wise Item—frequencies with reference to the response levels under Environmental Factors.

Sl. No.	Area	No. of items that received responses within the levels of										Total
		H.P.A.	%	M.P.A.	%	M.N.R. (i)	%	H.N.R.	%	M.N.R. (ii)	%	
1.	1. S.F.	2	(13%)	3	(20%)	3	(20%)	6	(40%)	1	(7%)	15
2.	2. S.A.	11	(44%)	2	(8%)	6	(24%)	6	(24%)	Nil	—	25
3.	3. E.A.	5	(33%)	Nil	—	2	(13%)	7	(47%)	1	(7%)	15
4.	4. (a) F.	Nil	—	2	(40%)	Nil	—	1	(20%)	2	(40%)	5
5.	(b) C.	2	(20%)	Nil	—	2	(20%)	2	(20%)	4	(40%)	10
6.	(c) V.S.	3	(30%)	Nil	—	1	(10%)	1	(10%)	5	(50%)	10

Index: H.P.A. : Highly Positive Acceptance.
M.P.A. : Moderately Positive Acceptance.
M.N.R. (i) : Moderately Neutral Response items on the Positive side.
H.N.R. : Highly Neutral Response items at the median level.
M.N.R. (ii) : Moderately Neutral Response items on the Negative side.

The figures within brackets reveal percentages of items in each area at the five levels.

Findings from Tables 56 and 57

1. Items that received positive responses with mean scores ranging from 2.5 to 3.0 seem to have received these responses at two levels, one under a highly positive Response (2.8 to 3.0) and the other under a Moderately Positive Response (2.5 to 2.7) . These items are in a larger number (66%).
2. In view of a wider range of the item mean-scores from 1.5 to 2.4 under the Neutral Response, items that received such responses seem to have received them, at three different levels; (a) A Moderately Neutral Response (i) on the positive side; (b) A highly Neutral Response at the median level, and (c) A Moderately Neutral Response (ii) on the negative side.
   (a) Items with a Moderately Neutral Response (ii) on the negative side may be, perhaps, treated as almost rejected. These are approximately 23% within the entire spectrum of the existing neutral response points, i.e., out of a total No. of 98 Neutral Response Points.
   (b) Items with a Moderately Neutral Response (i) on the Positive side may be perhaps, treated as almost accepted. These are approximately 44% within the entire spectrum of the existing Neutral Response Points i.e., out of a total No. of 98 Neutral Response Points.
   (c) Items with a Highly Neutral Response, may be, perhaps, treated as almost 'undecided'. These are approximately 33% within the entire spectrum of the existing Neutral Response Points i.e., out of a total No. of 98 Neutral Response Points.
3. Thus, on the whole, 76% items in the Teacher Factor seem to have received responses on the positive side, under the levels of (a) A High Positive Acceptance, (b) A Moderately Positive Acceptance, and (c) A Moderately Neutral Response on the positive side; but only 55% items of this type fell under the Environmental Factors. Evidently, Teacher Factor has more positive acceptance than the Environmental Factors as already observed, under the Section No. A (Table no. 13).
4. Similarly, 13% received a Moderately Neutral Response on the negative side under the Teacher Factor, while such items under the Environmental Factors are 16%. Probably, these two factors fared almost equally in this regard.

5. Then, 11% items received a Highly Neutral Response at the median level under the Teacher Factor while such items are as many as 29% under the Environmental Factors. So, Environmental Factors had more of these items than Teacher Factor, as already observed under Section No. A (Table no. 13).
6. Area-wise, under the Teacher Factor the following two areas appear to have received a larger no. of responses on the positive side:
   (i) Personality Factors
   (ii) Professional Aspirations.

Under the Environmental Factors, the area pertaining to School Administration alone received such responses.

7. Items with a Highly Neutral Response at the median level are the highest in the area of Teaching Ability, under the Teacher Factor, while this happened in the area of Educational Administration under Environmental Factors.

Items with a Moderately Neutral Response (ii) on the negative side are the highest in the area of Linguistic proficiency, under the Teacher Factor, while this happened in the area of Value-system under the Environmental Factors.

8. Item-wise, the sample seems to have given almost a Positive Opinion (with mean-scores of 2.1 to 3.0) to 105 items in the whole opinionnaire (nearly 66%) whose content refers generally to certain idealistic, simpler, more generalized and less complicated situations of Teacher behaviours as exemplified here-under:

Item No.	Statement
7.	I tolerate the errors in their (pupils')behavioural changes (inellectual and moral) in order to develop them constructively.
63.	I don't teach my subjects systematically. (N)
76.	I don't like to use simple sentences in my language. (N)
21.	I take part in additional duties such as polling, census work etc, willingly.

The above type of items are 62 in Teacher Factor and 43 in the Environmental Factors. So the Teacher Factor got the items of the above type, in a larger number, as already observed in the finding

No. 6. Besides, there seem to be in these 105 items, some items like the following three items altogether with simpler as well as less complicated Teacher- behaviour, which are assumed to be manifest more in the rest of the above 105 items. These seem to refer to certain highly idealistic situations which may not be actually as simple as the latter.

Item No.	Content of the Item
113	Availability of the Head Master's guidance to all the staff members.
114	Availability of the guidance of Head Master for all the teachers in preventing their errors.
119	Satisfying the needs of the school by managing body.

Thus, these 105 items appear to be, perhaps, heterogeneous in their content, slightly.

9. Again, under the Highly Neutral Response at the Median level with mean-scores of 1.8 to 2.00, the sample seems to have chosen, in general, items whose content refers, largely, to situations of Teacher behaviours which tend to be most idealistic in their nature but most difficult to translate into action at the grass-root level as exemplified here under for the sake of clarity.

Item No.	Content of the Item
4	Exchanging Teacher's ideas with pupils.
5	Encouraging the pupils to make their own decisions in class room management.
34	Taking decisions for the proper management of the classes.

Their No. is 32 in the two factors; which comes to 20%; their distribution in these two factors is as follows:

Teacher Factor—9

Environmental factors—23

There are thus a larger number of such items under the Environmental Factors as already observed above in the finding No.5.

10. In the case of items reclassified under Moderately Neutral Response (ii) on the negative side with mean-scores of 1.5 to 1.7, we find that their content, generally refers to certain

situations of Teacher behaviours which appear to be most ambitious and also less valuable from a practical point of view and mostly performed in a mechanical as well as ritualistic manner, as exemplified here under for the sake of clarity.

Item No.	Content of the Item
56	Utilising Leisure time for writing articles on Education.
58	Participating in the academic meetings held by Education Department and other agencies.

The total no. of such items comes to 23 (14%). They are 10 in the Teacher Factor and 13 in the Environmental Factors. They are thus distributed almost equally under the two constituent factors, as already observed in the finding no. 4.

Thus, the aforesaid reclassification of the Positive and Neutral Responses may be perhaps regarded, as not at all unreasonable in view of an attempt made in this section of Chapter IV to classify and analyse the Neutral Responses in a greater detail. This endeavour, together with the two levels manifest in Positive Responses, approximates almost to a 5 pt. scale which would help to enlarge the various shades of opinion manifest in the sample. This, however, does not mean that this investigator has abandoned the 3 pt scale adopted by him. In fact, he had adopted it in this study, inspite of its disadvantage of the restricted shades of opinion, mainly in view of its suitability for the study of a social phenomenon like Teacher Morale, as decided in Chapter No. III.

Thus, the above reclassification to categorize the Positive and Neutral Responses obtained in this study, into five groups, involves only a superimposition of 5 pt scale on this study mainly to help an analysis of the two types of Responses for the purpose of observing the various shades of opinion manifest in the Item Responses. Hence the significance of the five levels of opinion presented in Table Nos. 56 and 57 together with the findings therefrom.

These five levels are mainly based on Item Mean Scores. They, thus involve a reclassification of the 160 items as follows.

a) Items with a high level of Positive Opinion (2.8 to 3.0).

b) Items with a moderate level of Positive Opinion (2.5 to 2.7).
c) Items with a low level of acceptance (2.1 to 2.4).
d) Items with some type of indecisiveness (1.8 to 2.0).
e) Items with almost a negative opinion (1.5 to 1.7).

Besides, the above five categories of Item Responses seem to approximate the Integers of scores fixed in the 3 pt scale, positive opinion with its three levels being above 2.0, neutral opinion being nearer 2.0, and Negative opinion being moderately below 2.0. There is thus a replacement of all the 160 items on the 3 pt scale, by virtue of the above reclassification. All the above five categories of items have been listed above separately.

Skewness

The following are tables showing distributions of frequencies of responses and Skewness of the whole opinionnaire and its two Tools.

TABLE—58

Table showing the Frequency Distribution and Skewness of whole opinionnaire.

Class Interval	Frequency	Mid-value
220–250	27	235
250–280	41	265
280–310	55	295
310–340	62	325
340–370	134	355
370–400	174	385
400–430	59	415
430–460	40	445
460–490	38	475
Total	630	

	Mean	Median	S.D.	Skewness
Computerised	361.11	369.00	57.49	–0.41
Manual	362.67	369.1	58.8	–0.33

TABLE—59

Table showing the Frequency Distribution and Skewness of Teacher Factor Tool.

Class Interval	Frequency	Mid-value
80 - 100	0	90
100 - 120	10	110
120 - 140	48	130
140 - 160	56	150
160 - 180	129	170
180 - 200	187	190
200 - 220	123	210
220 - 240	77	230
Total	630	

	Mean	Median	S.D.	Skewness
Computerised	184.87	187.00	29.13	–0.22
Manual	185.30	187.7	29.18	–0.25

TABLE—60

Table showing the Frequency Distribution and Skewness of Environmental Factors Tool.

Class Interval	Frequency	Mid-value
80 - 100	0	90
100 - 120	25	110
120 - 140	68	130
140 - 160	90	150
160 - 180	157	170
180 - 200	125	190
200 - 220	98	210
220 - 240	67	230
Total	630	

	Mean	Median	S.D.	Skewness
Computerised	176.24	175.50	31.76	0.07
Manual	177.02	176.82	32.17	0.02

Note: The mean-scores, the median-scores and the S.D. measures under the above three tables, (Table Nos. 58, 59 and 60), are reckoned manually, quite distinct from those with computerised data. The mean-scores under the latter are given in Table No. 11. They thus differ from the former slightly. This variation is probably due to the fact that the computerised data (mean-score, median score, and S.D. measure) are based on ungrouped data, while the manually prepared data (mean-scores, median-scores and S.D. measure) are based on frequency distributions.

Based on the data in Table Nos. 58, 59 and 60, six diagrams are given herein, in order to present the related data graphically, through three polygons and three histograms vide the diagrams Nos. 5 to 10 in the list of figures. (Shown in Page nos. 230-235)

The curves in the diagrams under figures Nos. 5 to 10 are slightly symmetrical in a way and not bell-shaped. They exhibit how the Teacher–Morale frequencies of the sample under this study are distributed.

As stated by Garrett, one simplest approach to an understanding of the normal probability distribution is through a consideration of some principles of probability… . in statistics, the 'probability' of a given response is defined as the expected frequency of its occurrence among the responses of 'a like sort'… .

The normal distribution may not be "the actual distribution" of scores, but "is instead a mathematical model...frequency distributions of scores approach the theoretical distribution as a limit, but the fit is rarely perfect... (Normal) Distributions seem to express a general tendency of quantitative data to take the symmetrical bell-shaped form. This general tendency may be stated in the form of a 'principle' as follows : measurements of many natural phenomena and of many mental and social traits under certain conditions TEND to be distributed symmetrically about their means, in proportions which approximate those of the normal probability distribution... .In the normal probability curve, the mean, the median and the mode all fall exactly at the midpoint of the distribution and are numerically equal. Since the normal curve is bilaterally symmetrical all the measures of central tendency must coincide at the centre of the distribution." In a frequency polygon or histogram of test scores, usually the first thing which strikes the eye is the symmetry or lack of it in the figure. In the normal curve model the mean, the median, and the mode all coincide and there is perfect balance between the right and left halves of the figure

FIGURE—3

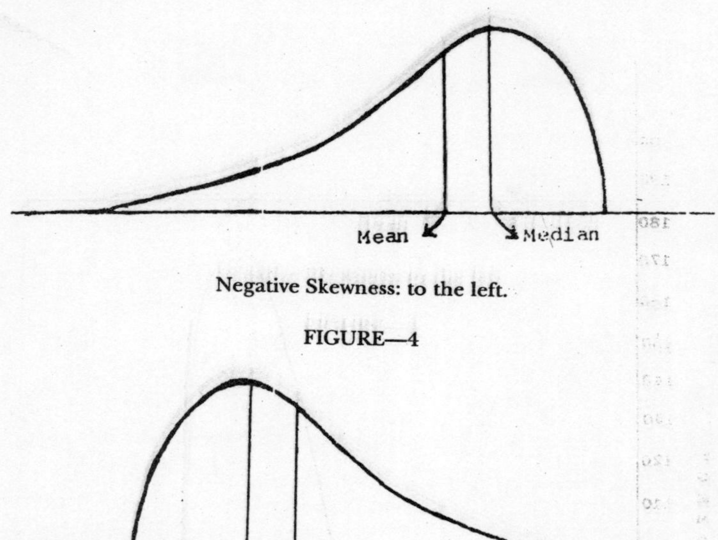

Negative Skewness: to the left.

FIGURE—4

Median
Mean

Positive Skewness : to the right.

A distribution is said to be 'skewed' when the mean and the median fall at different points in the distribution, and the balance (or center of gravity) is shifted to one side or the other—to left or right. In a normal distribution, the mean equals the median exactly and the skewness is, of course, zero. The more nearly the distribution approaches the normal form, the closer together are the mean and median, and the less the skewness. Distributions are said to be skewed negatively or to the left when scores are massed at the high end of the scale (the right end) and are spread out more gradually toward the low end (or left) as shown in Figure 3. Distributions are skewed positively or to the right when scores are massed at the low (or left) end of the scale, and are spread out gradually toward the high or right end as shown in Figure 4.

Note that the mean is pulled more toward the skewed end of the distribution than is the median. In fact, the greater the gap between mean and median, the greater the skewness. Moreover, when

FIGURE—5

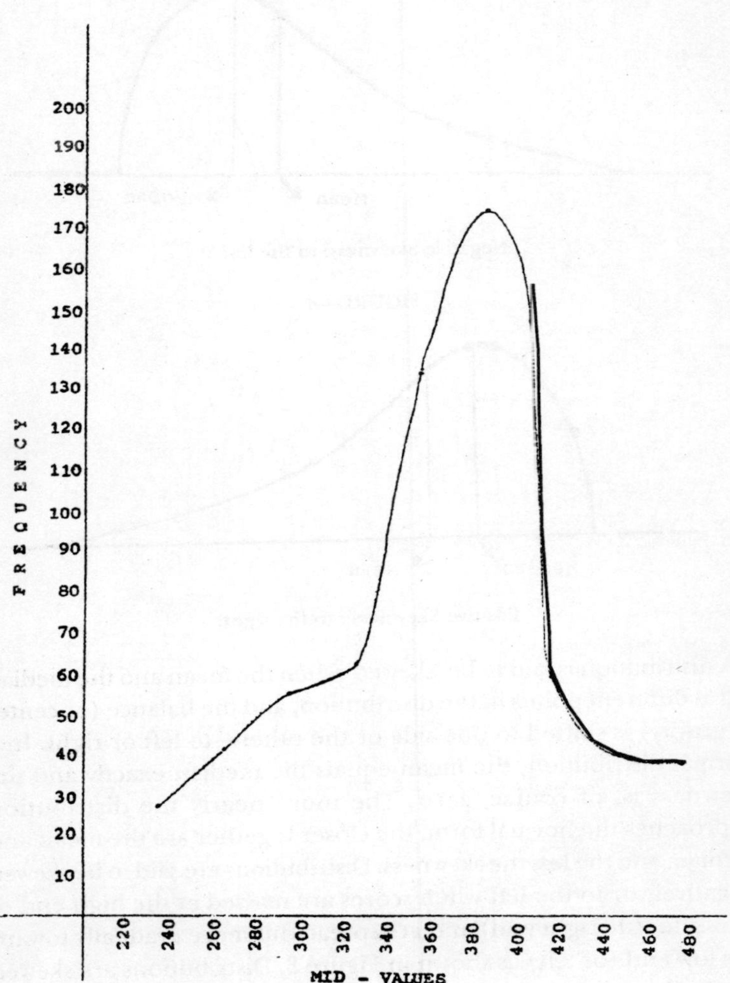

Smoothed Frequency Curve of the Distribution of Scores on whole Opinionnaire.

FIGURE—6

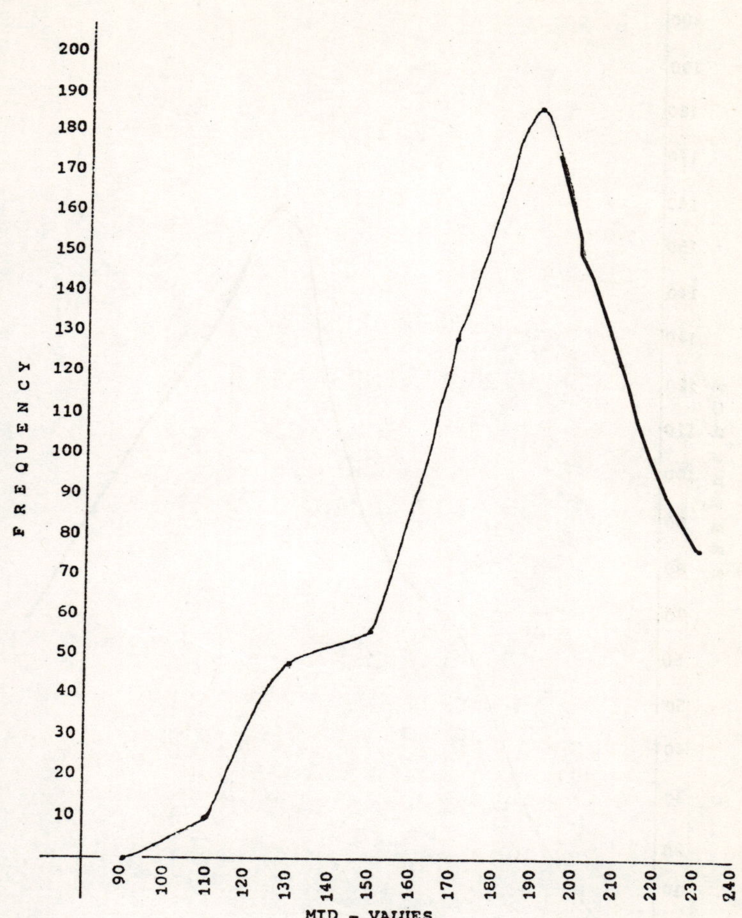

Smoothed Frequency Curve of the Distribution of Scores on Tool—I.

FIGURE—7

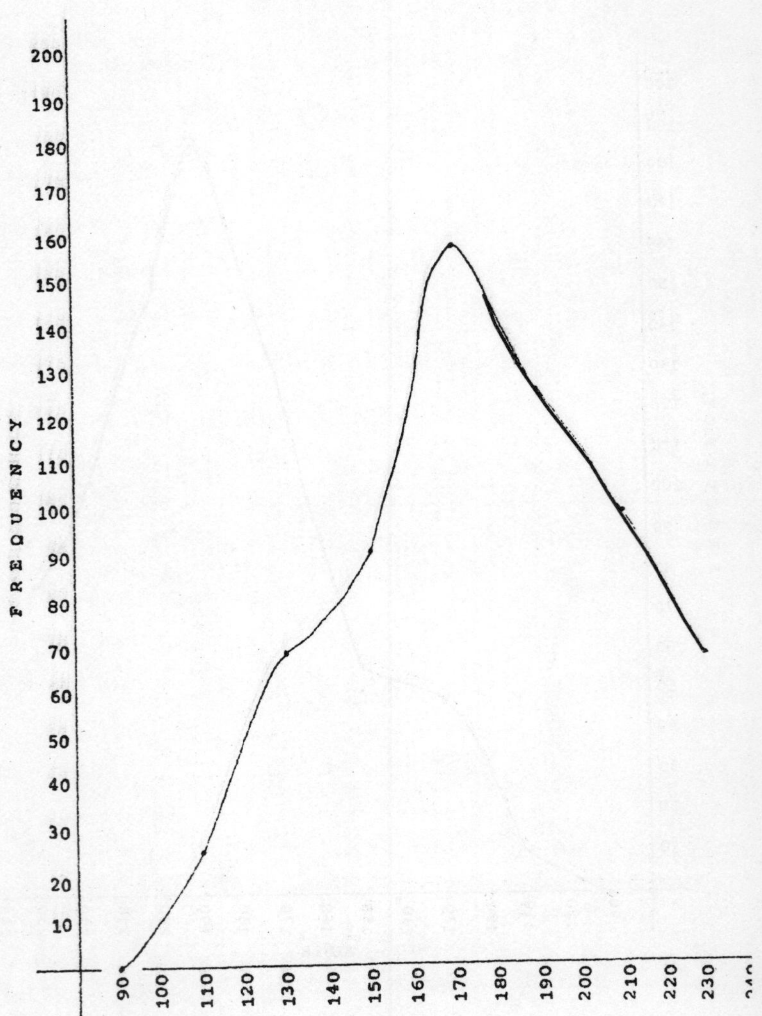

Smoothed Frequency Curve of the Distribution of Scores on Tool—II.

FIGURE—8

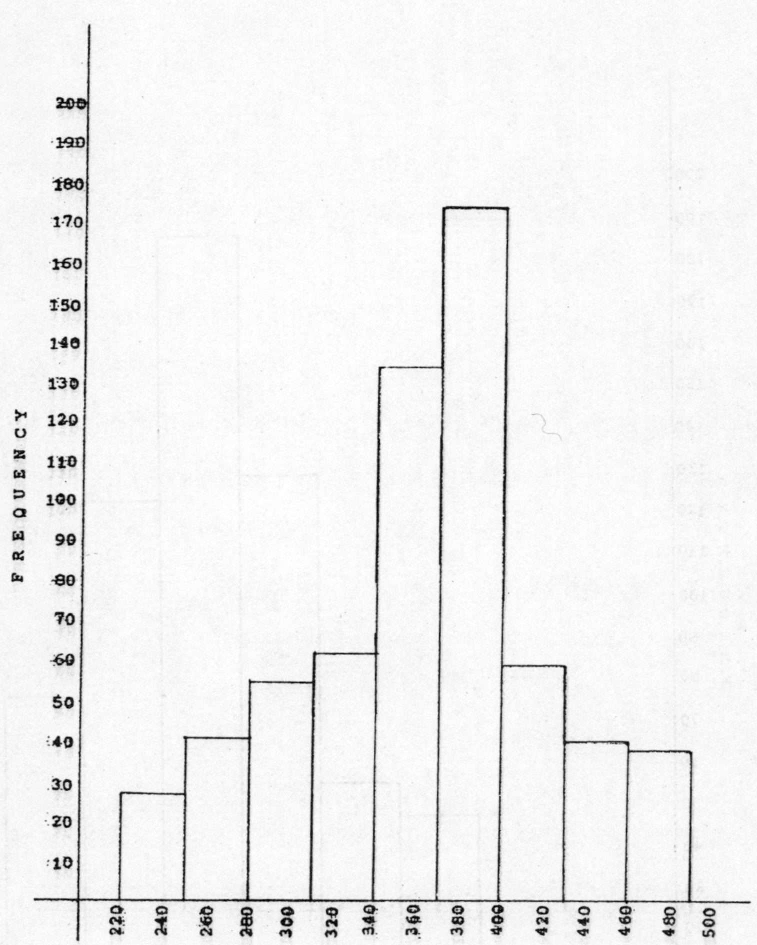

CLASS INTERVAL

Histogram (Whole Opinionnaire)

FIGURE—9

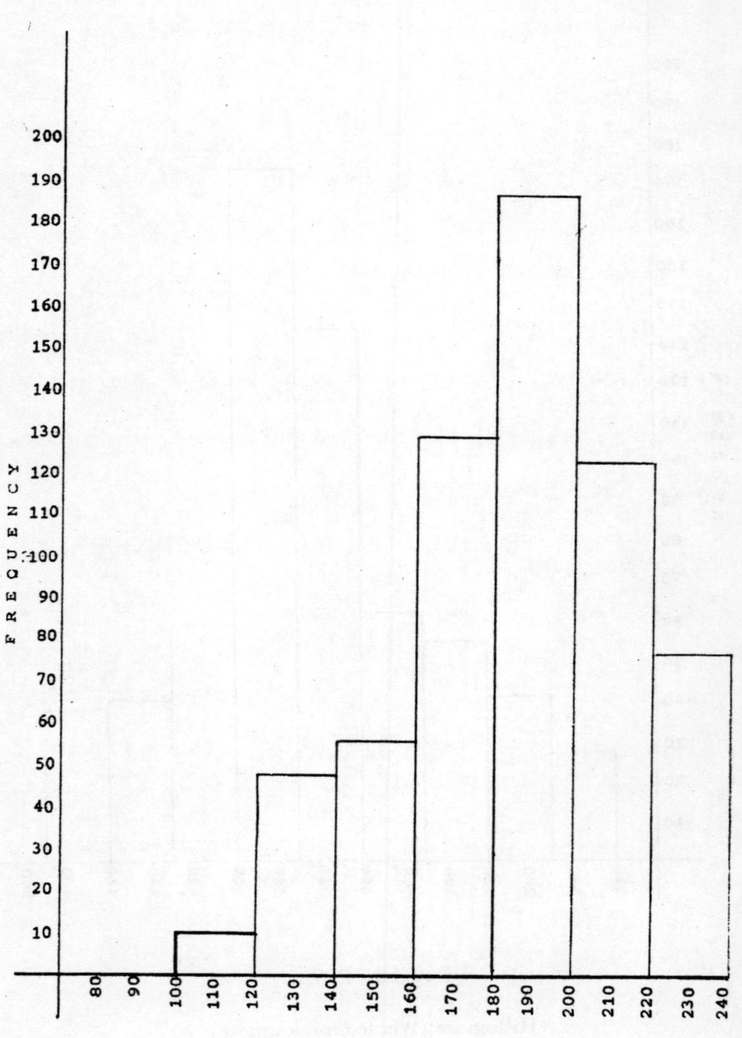

CLASS INTERVAL

Histogram (Tool—I)

FIGURE—10

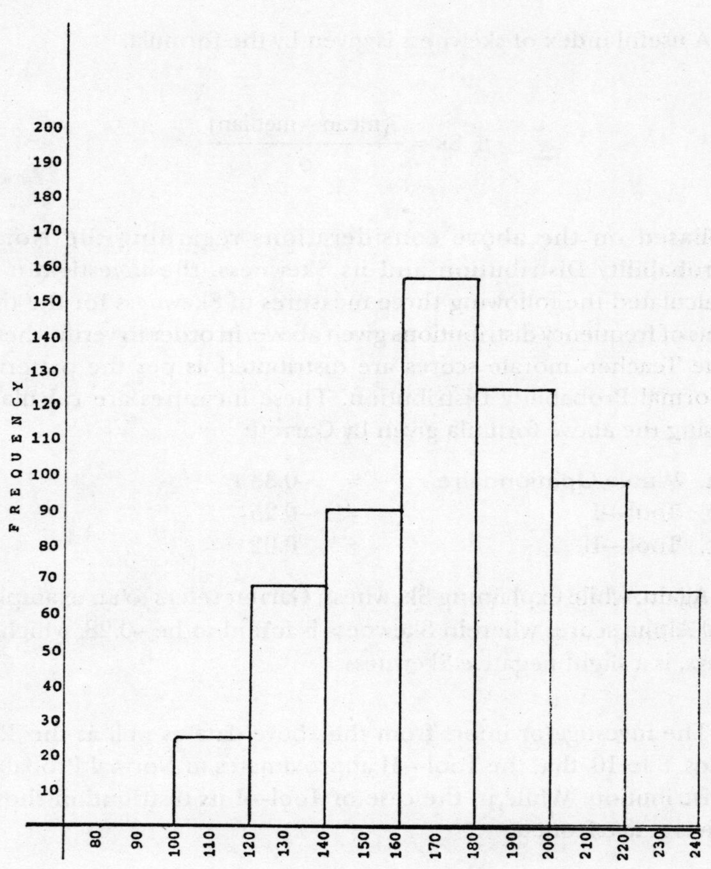

CLASS INTERVAL

Histogram (Tool—II)

skewness is negative, the mean lies to the left of the median; and when skewness is positive, the mean lies to the right of the median.

A useful index of skewness is given by the formula.

$$Sk = \frac{3(\text{mean} - \text{median})}{\sigma}$$

Based on the above considerations regarding the Normal Probability Distribution and its Skewness, the investigator has calculated the following three measures of Skewness for the three sets of frequency distributions given above, in order to verify whether the Teacher- morale scores are distributed as per the pattern of Normal Probability Distribution. These measures are calculated, using the above formula given by Garrett:

a. Whole Opinionnaire = –0.33
b. Tool—I = –0.25
c. Tool—II = 0.02

Again, while explaining Skewness, Garrett refers to an example of 50 Alpha scores wherein Skewness is found to be –0.28, which, he says, is a slight negative Skewness.

The investigator infers from the above data as well as the Table Nos. 8 to 10, that the Tool—II approximates to Normal Probability Distribution. While in the case of Tool—I its distribution shows a divergence from it.

Reliability

Reliability is the consistency and the accuracy with which a tool of Evaluation measures. For example the Opinionnaire with which an endeavour is made in this study to survey the Teacher Morale by measuring the opinions expressed by the .sample, should be considered as reliable, only when it helps us to measure consistently and accurately. The scores we have got with reference to the various items in this tool should be considered reliable when we have reasons for believing them to be stable and trustworthy. Garrett states as follows in this regard:

> *" A test score is called reliable when we have reasons for believing the score to be stable and trustworthy; stability and trust—worthiness depend upon the degree to which the score is an index of 'true ability'—is free of chance error."*
> (Garrett, 1981).

Methods of determining reliability

There are four procedures in common use for computing the reliability co-efficient (some times called the self-correlation of test). These are:

1. Test–Retest (repetition)
2. Alternate or Parallel Forms
3. Split-half Method
4. Rational Equivalance.

As it is not feasible to construct parallel forms of the opinionnaire or to readminister the opinionnaire to the sample, it is decided to employ the split-half method. In the words of Garrett, this situation occurs with many performance tests as well as with Questionnaires and inventories dealing with personality variables, attitudes and interests.

The Co-efficient of correlation between the two halves odd and even scores was computed. The obtained value of r ½ ½ is 0.91. Substituting this value in the Spearman-Brown formula and after simplification value of the reliability co-efficient of whole test was found to be 0.95 which shows that the Opinionnaire is a highly reliable tool.

Validity

Validity is a condition that makes a measuring instrument efficacious and strong. Reliability too is one such condition. But it indicates, as already stated above, a consistency or accuracy with which the tool measures.

In the case of the Opinionnaire on hand, the investigator will be happy if it has validity too as it has a high reliability as already reported. In otherwords, it would help him to measure the Teacher Morale through verbal responses and not any other phenomenon.

Thus, the validity of a test or any measuring instrument, depends upon the fidelity with which it measures what it purports to measure. And a test is valid when the performances which it measures correspond to the same performances as otherwise independently measured or objectively defined.

Validity is thus determined, as Garrett says, (a) by means of Judgement (b) experimentally (c) by factorial validity, and (d) with reference to the length of a test. When we determining it by means of judgement, the content of the tool should cover the related area.

The Validation of the content through competent Judgement is most satisfactory, when the sampling of items is wide and judicious and when adequate standardization groups are utilised.

An alternative to content Validity is the Judgement process called 'face validity'. A test or any measuring instrument is said to have face Validity when it appears to measure whatever the author had in mind, namely what he thought he was measuring.

Judgement of face validity would help an investigator to decide whether his test items are relevant to some specific situation. Face Validity should never be more than a first step in testing an item; it should not be the final word.

The Validity of a tool of evaluation may also be determined experimentally by finding the co-relation between that tool and some independent criterion. A criterion may be an objective measure of performance or a Qualification measure such as a Judgement of the character of excellence of work done.

Anastasi discusses the uses of the certain internal consistency under the head construct Validity. "Another application of the criterion of internal consistency involves the Correlation of subject scores with total score. Many intelligence tests, for instance, consist of separately administered subjects (such as vocabulary, arithmetic, picture completion, etc.) whose scores are combined in finding the total test score". (Anastasi). The investigator adopted this method to establish validity to his tool using product-moment Co-efficients of Correlation which were calculated for the scores obtained on the Opinionnaire as a whole with the 12 area-wise scores. The obtained 12 Co-efficients of correlation are presented in Table—61.

TABLE—61

Table showing the Co-efficients of correlation between the whole opinionnaire and the 12 areas.

S.No./ Areas	Opinionnaire and Name of the Area	Co-efficient of correlation
1.	Opinionnaire and Personality Factors	0.78
2.	Opinnionnaire and Professional Aspirations	0.85
3.	Opinionnaire and Academic Proficiency	0.91
4.	Opinionnaire and Teaching Ability	0.70
5.	Opinionnaire and Organising Skills	0.86
6.	Opinionnaire and Linguistic Proficiency	0.74
7.	Opinionnaire and School Facilities	0.82
8.	Opinionnaire and School Administration	0.71
9.	Opinionnaire and Educational Administration	0.87
10.	Opinionnaire and Family	0.79
11.	Opinionnaire and Community	0.76
12.	Opinionnaire and Value System	0.73

From Table—61, it can be noted that the Co-efficients of correlation for all the 12 areas and Opinionnaire as a whole are high to very high. From this it can be concluded that the tool possess construct validity at a higher degree.

Content Validity

As the items are selected after discussion with experienced teachers and Headmasters, it may be reasonably assumed that all items relevant to the aspect measured are included. This establishes the Content Validity of the instrument.

A Resume of the Findings

Thus, based upon the above presentation and interpretation of the data compiled in this investigation, the investigator hereby recapitulates the following important findings drawn from the data.

Section–A : Analysis of the Tool-wise Data

1. The distribution of Teacher Morale scores under Environmental Factors seems to approximate to the pattern of Normal Probability Distribution, while the distribution of the same under Teacher Factor seems to manifest a divergence from this pattern.
2. The Environmental Factors seem to manifest a more significant impact on Teacher Morale than the Teacher Factor, Vide the Table Nos. 9 and 10. *PROBABLY THE ENVIRONMENTAL FACTORS CONTRIBUTE RELATIVELY MORE TO THE TEACHER MORALE THAN THE TEACHER FACTOR.*
3. The two constituent factors of Teacher Morale thus seem to differ from each other, which is corroborated from Table No. 11 also, wherein significant mean differences between these two factors are revealed. However, these two factors manifest, in general, a very high positive correlation (0.783), Vide Table No. 14. Probably the impact of these two factors on Teacher Morale differs in their various areas, please see Table Nos. 31 to 35 for details.
4. Table No. 8 reveals that the distribution of morale scores in the whole Tool is relatively more normal than the same under Teacher-Factor. This phenomenon seems to be probably due to the relatively greater impact of Environmental Factors as revealed in Table Nos. 9 and 10.
5. As could be seen from the Table No. 13, a majority of the items in the opinionnaire received Neutral Responses, while a lesser number got Positive Responses. It is pertinent to note herein that none of the items got Negative Response. Evidently, the Neutral Responses are more heterogeneous. Furthermore, the item-responses do not seem to have reflected the various shades of opinion prevalent in the sample on a 3 pt scale. Under these circumstances, the investigator has endeavoured to reclassify the Neutral Responses to probe further into the Item-Responses, giving the results of this reclassification, in the findings under Section—D (Analysis of Item-wise Mean-Scores).

6. Positive Responses are found to be slightly more under the Teacher Factor, than under the Environmental Factors. (Vide Table No. 13).
7. The sample seems to have manifested a higher morale under the Teacher Factor than under the Environmental Factors, as could be inferred from the mean-scores under these two factors. (Vide Table No. 11). Evidently, the teacher has a tendency to manifest comparatively a greater morale under the Teacher Factor than in the Environmental Factors. This might be because the Teacher Factor is primarily concerned with Personality Factors, Professional Aspirations etc. which are directly concerned with Teacher-Morale, whereas the Environmental Factors pertain to the School Facilities, School Administration, etc. which become effective through the Teacher only. Hence the uniqueness of Teacher Factor as distinct from Environmental Factors.

Section–B : Analysis of Variable-wise Data

8. Table No. 15 shows that the sample has manifested, in general, a higher morale score in Teacher Factor than Environmental Factors, as already stated in the finding No. 7.
9. The higher morale manifest in the Teacher Factor is observed in all the eight variables of the sample. (Vide Table No. 15).
10. A majority of the various categories in the variables of this sample seems to have shown a higher morale in the Teacher Factor; with significant mean-differences (Vide Table No. 15). The rest of the sample seems to have shown their morale equally in the two factors i.e the Teacher Factor and the Environmental Factors.
11. However, in the case of the categories that manifested a higher morale in Teacher Factor, a greater variability is seen in Environmental Factors, as evidenced in their standard deviation measures. (Vide Table No. 15).
12. The categories that manifest higher morale in Teacher Factor do so, under all the eight variables. But they do not do so equally under all these variables. For example, Sex and Location show the highest Teacher Factor Morale. Age shows the lowest of it as can be found from Table No. 15.
13. Teacher's manifestation of an equal morale in the two factors i.e., Teacher Factor and Environmental Factors is not influenced

by the variables of Sex and School Location. (Vide Table No. 15). This is probably because these two variables appear to manifest a higher impact on Teacher Morale so as to prompt some of the concerned respondents i.e., Women Teachers and Rural Teachers to show a higher morale than their counter parts.

14. The categories that manifest equal morale in the two factors do so, only in six variables; there is therefore no impact for the variables of Sex and Location, on this phenomenon of equal morale in these two factors, as already observed in the finding No. 13. Besides, Age Variable shows a highest impact on this phenomenon. The next variable that shows a high impact after the Age Variable is Experience. The Qualifications Variable shows a low impact, the lowest being, in the variables of Sex and Location (Vide Table No. 15).
15. The sample appears to be more heterogeneous probably under the variables of Age, and also Experience than under the other variables. (Vide Table No. 15).
16. All the eight variables namely Age, Sex, Qualification, Designation, Experience, Location of the School, Type of Management and Size of the Class have shown impact on Teacher Morale under both the factors i.e., Teacher Factor and Environmental Factors. (Vide Table Nos. 16,17 and 18). This impact does not, however seem to manifest equally, in all the variables of the sample as well as all the areas of the opinionnaire.
17. As for the variable of Age, its impact is the highest in terms of Teacher Morale, only in the Age group above 50 years in the two factors. (Vide Table Nos. 16, 17 and 18).
18. Sex has a lot of impact on Morale, in view of the manifestation of a higher morale by Women Teachers in the two constituent factors of Teacher Morale. (Vide Table Nos. 16 to 18). This phenomenon couldn't be observed consistently in the related studies discussed in Chapter No. II. Besides, its manifestation might have been facilitated, in general, by the possible biological factors favouring a higher morale in Women than Men.
19. As for the variable of Qualification, its impact is higher among the Under Graduate and Post-graduate Teachers than among the Graduate Teachers in the two factors. (Vide Table Nos. 16 to 18).
20. As for the variable of Designation, the Head Masters show the highest morale under Environmental Factors, Vide Table No.

18. However, their morale has become equal to that of Secondary Grade Teachers, in the Teacher Factor. (Vide Table No. 17). Evidently, the impact of Designation is higher in Environmental Factors, than in Teacher Factor. Besides, Secondary Grade Assistants seem to have higher aspirations, on par with Head Masters under the Teacher Factor. This finding could be confirmed from Table Nos. 19 and 20, that pertain to Personality Factors and Professional Aspirations which are some components of the Teacher Factor, and which also reveal a higher morale when compared to the other components of this Factor.

21. B.Ed Assistants manifest a lower morale than Secondary Grade Assistants in the two constituent factors of Teacher Morale in spite of their higher qualifications. (Vide the Table Nos. 16 to 18). This finding seems to be in accord with the finding No. 19 wherein Graduate Teachers were found to have a lower morale than Under Graduate Teachers. This confirms also the finding No. 20 wherein the Secondary Grade Assistants were observed to have higher aspirations.
22. Certain imperceptible changes in Teacher Morale seem to occur gradually under the impact of Teaching Experience after one acquires the first five years' experience, (Vide Table Nos. 16 to 18). They probably remain latent until one acquires 15 years' experience in Teaching and seem to become manifest, only at that time.
23. Such imperceptible changes in Teacher Morale are observed more in Environmental Factors. (Vide Table No. 18).
24. Thus, the impact of 'Experience', is manifest more in Environmental Factors, than in the Teacher Factor.
25. The impact of Experience is manifest in the same manner, in the whole opinionnaire as well as the Environmental Factors i.e., without being limited as in the case of Teacher Factor.
26. In the case of School Location, the investigator has observed that Urban Teachers manifest a lower morale, probably due to their greater diversions, and greater sophistication.
27. In the case of School Management, its impact on teachers of schools under public management *i.e.,* Government and Local Bodies, seems to be equal; it is however higher, in the case of those working in schools under Private Managements. (Vide Table Nos. 16 to 18).

28. In the case of the variable pertaining to Class- Size, its impact on each of the 3 categories of Teachers under it is manifest very highly. Those with the lowest class size manifested the highest morale; next, come those with the median class-size; and last come those with the highest class-size manifesting the lowet morale. This phenomenon is found to be the same, in the two constituent factors of Teacher , (Vide the Table Nos 16 to 18). Evidently teacher with the lowest class-size have Professional Aspirations of a higher nature so as to be conducive to a higher Morale.

Section–C: Analysis of Area–wise Data

29. all the eight variables selected under this study seem to have influenced the Teacher Factor Morale in the areas of Personality Factors, Professional Aspirations and Teaching Ability. (Vide Tables. 19, 20 and 22).
30. The variables of Age, Sex and Experience, have not influenced Teacher Morale under the Area of Academic Proficiency (Vide the Table No. 21). Evidently, Academic Proficiency of the Teacher doesn't manifest in these three variables, as much morale as in the other variables such as Qualifications, Designation, School Management, School Location, and Class-size.
31. In the area of Organising Skills, Teacher Morale is not influenced by the variables of Sex and Location of the School (Vide Table No. 23). Probably, Teaching Skills are constant irrespective of Sex and School Location.
32. In the area of Linguistic Proficiency, the variables of Age, Designation, and Experience have not influenced Teacher Morale (Vide Table No. 24). The investigator may, therefore, infer tentatively, that Linguistic Proficiency of a Teacher doesn't depend upon Age, Designation, and Experience; on the other hand it seems to have a greater relationship with other variables such as Sex, Qualification, School Management, School Location, and Class-Size.
33. Environmental Factors Morale seems to have been influenced by all the eight variables in the areas of School Facilities, School Administration and Family. (Vide Table Nos. 25, 26 and 28).
34. Sex has not influenced the Environmental Factors Morale in the areas of Educational Administration, and Value System.

(Vide Table Nos. 27 and 30). Evidently, these two areas of Environmental Factors Morale have not developed like its other areas i.e., those pertaining to the School System, Community and Family) in order to promote the Professional Morale of Women Teachers.

35. Experience has not influenced the Environmental Factors Morale in the areas of Educational Administration and Community. (Vide Table Nos. 27 and 29). Evidently, the potential in these two areas of Teacher Morale is not tapped well, for promoting the Professional Morale of a Teacher by virtue of his Teaching Experience.
36. The variable of School Location, which seems to have boosted up the Morale of Rural Teachers, has not shown any impact, only on the area pertaining to Organising Skills, (Vide Table No. 23). Evidently, Rural Teachers don't manifest a higher perception of the Organising Skills than the Urban Teachers, while they could show such a higher perception in all the other areas of Teacher Morale. Probably the Teacher training of this group is not up to the mark.
37. All the eight variables of the sample have affected the various areas of Teacher-Morale in varying proportions. (Vide Table Nos. 31 to 35).
38. Besides, out of the twelve (12) areas taken up under the study on hand, the sample has manifested a higher morale in two areas of the Teacher Factor i.e., Personality Factors and Professional Aspirations.(Vide Table No. 36).
39. As for the subfactors of the Environmental Factors a higher morale is manifest in School Administration and School Facilities. (Vide Table No. 37).
40. Again, a low morale is manifest in Professional Skills under Teacher Factor. (Vide Table No. 36).
41. As for the low morale in the areas of the Environmental Factors, the investigator finds them under four sub factors i.e., Educational Administration; and those pertaining to Environmental impact i.e., Family, Community, and Value System. (Vide Table No. 37).
42. Academic Proficiency has a low correlation with Teaching Ability (0. 476) as revealed in Table Nos. 38 and 39. Evidently, all that teach well, need not necessarily have Academic Proficiency; converse also may be true. Barring these two correlates with

low correlation, all other correlates in the two constituent factors of Teacher Morale, which have developed 66 interrelations with one another Vide Table No. 39 show positive correlation ranging from 'modest' to 'high'. Besides, the above two correlates with a low correlation manifest their interrelations with the other correlates highly.

43. The highest coefficient of correlation is found under the Environmental Factors, (0.921) between School Facilities and School Administration. So, these two Factors are related most positively.
44. Under the Teacher Factor, the highest coefficient of correlation (0.797) is between Academic Proficiency and Organising Skills. Evidently, the sample finds these two factors are interrelated well.
45. The investigator finds a higher correlation, in general, in the areas of Environmental Factors, than in those of the Teacher Factor.

Section –D : Analysis of the item-wise Scores

46. Positive responses are found slightly more in the Teacher Factor (40%) than in the Environmental Factors (37.5%) (Vide Table Nos. 53 and 54) as could be observed in the finding No. 6. In other words, the Item Mean-Scores are slightly higher in the Teacher-Factor. Probably, these items in the Teacher-Factor indicate a slightly higher morale. This differentiation in the two constituent factors is most marginal. Besides, the sample seems to be indecisive either to accept or reject the statements in a majority of items which is evidently an indication of a high disagreement in them.
47. The sample could not perceive any lower morale in the two constituent Factors of Teacher Morale, as there are no negative responses in them. (Vide Table Nos. 53 and 54).
48. Thus, there is a compressed span of assessment by the sample in the present survey of Teacher- Morale. A majority of the items with Neutral Responses got their mean scores inclined towards the positive side. So, they may be probably treated as almost accepted by the sample. Besides, they fall mostly in the Teacher Factor. So, in a way, the Teacher Factor items seem to have received more acceptance than the Environmental Factor items. (Vide Table Nos. 56 and 57).

49. Nearly one-third of the items with Neutral Responses got their mean-scores inclined towards the negative side. So, they may be treated as reverberating into Negative Responses. Such items are slightly more under Environmental Factors. (Vide Table Nos. 56 and 57).
50. Nearly one-fourth of the items with Neutral Responses got their mean-scores at the median level i.e., without being inclined towards Positive and Negative sides. Evidently the sample is more undecided about these items. Such items fall more under Environmental Factors. (Vide Table Nos. 56 and 57).
51. So, items which received almost a positive acceptance, are under three levels of (i) a highly positive opinion (Item mean-scores of 2.8 to 3.0) (ii) a moderately positive opinion (Item mean-scores of 2.5 to 2.7), and (iii) a moderately Neutral Response inclined towards the positive side (Item mean-scores of 2.1 to 2.4). (Vide Table Nos. 56 and 57). They seem to refer to certain situations of Teacher behaviours, which are more idealistic, simpler, more generalised and less complicated as in the case of the following items:

Item No.	Item
53	I strive to enrich my knowledge of the content in the subjects i teach.
63	I don't teach my subjects systematically. (N)
76	I don't like to use simple sentences in my language. (N)
80	I always learn to use correct language, while communicating to the students.

52. Again, items which received a highly Neutral Response at the median level with mean-scores of 1.8 to 2.0 may be regarded as 'undecided', (Vide Table Nos. 56 and 57). They refer to certain situations of Teacher behaviours, which tend to be idealistic in their nature but difficult to translate int‹ action at the grass-root level as exemplified hereunder for the sake of clarity:

Item No.	Item
4.	I exchange my ideas with them (Pupils).
5.	I encourage them (Pupils) to make their own decisions in class room Management.
34.	I take decisions for the proper management of the classes.

53. Items which received a moderately Neutral Response on the negative side with mean-scores of 1.5 to 1.7, may be regarded as almost rejected with negative responses. (Vide Table Nos. 56 and 57). They refer to certain situations of Teacher behaviours which tend to be ambitious and also less useful to the School from a practical point of view, mostly performed in a mechanical as well as ritualistic manner, as exemplified hereunder:

Item No.	Item
56.	I utilise my leisure time for writing articles on Education.
58.	I participate in the academic meetings held by Education Department and others.

Results In Terms of Hypothetical Assumptions

Thus, the present study has yielded some information, based on the various objectives and hypothetical assumptions formulated by the investigator in Chapter No. 1. The following are the results of this study with reference to the various hypothetical assumptions:

Hypothesis No. 1	:	This is proved partially, vide the finding Nos. 1 to 4.
Hypotheses No. 2	:	This is proved partially, vide the finding Nos. 7 and 8.
Hypotheses No. 3 & 5	:	This is proved to be incorrect, vide the findings under Section No. B
Hypothesis No. 4 & 7	:	This is proved to be partly incorrect, vide the findings under Section No. C
Hypothesis No. 6	:	This is verified, vide the findings under Section No. D with the result that on an overall basis the Teacher-Morale manifest in this study does not conform to Normal Probability Distribution.

Corroboration with Previous Studies

In a nut shell the major findings of this investigation are presented hereunder, corroborating with the previous investigations.

This corroboration has been attempted hereunder, particularly after verifying in the present study in the above para no. 4.06 all the seven Hypothetical assumptions too, which had been formulated in Chapter No–1. Probably a follow-up of the present study at a depth level would help in finalizing the findings of this study in the light of the corroboration attempted hereunder.

Section—A : Analysis of Tool-wise Data

The findings under this section include those of the whole opinionnaire, its sectional tools pertaining to Teacher Factor and Environmental Factors. Mainly, these findings centre round a phenomenon wherein the distribution of Teacher Morale doesn't seem to conform to the pattern of Normal Distribution under the Teacher Factor, while its distribution under the Environmental Factors seems to approximate to this pattern. They also show that the Teacher Factor Morale scores are higher than those of Environmental Factors Morale scores. None of the previous studies makes references to phenomena like these under the above analysis in the present study.

Section—B : Analysis of Variable- wise Data

The above findings under this section mostly pertain to the significance of Mean-Differences under the eight variables selected in this study with reference to the whole opinionnaire and the sectional tools referred to above. None of the previous studies included the variable of class-size. Hence the findings pertaining to it, wherein the investigator found that teachers handling small size classes have better Environmental Factors has no relevance to the findings under the previous studies in Chapter II. The following is the position in the case of the other seven variables.

Age

This study has shown in general, that the higher is age, the higher is the morale, vide Table Nos. 16 to 18; this is found mostly in the age group of Teachers exceeding the age of 50 years.

This finding is, generally, in line with the one in the study by Chaya (1974), who found (Page No. 49) that age had a significant relationship with the effectiveness of Teaching and also in the study by Jain, B (P. 58) who found that there was significant positive relationship between the age of Teacher and religious values; Nair S. R. who found (p. 80) that positive relationship exited between the age of Teacher and his teaching ability. But in the case of a study by NCERT (1971) (Page No. 47) it was found that younger teachers found a more positive attitude towards the profession. The NCERT's; finding is in regard to an attitude towards the profession while the findings of the present study as well as the one by Chaya (P. 49) are in favour of the impact of Age on Teacher Morale and Teacher effectiveness respectively.

Sex

As per the present study, the female teachers have received higher mean-scores than the male teachers as can be seen from the Table Nos. 16 to 18, under this section. This finding is quite contrary to the one in the previous studies, by Nair S.R. (P. 49) Jayamma, M.S. (P. 46) and Jain, B (P. 58) who found no such significant impact for this variable. In the case of studies by NCERT (1971) (P. 47) by Chaya (P. 49) during 1974, by Chhabra, N. (P. 52) during 1975 and Puranic S.D (P. 61) during 1985 the above finding of the present Investigation is confirmed.

Qualification

Following are the findings of this study vide Table Nos. 16 to 18.

a) Graduate Teachers had a higher Teacher Factor Morale than Environmental Factors Morale, vide Table No. 15 under this study, while the other two groups of teachers showed an equal level in these two factors of Teacher Morale.

b) The Graduate Teachers seem to manifest a lower morale than the other two groups of teachers.

In the case of finding no. (a) no phenomenon pertaining the two factors of Teacher Morale in question (T.F and E.Fs) seems to have been studied in any of the previous investigations.

However the other finding No. (b) seems to be, generally, in line with the findings, in the previous studies by NCERT who found that Teachers with lower educational qualifications were having more positive attitude towards the profession than the teachers with higher educational qualification and by Savadamuthu, T. (1994) who found that there is no significant association between the qualifications of the Teachers and their morale. But in the study by Debnath, H.N. (P. 47) it was found that academic qualification would be an important correlate of teaching efficiency.

Designation

This study shows, vide Table No. 15, that the secondary grade and B. Ed., grade teachers have a higher level of Teacher Factor Morale than the Environmental Factors Morale, while the other group (Headmasters) manifests an equal level of Morale in these two factors. It also shows in Table Nos. 16 to 18 that Headmasters and Secondary Grade Teachers manifest Teacher Morale at a higher level than B.Ed., Teachers. However, it is necessary to note also that these two groups manifest an equal level in the Teacher Factor Morale rather than the Environmental Factors Morale, in view of their significant Mean Differences in the latter phenomenon, vide table no. 18.

Some of the previous studies by Dorsey S.M., Fosdick S.J., Rorer J.A., etc., show that Morale of teachers will improve with good salary which is an aspect related to the above variable of Designation. This finding from the previous studies corroborates partly with the finding from the present study, in favour of H.Ms. only; however, the finding in the case of B.Ed., Assts. revealed in the present study is not borne out in any of the previous studies. K. Sexana's study on professional factors influencing Teachers' Morale seems to show that Teachers' Morale is affected by teachers' status which is analogous, in a way, to Designation. Thus the findings of the present study in respect of Designation are not fully borne out by the previous studies.

Experience

Under this variable, table no. 15 in the present study shows a higher Teacher Factor Morale than the Environmental Factors Morale, in the case of teachers with above 10 years' experience, while the rest (those with less than 10 years experience) manifested an equal level in these two phenomena of Teacher Morale. This finding is supported by table Nos. 17 and 18 also.

The above finding on experience is in line with the one reported in 'Experiments in Education' of May, 1990 under a study on Job-satisfaction of Harijan Welfare school teachers in Tamilnadu by Dr. S. Sundararajan and Mr. A.M. Ashrafullah. However, in a study by Dekhtanwala, P.B. during 1977 (p. 55) it was found that experience didn't have a significant relationship with Teacher Morale.

Management

Under this variable, as already reported in this thesis teachers from three types of managements were selected. Two types of them (Government and Local bodies) belong to public management. The other type is private management. The table no. 15 of the present study draws a differential position in the case of local body schools as distinct from Government schools; the local body school teachers manifested a higher morale in the Environmental Factors than in the Teacher Factor; while Government school teachers showed an equal morale in these two types of factors.

In case of teachers under private management, they showed a higher morale than their counter parts under public management, in these two types of Teacher Morale Factors.

In a study by Baehr, M.E and Renck, R. it was found that organisation and management could be one of factors affecting Teacher Morale. In the study by Panda, U.N. (P. 60) and impact for this variable was reported, but it was altogether on certain different matters such as school facilities, public examination results, teachers' satisfaction with the school system etc. In another study by Pauranic S.D. (P. 61) also, a different finding was got indicating high morale in the case of Government School Teachers. Again in the study by Dr. S. Sundararajan and Sr. R. Vivekanandam on Job-satisfaction in some selected Higher Secondary Schools in the city of Madras, the variable of Management seems to have caused significant Mean Differences in Teachers' Job satisfaction in favour of schools under public management.

In the study by NCERT (1971) (P. 47) it was found that the attitude of teachers differed significantly under different managements. However, this variable seems to have much impact on Teacher Morale. Thus, the findings of previous studies don't corroborate with the one obtained in the present study.

Location

Under this variable, both rural and urban Teachers manifested a higher morale in Teacher Factors than in Environmental Factors, vide Table No. 15, when compared with each other the rural teachers' group manifested a higher morale than the other group.

This finding in favour of rural teachers is in the line with the one in study by Savadamuthu, T. on Teacher Morale and student Morale at Secondary Level in 1992. However, the study by Jayamma, M.S. (P. 46) reports that a teacher's professional success was in no way influenced by the locality of work, which doesn't support the finding from the present study. In another study by Chaya during 1974, it was found that rurality or Urbanality had no significant relationship with Teacher effectiveness. In the case of another study by Puranic, S.D. (P. 61) Urban locality was found to be conducive to Teacher Morale. Thus, there are conflicting findings on the impact of this variable.

The other sections (No. 3; Analysis of area-wise data and No. 4 analysis of item-wise data) are essentially based up on the above two sections of Tool-wise and variable-wise data. No reference is made in any of the previous studies, to the phenomena under the section Nos. 3 and 4, i.e. other than Section No. 2.

The results of the present study which have been analysed under the four sections referred to above, could be thus interpreted with reference to the findings of previous studies, only in the case of findings from seven variables, the variable of class-size being conspicuous by its absence in the previous studies; even in the case of the other seven variables, the corroboration of their findings with those of previous studies is limited as reported above; besides, even in the previous studies, there are conflicting findings under these seven variables; moreover the previous studies cover a wider spectrum of Teacher Morale by including aspects such as Teachers effectiveness, Job-satisfaction etc.; naturally, they give rise to conflicting findings; thus, the findings of the present investigation compare with those of the previous investigations, only in the case of the above seven variables.

So, the above endeavour for corroboration shows:

(i) that the variable-wise findings of the present investigation could compare well with the findings of the earlier studies; however, they are not fully borne out by the latter;
(ii) that the other findings of the present study under Sections No. 1, 3 and 4 referred to above could not have such a comparison for the reasons already stated above.

Therefore, a further follow-up study might be necessary by way of a thorough probe into all the findings of the present investigation, in order to confirm or reject them, as they couldn't be fully borne out in the previous studies. For example, the findings under the variable of 'age' is in line with three previous studies and doesn't tally with two others. In the same way, sex has shown a positive corroboration with reference to four previous studies, while three other studies showed a conflicting finding. In the case of Qualifications, the present investigator noted a singular phenomenon wherein out of three groups of teachers under this Variable, one manifested a higher level of morale under the Teacher Factor than under the other factor, which phenomenon didn't figure in any of the previous studies as for the other phenomenon manifest under this Variable in the Case of Graduate Teachers showing a lesser morale than the other two groups, one of which is less qualified, the other being better qualified, it seems to be indirectly in line with the findings from two previous studies; however, in one study, there is a contradiction.

In this way, in all the seven variables, wherein the above type of corroboration could be attempted herein between the findings of the present study and those of the previous studies, a cent per cent corroboration couldn't be observed; on the other hand there are some conflicting findings too like the above. Besides, the phenomena observed in the present study under the Section No. 1, 3 and 4 mentioned above couldn't be observed in the previous studies. Though a few recommendations could be worked out separately on the basis of the present study in Chapter—V, yet there seems to be a dire necessity for a follow-up study for the present investigation, as already stated above for the purpose of positivizing or negativizing the above corroboration attempted herein.

5

SUMMARY, CONCLUSIONS AND RECOMMENDATIONS

The morale of an individual is affected by a variety of factors. The morale held by an individual has direct relationship with his level of efficiency. In industry, production is affected by worker morale. Though education is not an industry but yet this is also a process where the teacher occupies a pivotal place. Educational standards can be achieved, only through the teachers who are sincere, dedicated, satisfied with the job and possess the right morale. A variety of factors contribute to the morale of the teacher.

In this study, we have analysed these factors broadly into two categories:

(a) Teacher Factor which pertains to his personality, professional aspirations and professional skills.
(b) Environmental Factors which are taken up under, (i) School Facilities (ii) School Administration (iii) the system of Educational Administration obtaining in the present set-up, (iv) Environmental forces such as Family, Community, and Value-system.

Let us look at the summary given hereunder for the study made in this investigation, for the sake of our convenience to peruse its conclusions in a proper perspective.

INTRODUCTION

The prosperity and well-being of a nation exclusively depends upon the quality and quantity of Education that it provides to its youth. All the nations in the world are giving priority for the development of Education including the countries which have hitherto paid scant attention for the development of Education. The contribution of science and technology has become an inseparable part in the nation building process. Naturally, Education that provides a general background at 10+2+3, should be improved on a top priority-basis in view of the background of learning which it provides particularly at the School and Intermediate Stages of Education, for the training of most of our Technicians, as also all the citizens of a Modern Society.

Consequently, every nation in the world has been voting crores of rupees from their parliaments for the development of Education.

The number of educational institutions which have been thus fast developing have increased today the strength of their staff and students, enormously; in order to quench the quest of public for acquisition of modern knowledge and for the development of education, the private institutions are increasing day by day raising the strength of their staff and students. Consequently, the contribution of the Government and the Private Organizations has been quite significant which in turn makes the system of education a huge organization in its in-take, infrastructure and the required teaching and non-teaching material. Proper management of these institutions has become a problem in the present days.

The very purpose of an educational institution and its existence will be evaluated to a maximum extent on the basis of its products. So, for obtaining good products from the institution all the other factors should contribute their share satisfactorily. Some of these factors are the reading and writing materials made available to it, its infrastructure, the teaching aids, proper financial assistance etc. But almost all the institutions are being equipped in one way or the other with the required facilities, but yet the results are not very satisfactory to-date.

A lot of research has been made to analyse the factors contributing positively or negatively for the successful functioning of the Educational Institutions. The contribution of academic, administrative, psychological, sociological and economic factors has also been analysed in detail to measure their degree of contribution to making an institution successful. Almost all the aspects contributing to the successful functioning of an Educational Institution were analysed to identify their share, but the contribution of the teacher who is the king-pin in the system has not been evaluated satisfactorily.

The teacher and his personal traits apart from his conscious commitment to his profession must also be treated as a major factor that contributes to determine the destiny of the institution, Whatever the other factors like teaching aids, audio-visual equipment and financial assistance do, they are all subsidiary when compared with the teacher and his commitment. A committed teacher is an asset to the system. The contribution of a committed teacher will certainly over-ride the absence of other factors to a large extent. Ample evidence is available in Indian Education system, even today in rural areas, where the institutions are suffering from all deficiencies but the contribution of a committed teacher is the only reason for which the institutions are living and enjoying the appreciation of the society.

The factors conducive to making the teacher contribute consciously to his profession have also been analysed by different scholars. Proper remedial measures were also suggested to rectify the defects for creating a healthy environment for the teacher. In spite of all these efforts, the institutions are not functioning properly. The standards are deteriorating day-by-day. The management of the institutions, is subjected to criticism. The maintenance of the institutions is still in a questionable state. No doubt the centre and the state Governments are contributing their mite, perhaps, more, for the proper financing of these institutions. But the results are not commensurate at any stage in terms of their inputs like men and material. Why are they not producing good results? Besides, the material conditions of the Teacher have been bettered than before. But the out-put is not that satisfactory.

So, if one critically analyses the factors contributing to the successful functioning of educational institutions, one may certainly come to a conclusion that the lack of consciously committed teachers is the main reason for not producing the good students. Teacher and his conscious commitment must be therefore analysed in detail in these changing circumstances. Even if all facilities other than this in-put, are available in an institution, it may not lead to much success. Thus, failure to have teachers with highest morale should be avoided without fail. A teacher with highest morale is the need of the hour.

So in order to identify the inability of the institutions for not producing good students, a critical analysis of the teacher and his morale is essential. No research has been conducted so far to analyse the teacher morale in all forms. Providing all facilities in the absence of committed teachers to an educational institution will be an unsuccessful venture. So the researcher has taken up the problem of studying the factors that contribute to the teacher morale.

Status of the Teacher in India

Teacher was regarded as a holy person in ancient India; he was compared to a God. He is to be treated as a combination of the Trinity, (Brahma, Vishnu, Maheshwar) as well as the supreme ONE. Thus, teacher was regarded as the most perfect Being in those days and teaching was considered to be a holy duty.

In the modern age, the functioning of a teacher is regarded as transmitting the knowledge contained in the texts to the students. Apart from his academic work, other activities of para-academic and non-academic nature, were also entrusted to him.

Kothari Commission has stated, that the destiny of the nation is shaped within the four walls of the class-room. Hence, the teacher is considered to be the Nation builder and moulder of the personalities of the children.

Teacher's Functions

In the present-day society where there is a heavy explosion in knowledge and rapid social change, the teacher is required to perform multifarious functions. The duties and functions of a teacher can be categorised as—planning, Educating, Organising, Supervising, Guiding, Recording, Evaluating and Maintaining good relations.

Teaching is his first and foremost duty. It is his duty to have a thorough knowledge of the subject he teaches. A teacher has to organise various curricular and co-curricular activities. He has to organise the School plant, Library work of the pupils and instructional work.

Thus, the teacher's role is most crucial at the school stage. Unless and until his morale is high, he can't be motivated well for playing this role effectively.

Teacher Morale

But teachers are entrusted with society's most valuable asset, the children and they have the responsibility of moulding their character and citizenship. The future of democratic education and consequently the future of our democracy depends upon the teacher's success in his profession. It is determined largely by his morale. The morale of a teacher is indispensable for the successful implementation of educational programme. Hence, the morale has come to be regarded as a prime requirement for effective organisation in industry as well as in education.

The definitions given by Leighton, A.A.S.A. and Spalding considered 'Morale' as a group understanding to put forth its co-operative efforts. This approach may be understood as co-operative or group approach of morale.

Redefer referred to Morale, as the rate of work or an individual efficiency. In the present study of Teacher Morale, the definition referred to above as 'the teaching rate of teachers' has been considered as a workable definition. If it is further analysed—'rate' means 'standard' that means the standard or the efficiency of teaching. Thus, the teacher morale in this study referred to as the teaching efficiency of teachers. The morale obligation of the teacher is to provide effective teaching to shape his wards entrusted to him by the society. A large number of factors such as Personal, Professional, Intellectual, Social, Moral, Economic, etc. affect the teaching rate or the efficiency of teachers. To some extent Teacher's environment too affects his morale.

Thus, the Teacher Morale may be regarded not only as the behaviour of an individual teacher but also as the work environment provided to him in the school; the latter pertains to the group behaviour mostly at the institutional level that would influence his individual behaviour, and consequently his professional efficiency.

Significance of the Problem

The present problem is one of primary importance from social as well as educational points of view, for it pertains to Teacher effectiveness which appears as a mirage as well as the need of the hour in the present-day society.

The investigator may probably assume that Teacher morale is an important factor which would in fact, determine Teacher Effectiveness. In all human societies, the teacher occupies a pivotal position, for, he moulds the destiny of the future citizens by educating them. Naturally, his role in shaping their destiny is very significant. We are also aware that the Kothari Commission has stated that the destiny of the nation is shaped within the four walls of the class-room. Hence, the teacher is considered to be the nation-builder and the moulder of the Personalities of children. He is responsible for shaping character of the students and protecting the democracy. So, the importance of the teacher even in this new era is multidimensional. Thus, the problem on hand is very significant not only for the Teacher, but also for the society.

Statement of the Problem

In the present society, Teacher morale is reducing due to several factors. Consequently, standards of education are also reduced. A part of responsibility for this deterioration, rests on the Teacher. His morale is thus one major factor responsible for this deterioration. Morale is a psychological and sociological issue dependent on certain factors. It is a comprehensive system with certain contributory subsystems.

It may therefore reasonably assume that among all the academic, para-academic and non-academic factors contributing to the successful functioning of an Educational system, Teacher Morale may be regarded as a pivotal force. So, for strengthening it, it is better to study the factors promoting it and their contribution in order to keep up the academic standards. With this object in view, the researcher has taken up the problem on hand with the following title:

"A Study of the Factors Contributing to
the Teacher Morale in Secondary Schools".

Morale is influenced by certain factors like Personality and Environment. In other words, it involves a system from psychological point of view, and becomes manifest, merely from a sociological point of view, with reasonable contributions from all its sub-systems. It is proposed to study in this investigation these factors contributing to Teacher Morale.

A study of these factors might help us to follow up this the investigation, in order to suggest certain steps for increase of Teacher Morale. Hence the present title of the problem.

Operational Definitions of the Title of the Study

The problem taken up in this investigation is studied with the following title with a view to focus the attention of the investigator mainly on certain aspects of this subject: "*A Study of the Factors Contributing to the Teacher Morale in Secondary Schools*".

Study : The term 'Study' is used in this investigation, in order to indicate the process by which the investigator will be able to identify and analyse the factors assumed for the purpose of this investigation.

Factors: The term 'Factors' includes the two dimensions, formulated for the purpose of this study; one of them comprises the two major factors i.e., Teacher Factor and Environmental Factors. It includes also the variables selected in the sample.

Teacher Morale: The term 'Morale' used in this study, to indicate the conscious commitment of the teacher to his profession in order to promote effectiveness of teaching and thereby provide qualitative education in the society.

Secondary Schools: The term 'Secondary Schools' is used in this study to include high schools functioning in Andhra Pradesh with classes VI to X to impart education at two different stages : (a) Upper Primary, and (b) Secondary.

Secondary School Teachers: This term is used to indicate teachers handling the classes VI to X in Upper Primary and Secondary Stages of Education i.e., Secondary Grade Teachers and B.Ed., Assistants.

Thus, the selected problem has been titled as shown above in a simplified manner with the above terminology for the purpose of the above investigation which is taken up with certain objectives and hypothetical assumptions for studying the phenomena of Teacher morale.

OBJECTIVES

The investigation has been designed with the following specific objectives:

1. To identify the distribution of morale in the Teacher population.
2. To find out whether the teachers manifest their morale equally in Teacher Factor and Environmental Factors.
3. To identify whether the morale scores in Teacher Factor and Environmental Factors are equal in each of the subsamples.

4. To identify the influence of the variables selected under this study on Teacher Morale.
5. To identify whether all the areas included under the Teacher Factor manifest Teacher Morale equally.
6. To identify whether all the areas included under the Environmental Factors manifest Teacher Morale equally.
7. To find out whether the morale components (areas) of Teacher Factor and the morale components of Environmental Factors have any relationship.
8. To study the teachers' responses item-wise under the Teacher Factor and the Environmental Factors, and thereby identify the items and their areas falling in each of the points with the 3 pt scale.

Hypotheses

The following tentative hypotheses are formulated to study the present problem of investigation.

1. Teacher Morale is distributed in any given group as per the pattern of Normal Probability Distribution.
2. Morale in terms of Teacher Factor does not necessarily differ from the one in terms of Environmental Factors.
3. Morale scores under the Teacher Factor do not differ from those under the Environmental Factors, in any of the subsamples.
4. All the areas included in the Teacher Factor and Environmental Factors reveal the Teacher Morale, equally.
5. The impact of the several variables selected in this investigation would be the same on Teacher Morale.
6. Teacher-Morale which would be surveyed in this investigation, would be revealed consistently item wise also.
7. Morale components (areas) of the two constituent factors of Teacher Morale are related positively.

Limitations of the Study

1. Certain factors like marital status, religion, income, family size and the other aspects of private life are not taken into account in the present study, due to Time-constraint.
2. The researcher limited the study only to the Secondary School Teachers, handling the classes VI to X working under different

educational managements in the Krishna District of Andhra Pradesh.

3. The area of investigation is also limited to one district i.e., Krishna District only because of certain administrative conveniences to the investigator. Moreover this is one of the few districts in Andhra Pradesh with high rate of educational growth.

Review of the Related Literature

The previous researchers and experts expressed different factors which develop morale among the teachers. The investigations and opinions expressed by Indian and Foreign educationalists reviewed under second chapter helped the investigator in preparing the plan of action. Keeping in view these research works and opinions, the investigator formulated the theoretical constructs and selected the method of research, the sample of the study, the tools of investigation, collection of data, analysis and interpretation of results.

Type of the Research Method Adopted

In the light of the over-view of the related literature, the investigator fixed up the design of the study. The problem for the present investigation is *"A Study of the Factors Contributing to the Teacher Morale in Secondary Schools"*.

The problem involves a study of the opinions expressed by the subjects about the factors which are contributing to the promotion of Teacher Morale. As such the present piece of research falls under the Normative survey type of research, referred to above.

Sample for the Study

This study was confined in Krishna District only. There are 203 rural schools and 79 urban schools, in this district. For the present study the investigator has taken up only 54 rural schools and 46 urban schools by applying the method of stratified random sampling.

From urban area the investigator has selected 46 schools, out of which 5 are under Government, 12 under municipal, 28 under private aided and 1 under Zilla Praja Parishad managements.

From rural area 54 schools were selected, out of which 5 are under government, 39 under Zilla Praja Parishad, and 10 under private aided managements.

The required data were collected from the above schools. For each school 7 staff members were selected on an average. Of these 4 are males and 3 are females. However the total sample came down to 630 teachers drawn from 100 schools i.e., 46 urban, and 54 rural schools, as data in full shape could be got only from them.

Variables of the Study

In the selection of the sample for this study, the following eight variables were selected.

1. Age	:	Between 26–30 / Between 31–40/ Between 41-50/Above 50 Years
2. Sex	:	Male /Female
3. Qualification	:	Under Graduate /Graduate/ Post-graduate.
4. Designation	:	Secondary Grade Teachers / B.Ed., Teachers / Head Masters.
5. Experience	:	Below 5 Years / Between 6 and 10 years / Between 11 and 15 years / Above 15 Years.
6. Management	:	Government Schools /Local Body Schools/ Private Schools.
7. Location of the School	:	Urban / Rural.
8. Size of the Class	:	50 or more students in the section/ 30–49 students in the section / Below 30 Students in the section.

Tools of Research

For the purpose of the investigation, the researcher has adopted the opinionnaire developed on the Likert method of summated ratings for testing the hypotheses and collection of data.

In order to collect the data for making a study of the factors contributing to teacher morale, the researcher has constructed a opinionnaire with 170 statements.

The opinionnaire was divided into two major parts, grouping all the identical statements under one part. Each part was treated as separate Tool. So, the first part (Tool—I) was named as Teacher Factor and the Second part (Tool—II) was named as Environmental Factors.

Description of the Tools of Investigation

For the study of the factors contributing to the Teacher Morale in secondary schools, the investigator divided the problem of the study into two major factors, i.e., Teacher Factor and Environmental Factors. These two major factors are further sub-divided with identical factors as sub-factors, as they did not receive much focus in the previous investigations and are at the same time very important in Teacher Morale. An area-wise discussion is made. While formulating the items, the researcher has consulted the experts in the field and also some of the experienced teachers and Head of Institutions. The researcher has selected the 3 pt scale on Likert type to collect the opinions of teachers. For each item included in the opinionnaire, three alternative responses viz., Agree (A) Neutral opinion (N) and Disagree (D) are given and the subjects were asked to encircle one of those with which they concur.

Pre-Tryout

The opinionnaire was got duplicated and pre-tryout was conducted. It was administered to a sample of ninety teachers of Secondary Schools belonging to different Age groups, Sex, Qualifications, Designation, working under different Managements, School location, Experience and Size of the class of Krishna District of Andhra Pradesh.

Item Analysis

These ninety filled in opinionnaires were analysed and all the one hundred and seventy (170) items were put to chi-square $(X)^2$ test.

The obtained chi-square values in respect of ten items fell below 9.210. As such, the ten items were deleted and the final opinionnaire was prepared with one hundred and sixty items for final administration and collection of data.

The Teacher Morale opinionnaire consists of fifteen pages. In the first page, an appeal was made to the subjects to give their free and frank opinions, space for personal data was also provided. In the second page, particulars of various variables selected under this study and instructions as to how to fill in the opinionnaire was given. Statements under Tool—I and Tool—II were given on pages third to fifteenth.

Administration

The Teacher Morale opinionnaires were issued to seven hundred (700) teachers working in Secondary Schools in Krishna District of Andhra Pradesh. The investigator visited a number of Secondary Schools and administered the opinionnaire personally and in some cases mailed it. The investigator received back only six hundred and fifty (650) opinionnaires. Of these, some are not filled completely and some are defective. So, the investigator eliminated them to the tune of twenty in number and took only six hundred and thirty filled in opinionnaires which are fool-proof.

Scoring

The responses of the subjects on the different items of the opinionnaire are quantified duly assigning numerical values 3,2, and 1 for A,N and D respectively in case of positive items and they are reversed in the case of negative items.

Analysis and Interpretation of Data

To measure the overall distribution of scores in the Teacher Morale Opinionnaire and its two constituent areas, i.e., Teacher Factor Tool and Environmental Factors Tool, chi-square values were calculated. The level of significance chosen for statistical interpretation of this study is 0.01 level.

In order to find out the difference in the opinions expressed by the subjects belonging to different variables, the researcher applied the 'T' test and the C.R. Values were tested for significance at 0.01 level.

Since each of the areas had unequal number of items and in order to make a comparison of the areas of the whole Tool, the area mean scores were averaged by the number of items of the area.

Since the Tool consisted of 12 areas the correlations of each area with other areas were calculated and a correlation matrix was presented. The correlations were arranged in Rank order and patterns of interrelationships identified.

Findings

Based upon the data presented in Chapter IV, a number of findings were drawn with reference to the hypothetical assumptions and objectives of the study on hand. They were discussed throughout the chapter no. IV. To facilitate an easy reference to them, they have been recapitulated and summarised under the resume at the end of the Chapter IV. Based up on the same, the results of this study in terms of the hypothetical assumptions are also given.

However, a resume of the findings given in Chapter IV is briefly given hereunder for a review.

Section—A : Analysis of Tool-wise Data

1. Teacher Morale manifest in the sample under Environmental Factors seems to confirm to the pattern of Normal Probability Distribution.
2. Teacher Morale manifest under Teacher Factor does not confirm to the Normal Probability Distribution. Probably its impact has less significance than that of Environmental Factors.
3. The sample has shown a greater perception in the Teacher Factor Morale than in the Environmental Factors Morale Evidently, the sample believes that Teacher Factor is more important than Environmental Factors in the Teacher Morale.

4. A very high positive correlation exists between the Teacher Factor and Environmental Factors (0.783).

Section—B : Analysis of Variable-wise Data

5. A majority of the sample seems to have shown a higher morale in the Teacher Factor. The rest of the sample seems to have shown their morale equally in the two factors i.e., Teacher Factor and Environmental Factors.
6. The categories that manifest higher morale in Teacher Factor do so, under all the eight variables. But they do not do so equally under all these variables. For example, Sex and Location show the highest Teacher Factor Morale. Age shows the lowest of it.
7. As for the variable Age, the highest Age group manifests a higher level of Teacher Morale in the two factors i.e., Teacher Factor and Environmental Factors.
8. As for the variable Sex, higher morale manifests in Women Teachers than in Male Teachers in the two constituent factors of Teacher Morale.
9. As for the variable Qualifications, a higher morale manifests in Under Graduate Teachers and Post-graduate Teachers equally, while lower morale manifests in the Graduate Teachers.
10. As for the variable Designation, the Head Masters have shown the highest morale under Environmental Factors and equal morale to that of Secondary Grade Teachers in the Teacher Factor.
11. A lower morale manifests in B.Ed., Assistants than in Secondary Grade Teachers and Head Masters in the two constituent factors of Teacher Morale.
12. In case of the variable Experience, its impact is more in Environmental Factors, than in the Teacher Factor.
13. In case of School Location, a higher morale manifests in Rural School Teachers than in Urban School Teachers.
14. In case of School Management, Teachers of schools under private managements have shown a higher morale than those of Local Body and Government Schools, the latter maintaining more or less the same level of morale.
15. In case of variable pertaining to Class-size, Teachers of small size classes have shown the highest morale; next comes those of median size classes and large size classes in Rank order, in terms of their morale.

Section–C : Analysis of Area-wise Data

16. All the eight variables selected in this study seem to have influenced the Teacher-Morale under the areas of Personality Factors, Professional Aspirations, and Teaching Ability under the Teacher Factor; School Facilities, School Administration and Family under Environmental Factors.
17. The variables Age, Sex and Experience have not influenced the Teacher Morale under the area of Academic Proficiency.
18. In the area of Organising Skills, Teacher Morale is not influenced by the variables of Sex and Location of the School.
19. The variables Age, Designation and Experience have not influenced the Teacher Morale in the area of Linguistic Proficiency.
20. Sex has not influenced the Environmental Factors Morale in the area of Educational Administration and Value System.
21. The variable Experience has not influenced the Environmental Factors Morale in the areas of Educational Administration and Community.
22. Personality Factors and Professional Aspirations under the Teacher Factor; School Administration and school Facilities under the Environmental Factors show a relatively higher morale, when compared to the other areas.
23. Professional Skills under Teacher Factor; Educational Administration, Family, Community and Value System under Environmental Factors show a relatively low morale, when compared to the other areas.
24. Academic Proficiency has a low correlation with Teaching Ability. (0.476)
25. The highest coefficient of Correlation is found under the Environmental Factors (0.921) between School Facilities and School Administration.
26. The areas of Environmental Factors have more positive interrelations than those of the Teacher Factor.

Section—D : Analysis of the Item-wise Mean-Scores

27. Positive Response are found slightly more in the Teacher Factor than in the Environmental Factors.
28. The sample could not perceive any lower morale in the two constituent factors of Teacher Morale.

29. Thus, there is a compressed span of assessment by the sample in the present survey of Teacher Morale. A majority of the items with Neutral Responses got their mean scores inclined towards the positive side. So, they may be probably treated as almost accepted by the sample. Besides, they fall mostly in the Teacher Factor. So, in a way, the Teacher Factor items seem to have received more acceptance than the Environmental Factor items.
30. Nearly one-third of the items with Neutral Responses got their mean-scores inclined towards the negative side. So, they may be treated as reverberating into Negative Responses. Such items are slightly more under Environmental Factors.
31. Nearly one-fourth of the items with Neutral Responses got their mean-scores at the median level, i.e., without being inclined towards Positive and Negative Sides. Evidently the sample is more undecided about these items. Such items fall more under Environmental Factors.

CONCLUSIONS

Basing on the findings given in the Chapter—IV the researcher draws the following conclusions under Sections A to D.

Section—A : Analysis of Tool-wise Data

1. The distribution of Teacher Morale under sample in this study seems to approximate to the pattern of Normal Probability Distribution under the Environmental Factors. However, the same under the Teacher Factor manifests divergence from it.
2. The sample seems to have shown a greater perception of the Teacher Factor than the Environmental Factors. However, there appears to be a very high positive correlation between those two factors, as revealed in the Table No. 14. Evidently these two factors appear to be different in their impact on Teacher Morale in their various areas.
3. Again, the Teacher Factor seems to have received slightly more positive responses than the Environmental Factors.
4. The positive responses found in this study seem to be less in heterogeneity as well as number, when compared with Neutral Responses.

Section—B : Analysis of Variable-wise Data

5. The higher morale manifest in the Teacher Factor could be observed in all the eight variables of the sample which might mean that all the sub-samples consistently manifest in certain categories, a higher morale under the Teacher Factor when compared to the Environmental Factors.
6. A few categories of respondents under certain variables seem to favour an equal morale in the Teacher Factor, as well as Environmental Factors. Thus, the sample seems to have some difference of opinion in its preference to the Teacher Factor.
7. It is pertinent to note that the variables of Sex and School Location have not had any impact upon the manifestation of equal morale in the two constituent factors of Teacher Morale.
8. The sample appears to be more heterogeneous under the variables of Age and Experience.
9. Under the variable of Age, elderly teachers (above 50 years) seem to manifest a higher morale when compared to the other age groups. Probably, age ripens, so as to warrant a higher morale as age advances.
10. Under the variables of 'Qualifications' and 'Designation', perhaps certain negative factors of service incentives are manifest, with the result that Graduate Teachers (B.Ed. Assistants) seem to show a lower morale than the Under Graduate Teachers (Secondary Grade Assistants). However, Post-graduate Teachers, seem to manifest higher aspirations, when compared to Graduate Teachers. Similarly, Head Masters seem to manifest higher aspirations, particularly under the Environmental Factors when compared to both Secondary Grade Assistants and B.Ed. Assistants. But in the case of Teacher Factor, Head Masters do not have such superiority over Secondary Grade Assistants. In other words, both manifest an equal level of Teacher Morale in these groups under Teacher Factor Morale. Thus the Teacher Factor Morale seems to indicate, under these two variables, a phenomenon quite different from the Environmental Factors Morale, which may, perhaps, be attributed to some possible stagnation among B.Ed. Assistants, who seem to have lesser promotional opportunities for their Grade, when compared to the Graduates that joined service in some other Departments such as Revenue, Commercial Taxes, or the Secretariat at Governmental level. In

addition, their promotional opportunities as Head Masters seem to vary under the public and private managements of schools. But there are no data available to examine this aspect, in a greater detail, with the result that this observation is more in the nature of a consequential hypothetical assumption which warrants a further verification.

11. In the case of the variable of Experience its impact on the Teacher Factor is comparatively limited when compared to the Environmental Factors. Evidently, the two constituent factors of Teacher Morale present two different phenomena in the impact of Experience.
12. Teachers under the two types of Public Management (Government and Local Body) seem to manifest a lower morale than their counterparts under Private Managements. Probably, the investigator may attribute this observation to the prevalence of a possible politicisation among the former.
13. It is very interesting to note that Women Teachers and Rural Teachers manifested a higher morale in the two constituent factors of Teacher Morale.
14. As for the variable of Class-Size, it seems to be one important factor with much impact on Teacher Morale; and naturally teachers handling classes below 30, manifest a higher morale, when compared to the other teachers, such as those handling classes between 30 and 50, as well as above 50. In this connection, the investigator recalls that at some time in the past the class-size in a Secondary School was fixed as 40. Evidently, it is an optimal class-size.

Section—C: Analysis of Area-wise Data

15. Out of the total number of 12 areas of study selected in this investigation, six areas manifest the impact of all the eight variables on Teacher Morale. They are Personality Factors, Professional Aspirations, Teaching Ability, School Facilities, School Administration and Environmental impact through Family. This impact is distributed in the two constituent factors of Teacher Morale, almost equally.
16. Evidently, the sample didn't accept under the Teacher Factor, Professional Skills other than Teaching Ability, as conducive to Teacher Morale. Probably this situation points to a dire necessity of some Professional Skills for their scientific development in

2. Morale in Terms of the two Constituent Factors of Teacher Morale

The investigator assumed in this study, broadly two major factors *viz.*, (Teacher Factor and Environmental Factors), and analysed them into a series of some sub-factors (Six under each of the two major factors). Under objectives no. 2, it was proposed to study how these two factors have affected the Teacher Morale. Furthermore, the investigator hypothesized that Teacher Morale may not differ significantly in these two factors, vide the hypothesis no.2. However, the study on hand has revealed that *the sample has preferred in their verbal responses, the Teacher Factor to Environmental Factors.* For this purpose, they gave slightly more positive responses, in the former than in the latter. Besides, more than half the categories in the sample under this study, showed their preference to the former. *However, there is a high positive correlation (0.783) between these two factors.* Besides, *some of the categories of respondents treated the Teacher Factor Morale, and the Environmental Factors Morale equal.*

The Related Recommendations

(a) In view of the above observations regarding the two constituent factors, the *Teacher-Factor Morale may be, perhaps, regarded as the base for the development of the Environmental Factors Morale.* Doing so might help to promote Teacher Morale duly founded in the Teacher-Factor.

(b) Besides, steps should be taken up, to *step up the Teacher Morale in terms of Environmental Factors as contra-distinct from the other Factor,* as its ramifications seem to be much wider as could be seem from a greater variability in the Environmental Factors Morale, and also in view of the least divergence of this morale from the normal form in its distribution in the sample, when compared to the Teacher Factor Morale as well as the whole Teacher Morale.

(c) It might also be necessary *to probe further into the Teacher Factor, and its various sub-factors* for the purpose of observing their factor-loadings by factorial analysis.

(d) *This further study might also help to identify, in detail, the steps to be taken* to *safeguard and strengthen the Teacher-Factor* in which the present study revealed a greater potential in the Teacher.

(e) *If the Teacher Factor is taken care of,* it might be possible to strengthen the Environmental Factors Morale to some extent. in view of the Correlation found between them.

3. Impact of Variables on Morale

The investigator proposed also to study the impact of variables on the Teacher Morale, Vide the objectives no. 3 and 4. Accordingly he assumed by way of hypothesization, in the hypothesis no. 3, that Morale Scores under the Teacher Factor may not differ from those under the Environmental Factors, in any of the subsamples. The study has revealed that there is some *impact of these variables, on Teacher Morale under its two constituent factors, in varying proportions.*

The Related Recommendations

(a) The Educational Authorities should endeavour to *promote some type of guidance in a positive manner, from the Senior Teachers who are elderly in age as well as those who are very much experienced in the profession,* in order to guide the Junior Teachers, with a view to helping them to realize and manifest a higher morale.

(b) *In view of the manifestation of a higher Morale by Women Teachers and Rural Teachers,* the State should provide certain amenities to them, in matters pertaining to Accommodation, Incentives in Service, etc., as most of them find many inconveniences in matters such as their Residence, etc., particularly in rural areas. *Probably more facilities for Teacher-Training too may be offered to these two categories of Teachers.*

(c) *A depth-study might be taken up in order to analyse why the Graduate Teachers as well as B.Ed., Grade Teachers manifested lower morale* than the Under Graduate Teachers as well as Sec. Grade Teachers. This depth study might also be developed as a follow-up study for the present investigation with reference to the section on corroboration with previous studies.

(d) In view of a *higher morale on the part of Teachers of Private Institutions, steps should be* taken in order to *probe* into the matter *further,* by way of an additional research as well as an inquiry by experienced Educationists and *consider also some type of steps such as bringing all Educational Institutions under one umbrella with some autonomy*, as well as Incentives of Promotion opportunities etc., to the Teaching Personnel of all the managements. At present, Educational Institutions are managed at school level, mostly by local bodies, as well as some other agencies. *By bringing all the Educational Institutions under one umbrella, it will be possible to co-ordinate the Institutions under different managements.* The Kothari Commission too recommended a similar proposal, suggesting several steps to implement the same. One of these steps taken up recently by the Centre as well as the States in Indian Union under the New Education Policy is to set up a village level committee. *As for the role of Panchayati Raj Bodies, their prominent role in Education is not much* except for (a) opening new schools and expanding the existing schools subject to funds, and (b) appointing and transferring teachers. *As for the role of Education Department, its existing major function is only to inspect and exercise some control* over the schools imparting primary and secondary education more or less *on the lines of a colonial policy*, in several matters concerning education. *But there is not much co-ordination between these two organisations. The proposed umbrella for bringing all educational institutions under it is, perhaps, intended to co-ordinate the above two organisations (P.R. Bodies and Education Dept. of State Government).* Want of an effective coordination will result only in failure to solve the problems concerning Teacher Morale. So, the Centre and States in our Country may take steps to effectivise action to bring all Educational Institutions under one single umbrella by co-ordinating the above two powers of control over Education, if Teacher Morale is to be strengthened. *Without establishing such committees at District and State levels, there will be no effective co-ordination* between the different agencies managing the various institutions. Doing so will be useful to reduce the bureaucratic functioning of Education Department and also co-ordinate with the P.R. Agencies managing the schools at Primary and Secondary levels, effectively by setting up an umbrella like the above.

(e) Besides, *in view of a higher impact of class-size on the Teacher Morale*, particularly under the Environmental Factors Morale component of it. the State might consider certain steps to *optimize the Class-strength in each section, at 40* as it appears to be an optimal Class-size between 50 and 30, which are respectively the upper and the lower limits hypothesized in this study for the different categories of Teachers under this variable.

4. Morale in terms of the Areas of Study under Teacher Factor and Environmental Factors

Another objective of this study was to identify the areas influenced by the different variables (Objective Nos. 5, 6, 7). The investigator assumed by was of hypothesization that all the 12 areas selected in this study may reveal this influence equally. The investigation didn't prove this hypothesization.

The Related Recommendations

(a) In view of the manifestation of a higher morale in certain areas like Personality Factors and Professional Aspirations under the Teacher Factor, School Facilities and School Administration under the Environmental Factors, steps might be taken to *strengthen these four areas for promotion of Teacher Morale. One of these steps may be to identify Teachers with a high Professional morale* and encourage them so as to serve as standing examples and beacon light to the other Teachers. *It would also be necessary to develop, under the Environmental Factors, the aspects pertaining to School Facilities and School Administration,* so that Teachers utilise them in performing their task with a higher morale.

(b) Similarly, it would be desirable to *develop the Professional Skills of a Teacher,* which reveal at present a lower morale; further studies might perhaps, be taken up, to analyse the low morale phenomena manifest in the areas comprised in the Professional Skills and work out certain remedial steps.

(c) *As for Educational Administration, it could not manifest in this study highly favourable verbal responses from the Teachers in terms of their Morale. So, we can't afford to neglect, probably, this area in the existing Education system,* say, in a Country like India where it still continues as a legacy from the British rule prior to 1947, with a lot of centralized control over Education.

It is quite essential to make further studies to *analyse why Teachers are not favourable in their responses to this area,* even in Independent India, as conducive to Teacher Morale. We may probably observe here that *Educational Administration, still centralized as it is, seems to be carried on, as in a colonial organization,* in the most wooden and unresponsive manner that does not befit it in a Democratic State. Thus, it would be highly essential to study this phenomenon pertaining to Education system, and develop it by way of remediation, so as to be conducive to promotion of Teacher Morale.

(d) As for the other areas pertaining to Environmental impact of Family, Community and Value-System, we may have to *develop further studies in these areas too,* so that the potential of these areas might be tapped well for promotion of Teacher Morale, *in order that the Theorization developed on the impact of these three forces on Education, is rendered more and more practical and functional* in it value.

(e) Besides, in view of the low correlation found between Academic Proficiency and Teaching Ability, further studies might be useful as it would be highly valuable to *strengthen the Academic Proficiency of Teachers, in addition to their Teaching Ability.* Teachers with a higher morale in these two components might manifest a higher morale; the present set-up seems to be deficient in this regard. So, steps might be essential to develop such teachers for the present set-up.

5. Item-wise Teacher Morale

The investigator proposed to observe this phenomenon under the study on hand, with reference to the objective no.8 and the hypothesis no. 6 (Please see the related sections in the first chapter). Accordingly he studied the same, under Section—D. Keeping in view (i) the findings obtained on this phenomenon, the investigator formulated the following recommendations in this regard:

(a) *Teachers should develop their awareness of the Environmental Factors most positively* as they too influence their Morale, in addition to the Teacher-Factor.

(b) As already stated above, *Academic Proficiency of the Teacher should be strengthened,* in order to step up the Teacher Morale, particularly in view of the highest number of Positive Response manifest in this area.

(c) As already stated above, *the Professional Skills such as the Teaching Ability should be developed much, in the teacher,* in order to make it conducive to promotion of Teacher Morale in view of the Neutral Responses being more in this area.

(d) *School Administration should be strengthened* so as to make it positive for promotion of Teacher Morale, by increasing the status of Head Master, so as to make his functions supportive conducive to the manifestation of Teacher Morale.

(e) Steps might also be taken up to *focus in the Inservice Programmes of Teacher—Training, on certain situations of the Teacher-Behaviour with a relevancy for Teacher-Morale, which tend to be most idealistic but at the same time most difficult to be translated into action at grass root level,* like those identified in the Finding No. 52.

(f) In view of the Finding No. 44 *steps conducive to promotion of higher values* in the Teacher might be identified.

The investigator has thus highlighted in this section some ways and means of strengthening Teacher Morale. Partly, they involve further studies to focus a greater attention on some of the vital aspects revealed in the study on hand. Besides, they involve certain Administrative steps, mostly with the aim of promoting the Teacher Morale.

BIBLIOGRAPHY

BOOKS

Aggarwal, J.C.; *Teacher's Role, Status, Service Conditions and Education in India.* Delhi: Doba House, 1988.

......; *National Policy on Education, 1986 and Main Recommendations of National Commission on Teachers,* Delhi : Doba House.

.......; *Education Policy in India 1992,* Delhi; Shipra Publications.

.. ....; *Educational Research—An Introduction,* New Delhi; Arya Book Depot., 1975.

American Association of School Administrators; *Staff Relations in School Administration—33rd Year Book,* Washington D.C., National Education Association of the United States, 1955.

Anand, C.L.; *et.al., The Teacher and Education in Emerging Indian Society,* New Delhi, National Council of Educational Research and Training, 1983.

Barr, A.S.; *et.al., Supervision,* New York: Appleton Century Crofts, INC, 1947.

Best, J.W.; *Research in Education,* New Delhi: Prentice Hall of India (Pvt.) Limited, 1963.

Carroll, E.R.; *et.al., Morale for a Free World,* American Association of School Administrators, Washington D.C. : National Education Association of the United States, 1944.

Childs, J.L.; *Education and Morale,* New York: Appleton Century Crofts, INC, 1953.

David, G.R.; *Characteristics of Teachers—A Research Study,* Washington D.C.: American Council of Education, 1960.

Garrett, H.E.; *Statistics in Psychology and Education,* Bombay, Allied Pacific (Pvt) Limited, 1981.

Gilbert, H.; *The Art of Teaching,* New York, Alfred. A. Knot, 1950.

Good, C.V., Barr, A.S. and Scates, D.E.; *The Methodology of Educational Research,* New York; Mc Graw Hill Book Co., p. 617.

Guilford, J.P; *Psychometric Methods,* New York: McGraw Hill Book Company, INC, 1959.

...... *Fundamental Statistics in Psychology and Education,* New York: McGraw Hill Book Co., INC, 1956.

Hocking, W.E.; *Morale and Its Enemies,* New Haven: Yale University Press, 1918.

Huggett, A.J.; and Stinnett, T.M.: *Professional Problems of Teachers,* New York: The Mac Millan Company, 1956.

Joseph, T.; *Industrial Psychology,* New York: Prentice Hall, INC, 1952.

Kochar, S.K.; *Pivotal Issues in Indian Education,* New Delhi, Sterling Publishers (Pvt.) Limited, 1984.

Moore, H.E. and Walters, N.B.; *Personal Administration in Education,* New York: Harper and Bros., Publishers, 1955.

Murty, S.K.; *Contemporary Problems and Current Trends in Education,* Ludhiana, Parkash Brothers, 1982.

Nelson, B.H.; *The 45th Year Book of the National Society for the Study of Education (Part-II),* Changing Conceptions in Educational Administration.

Raghunath Safaya; *Development, Planning and Problems of Indian Education,* Delhi, Dhanpat Rai and Sons, 1977.

Raghunath Safaya and Saida, B.D; *School Administration and Organisation.* Delhi: Dhanpat Rai and Sons, 1977.

Rorer, J.A.; *Principles of Democratic Supervision,* New York: Bureau of Publications of Teachers College, 1942.

Sukhia, S.P., Mehrotra, P.V. and Mehrotra, R.N; *Elements of Educational Research,* New Delhi: Allied Publishers (p) Limited, 1980.

Wiles, K.; *Supervision for Better Schools.* New York: Prentice Hall, INC, 1955.

Research Reports

Chaya, *An Investigation into Certain Psychological Characteristics of an Effective School Teacher.,* Ph.D. in Psychology, Karnataka University, Dharwar, 1974.

Chhabra, N; *A Study of certain Social Psychological Variables relating to Teachers Morale at Secondary and College levels,* Ph.D. in Education, Meerut University, Meerut, 1975.

Debnath, H.N.; *Teaching Efficiency: Its Measurement and Some Determinants,* Ph.D. in Education, Viswa Bharati University, Shanti Niketan, 1971.

Dekhtawala, P.B.; *Teacher Morale in Secondary Schools of Gujarat,* Ph.D. in Edu., M.S. University, Baroda, 1977.

Franklin, I.; *A Study of Organisational Climate and Teacher Morale in Colleges of Education in Gujarat,* Ph.D. in Education, M.S. University, Baroda, 1975.

Jayamma, M.S.; *Construction and Standardization of an Inventory* for Predicting Teacher Efficiency (for Primary school teachers of Karnataka State), Ph.D. in Education, M.S. University, Baroda, 1962.

Jain B.; *A Study of Classroom Behaviour Patterns of Teachers in relation to their Attitude towards Profession, Morale and Values,* Ph.D., JMI, 1982.

Mehta, A.V.; *Institutional Climate as a Factor of Staff Morale and Student Control Ideology in the Affiliated Colleges of Gujarat University,* Ph.D. (Edu), M.S. University, 1977.

Mahatma, C.M.; *Classroom Ethos and their Relationship with Teacher Behaviour, Characterstics and Teacher Morale,* Ph.D. in Education, S.G.U. 1980.

Pandey, G.S.; *A Study of Teachers Adjustment in Relation to Professional Efficiency,* Ph.D. (Edu), Gorakpur University, Gorakpur, 1973.

Panda, U.N.; *A Study of Management, Organisational Climate and Teachers' Morale in Orissa Schools, Ph. D. in Education Utkal University, 1985.*

Pandey, Saroj; *A Study of Leadership Behaviour of the Principal, Organisational Climate and Teacher Morale of the Secondary Schools.* D.phil. in Education, Aligarh University, 1985.

Puranik, S.D; *A Study of the Relationship of Social Maturity of Pupils with Organisational Climate and Teachers' Morale in the Primary Schools of Bangalore City.* Ph.D., Education, Mysore University, 1985.

Samron Pengnu; *A Study of Organisational Climate and Teacher Morale in Secondary Schools in Central Zone of Thailand,* Ph.D (Edu), M.S. Univ., Baroda, 1976.

Sharma, M.L.; *An Investigation into Organizational Climate of Secondary Schools of Rajasthan,* Ph.D. (Edu), M.S. University, Baroda, 1974.

Sharma, R.C.; *Teaching Aptitude, Intellectual Level and Morality of Prospective Teachers:* Ph.D. (Edu), M.S.U., 1984.

Singh, S.A.; *A Study of some Personality Variables related to Teaching Effectiveness.* Ph.D. (Edu), Patna University, Patna, 1976.

Reports on Education

Report of the University Education Commission, 1948-49, New Delhi: Ministry of Education, Government of India.

Report of the Secondary Education Commission, 1952–53; New Delhi: Ministry of Education, Government of India, 1954.

Report of the Education Commission, 1964-66; New Delhi: National Council of Educational Research and Training.

10+2+3—A Major Change in School Education. New Delhi: Ministry of Education and Social Welfare, Government of India, 1975.

Reference Materials

Buch, M.B.; *"A Survey of Research in Education,"* Baroda, Society for Educational Research and Development.

......; *Second Survey of Research in Education,* Baroda, Society for Educational Research and Development.

......; *Third Survey of Research in Education,* Baroda: Society for Educational Research and Development.

......; *Fourth Survey of Research in Education,* Baroda: Society for Educational Research and Development.

Barris Chester, W. and Lisa, M.R.; *Encyclopaedia of Educational Research,* New York, The Mac Millan Co., 1960.

Little, W and Onions, C.T.; *The Shorter Oxford Dictionary on Historical Principles,* Oxford: The Clarendon Press, 1933.

Journals

Alexander, L.; "Applied Science of Human Relations", *Personal Administrator,* July, 1947.

Behr, M.E. and Renck, R.; "The Definition and Management of Employee Morale", *Administration Scientific,* Quarterly, 1950.

Dorsey, S.M.; "Promoting Friendliness in School Relations" *The Nation's Schools*—April, 1930.

Handel, H.; "Keeping Morale where it should be up", *The School Executive*—June, 1957.

Hunter, E.C.; "Attitudes and Professional Relationships of Teachers—A Study of Teacher Morale", *Journal of Experimental Education,* June, 1955.

Mathis, C.; "The Relationship between Salary Policies and Teacher Morale", *The Journal of Educational Psychology,* December, 1959.

Ogden, L. and Stoops, E.; "Staff Morale—What is it? How do we get it?" *Educational Administration and Supervision,* December, 1957.

Redefer, F.L.; "Studies on Teacher Morale and Quality of Education", *The Nation's Schools*—February, 1957.

Shamusuddin; "Teaching as a Career", *Educational India*—April, 1968.

Swami Atmaramananda, Editor of *Prabuddha Bharata,* a monthly journal of the Ramakrishna Order, started by Swami Vivekananda in 1896, with its Editorial Officer, P.O. Mayavati, Via Lohaghat, Dt. Pithoragarh—262 524, U.P., May, 1994.

Wadhera, R.C.; "Code of Conduct" published under Editorial in the *Journal of Educational India,* November, 1976; page. 217.

Prahallada, N.N.; "Moral and Spiritual Education in Teacher Education", (*The Journal of Educational India,* March 1977).

Sexena, K.; "Professional Factors Influencing Teacher Morale" in the Colleges of Garhard University, U.P., *(The Education Review*-October, 1988, page. 173.)

Sundararajan, S. and Ashrafullah, A. M.; made a study on "Job Satisfaction of the Harijan Welfare School Teachers in Tamilnadu" (*The Journal of Experiments in Education,* May, 1990, page–131).

Sundararajan, S. and Vivekanandam, R's study on "The Job Satisfaction of Teachers Working in Higher Secondary Schools in the City of Madras." *(Journal of Experiments in Education,* September, '90; page–234).

Mehta, P.M.; "Teacher Morale as Determinant of Teacher Perception of Supervisory Behaviour "in the High Schools of New York City. *(Journal of Indian Educational Review,* Volume–27 Jan., 1993, Published by N.C.E.R.T., page No. 36-46).

S.C.E.R.T.; "A Study on Character Development in Children of 4-8 years", *(Research Bulletin of Maharashtra, S.C.E.R.T.,* Pune, March–June, 1993.

Savadamuthu, T.; "Teacher Morale and Student Morale at Secondary School Level in Dindigal Anna District of Tamilnadu; Ph.D. Education., Alagappa University., 1992 *(Indian Educational Review,* Volume 29, July-October, 1994, Published by N.C.E.R.T.) page No. 179-182.

"Education For All–"Data Base" for "Certain Innovative Basic Education Projects in Developing Countries", Published by UNESCO, Published in 1992, page-37.

Dr. Mishra., A.N. and Jaya Mishra; "Leadership Behaviour of the Heads of the Secondary Schools" in the *Journal of Educational Review* of October, 1993; page 165.

•••